GRAPHIC MEMORIES OF
THE CIVIL RIGHTS MOVEMENT

WORLD COMICS AND GRAPHIC NONFICTION SERIES

Frederick Luis Aldama and Christopher Gonzalez, Editors

The World Comics and Graphic Nonfiction series includes monographs and edited volumes that focus on the analysis and interpretation of comic books and graphic nonfiction from around the world. The books published in the series use analytical approaches from literature, art history, cultural studies, communication studies, media studies, and film studies, among other fields, to help define the comic book studies field at a time of great vitality and growth.

GRAPHIC MEMORIES OF THE CIVIL RIGHTS MOVEMENT

REFRAMING HISTORY IN COMICS

JORGE J. SANTOS, JR.

UNIVERSITY OF TEXAS PRESS ꙮ AUSTIN

Requests for permission to reproduce material from this work
should be sent to:
    Permissions
    University of Texas Press
    P.O. Box 7819
    Austin, TX 78713–7819
    utpress.utexas.edu/rp-form

♾ The paper used in this book meets the minimum requirements
of ANSI/NISO Z39.48–1992 (R1997) (Permanence of Paper).

LIBRARY OF CONGRESS CATALOGING-IN-PUBLICATION DATA

Names: Santos, Jorge, 1980–, author.
Title: Graphic memories of the civil rights movement : reframing
    history in comics / Jorge Santos.
Other titles: World comics and graphic nonfiction series.
Description: First edition. | Austin : University of Texas Press,
    2019. | Series: World comics and graphic nonfiction series |
    Includes bibliographical references and index.
Identifiers: LCCN 2018034573
    ISBN 978-1-4773-1826-3 (cloth : alk. paper)
    ISBN 978-1-4773-1827-0 (pbk. : alk. paper)
    ISBN 978-1-4773-1828-7 (library e-book)
    ISBN 978-1-4773-1829-4 (nonlibrary e-book)
Subjects: LCSH: Comic books, strips, etc.—History and criticism. |
    Graphic novels—History and criticism. | Civil rights
    movements in literature.
Classification: LCC PN6714 .S26 2019 | DDC 741.5/3587392—dc23
LC record available at https://lccn.loc.gov/2018034573

doi:10.7560/318263

Contents

*Dedicated to Dr. Shirley Moore of Texas Southern
University, my personal Professor X*

Acknowledgments

This book started in 2012 in the office of Cathy Schlund-Vials, one of my mentors at the University of Connecticut, with a single question. After pitching her a nascent idea about a book on contemporary civil rights comic memoirs, Cathy asked me a research question that created an itch I have been scratching ever since—"Why draw comics about civil rights when we have so many pictures and film reels about it?" To this day, I do not know whether the question was offhand or strategic (knowing Cathy, it was somehow both), but without it, *Graphic Memories of the Civil Rights Movement* would not exist. The encouragement of my other intellectual mentor at the University of Connecticut, Martha Cutter, to work on an article on the comics series *Pablo's Inferno* (which became my first publication) put me on the path I find myself today. They both later encouraged me to contribute to their edited comics studies collection *Redrawing the Historical Past: History, Memory, and Multiethnic Graphic Novels* (2018); my essay on *Darkroom* became the first written chapter of *Graphic Memories* (also, much of chapter 3 originally appeared in this collection). While this book is not dedicated to you, my career is.

I would not have made it this far without the support of innumerable ethnic studies and comics studies colleagues. It was at a MELUS (Multi-Ethnic Literature of the United States) conference in Santa Clara in April 2012 that a fellow graduate student (and the Batman to my Superman), Patrick Steppenwolf Lawrence, introduced me to Christopher Gonzalez, a fellow comics lover and an emerging scholar in his own right. Years later, at a MELUS conference in Athens, Georgia, Chris asked whether my presentation on Weaver's *Darkroom* was laying the groundwork for a potential book project. When I told him I would write it "someday," he convinced me to call Frederick Aldama of Ohio State University and pitch him my idea. After about an hour-long conversation with Frederick, someday became tomorrow and I started working on a book proposal for Chris and Fred's book series on comics for the University of Texas Press. That book proposal eventually became *Graphic Memories of the Civil Rights Movement*.

I must thank the College of the Holy Cross for financially and intellectually supporting this project. In the spring of 2017, I was awarded a one-semester course release, during which I wrote nearly the entirety of the initial manuscript. The English Department embraced my project, and I have presented on it in multiple venues across campus. In particular, my colleagues Beth Sweeney, Sarah Luria, Christine Coch, Lee Oser, Leila Philip, Jonathan Mulrooney, Oliver De La Paz, Maurice Geracht, Pat Bizzell, and K. J. Rawson have all contributed resources, time, or encouragement. I am also indebted to Holy Cross colleagues from outside the English Department as well. My writing group with Stephanie Crist, Min Kyung Lee, Jennifer Leib, and Amanda Luyster helped me shape the early pages of *Graphic Memories*. Alvaro Jarrin, Susan Schmidt, and Stephanie Yuhl have offered me opportunities to present my work in a number of classrooms and venues across campus. Last, but certainly not least, my students in the "Graphic Novels: History and Form" senior seminar shaped my theorization of comics and offered me feedback on one of my campus research presentations. Shouts to Dan Apadula, Jackie Bashaw, Patrick Eberhard, Evan Grogan, Khorally Pierre, Bryan Rodriguez, Chris Saeli, P. J. Van Galen, Zach Williams, and my research assistant Jack Barton—without your hard work, all my scholarship would be meaningless.

Additionally, I want to thank the scholars who supported my work from outside the College of the Holy Cross. Frederick Aldama, Patrick Steppenwolf Lawrence, and Maria Seger read and commented extensively on multiple chapter drafts of *Graphic Memories*. Jason Berger helped me write my initial book proposal, and Cathy Schlund-Vials, Martha Cutter, Katherine Capshaw Smith, and Chris Gonzalez graciously responded to my sounding-board emails and questions with patience and generosity. In this spirit, I must also give shouts to the amazing Comic Scholars listserv not only for answering my research questions, but also for simply existing and generating so much excitement for both my own work and the field I am entering. I must also thank the organizations of MELUS, the American

Literature Association, the MLA, the Word and Image Conference, and the Canadian Society for the Study of Comics for allowing me to present my work on comics at their conferences. I must thank Paul Childs III, my undergraduate professor at Sam Houston State University, for reminding me how much I love literature as a field and as an aesthetic phenomenon. And I would be nowhere without Shirley Moore of Texas Southern University, who gave this overly ironic Gen Xer a chance at graduate school despite my mediocre undergraduate grades. Above all, I must thank my darling wife Kristina Reardon for commenting on every chapter and for generally supporting the ebb and flow of any large project. She supported me from my imposter-syndrome angst to my overconfident bravado about how this book is going to change the field, or even just coming downstairs so I could geek about whatever page of comics art I was currently obsessing over.

Finally, I must thank my loving family back in Houston, Texas, for their unwavering support over the years. I am incredibly blessed that my immigrant Latinx parents bravely persevered through all the bullshit that immigrants put up with just so their children could have the opportunities they never did. Big love to my little sister Jessica for her consistent inspiration and emotional support. And to all the friends and family that cheer for me as loud as the humidity in Houston allows, I thank you. I miss you. I love you.

GRAPHIC MEMORIES OF
THE CIVIL RIGHTS MOVEMENT

Graphic Memories in "Black and White"

D arkroom: A Memoir in Black and White (2012), Lila Quintero Weaver's graphic memoir of growing up Latina in 1965 Alabama, opens with a meditation on media, memory, and the movement. Watching home movies in the family living room, the Quinteros marvel at the ability of their father, Nestor, a pastor and photojournalist, to manipulate the footage by playing the film backward. Though the narration tells us that the family watches the movies in reverse, the reader becomes acutely aware of the materiality of the comics page, since the reversal effect can only be approximated through a variety of panel arrangements. Moments from these films are arranged in panels that must be read from both left to right and in reverse, inviting readers to symbolically fill the role of Nestor; they can read the panels in the order they wish, at the pace they desire. Darkroom expects readers, like the children laughing at the films, to delight in their ability to control the orientation of the narrative unfolding before them—a feature integral to the magic of graphic narrative storytelling. Despite these comic dimensions, "not everything tickled our funny bones," Weaver tells us as the narrative shifts to her father's footage of a civil rights protest gathering at the United Methodist Church in Marion, Alabama (3). In Weaver's depiction, the protesters move backward, away from the Perry County Courthouse, simulating a return to

–

1

a previous point in their movement's history, both literal and figurative. Weaver's narrator on the following page wistfully notes, "The march took them around the courthouse I don't know how many times" (7). Moreover, Weaver begins to wonder what the camera may have missed entirely: "The movie doesn't show how white people reacted. But having lived among them, I can make an educated guess" (7). A white supremacist voices what many might imagine, staring directly at the reader as he says menacingly, "They're looking for trouble, boys. Let's not disappoint them" (7).

In a sense, *Darkroom* itself deliberately looks for trouble, revisiting the tribulations of the civil rights era and seeking to unsettle how those troubles are remembered, restoring what may have been missed, forgotten, or erased. Likewise, Weaver asks readers to return to their memories of the civil rights movement, to go "looking for trouble"—a challenge to reconsider their received versions of this history. The visuals that accompany this observation fill the gaps in Nestor's documentation, and the memoir's graphic composition invites readers to reassess their own relationship to civil rights cultural memory. Like so many other authors, artists, and author-artists committed to graphically narrating memories of the movement, Weaver hopes to trouble our collective memories, vicariously asking us to do the same through active reading of her work. Like Nestor, the reader is expected to take control of the narrative, always aware of its composition and arrangement as well as the editorial process behind both.

Darkroom's prologue encapsulates many of the ideas that have motivated my research and this study. It began with a question—why, given the abundance of footage left to her by her father, did Weaver choose to draw the images he captured, rather than simply reproduce them? Since the civil rights movement is perhaps the most documented, photographed, and televised political phenomenon in US history, why did the author-artists covered in this study compose graphic narratives at all? And why did so many of them draw the photographs through which the movement has come to be known? Initially, the answer may seem apparent: *Darkroom*'s inclusion of the white-supremacist agitators threatening the protest marchers from United Methodist highlights the limitations even of an archive as extensive as that documenting the civil rights movement. One must not move past this observation too quickly, however, since the desire to fill the gaps in the narrative record of the movement—as well as the collective memories that the record contains—motivated many of the graphic memoirs and novels under study here. For example, much of John Lewis's *New York Times* best-selling memoir *March* (3 vols., 2013, 2015, 2016) resurrects the names and faces of important contributors rarely mentioned in popular accounts of the movement.

Mark Long's *The Silence of Our Friends* retells the story of the TSU Five, five students at Texas Southern University who were accused, and later acquitted, of murdering a Houston police officer, and simultaneously laments a civil rights narrative that elides stories from outside the Dixie South. *Darkroom* looks to write in Weaver's Latina immigrant perspective from outside the black-white battle lines of the movement in hopes of moving from observer to participant. In all these narratives, inclusion in the collective memories of the civil rights era often takes a visual form expressed via a multiplicity of graphic narrative techniques that purposefully depict what is missing from the master narrative of the civil rights movement. Even if, as Weaver says, "the camera didn't miss much," the graphic narratives included in this study hope to provide the essential people, places, and events missing from our collective memory.

There is much more at play in these texts than historical supplementation. At stake in all these narratives is a revelation of the process by which history is told and retold, produced and reproduced, and narrativized and renarrativized before becoming enshrined in our memories and disseminated for sociopolitical purposes. As *Darkroom*'s manipulation of the family's home movies allegorizes, narratives of history are built from fragments, still moments collected, edited, and arranged to give the appearance of a cohesive narrative. Given the extensive photographic and film records from which these comics both draw from and draw against, graphic narrative not only reveals the process by which histories are told and retold, but also allows readers to participate in this memory-making process through the materialization of history on the comic's page. As Hillary Chute observes: "'Materializing' history through the work of marks on the page creates it as space and substance, gives it corporeality, a physical shape—like a suit, perhaps, for an absent body, or to make evident the kind of space-time many bodies move in and move through; to make, in other words, the twisting lines of history legible through form (Disaster Drawn, 27). Along these lines (or, perhaps, gutters), graphic narratives can make "the absent appear," as Chute puts it, by introducing people and places missing, elided, or erased from our memories. More importantly, civil rights graphic memories, as I have dubbed them, foster in their readers a metacritical awareness of history as an editorial and curative process, simultaneously calling them to question what evidentiary forms, like the photograph or the film reel, we accept as truth. In doing so, these narratives draw our attention to which version of the civil rights movement has achieved cultural consensus and to our participation in that historical narrative's dissemination and political dispensation.

Invoking memories of the civil rights movement is as politically charged as it is commonplace. Street signs, monuments, and holidays all construct a "consensus memory" of the movement, to borrow a term from Renee C. Romano and Leigh Raiford's excellent *The Civil Rights Movement in American Memory*, one constructed by memoirs, films, and popular fiction. But "remembrance is always a form of forgetting," as Jacquelyn Dowd Hall reminds us, and all narratives of civil rights history elide as much as they recall ("Long Civil Rights Movement," 1233). The process is also political, subject to the shadows and smoke of subjective memories, the agendas and goals of competing ideologies, and the machinations and distortions of political contestations. *Graphic Memories of the Civil Rights Movement* explicates how the theoretical approaches of graphic narratives interrogate and illuminate narrative strategies used to push against the confines of our consensus memory of the movement. This consensus memory is a historical narrative recalled through popular memory, sanctioned by the state, and subject to appropriations and revisions by a wide variety of political ideologies. Of specific interest to the analysis in *Graphic Memories* is the growing corpus of graphic novels and memoirs that reflect on what Dowd refers to as the "classical era" of the civil rights movement, roughly from the mid-1950s to the late 1960s. *Graphic Memories* investigates graphic novels and memoirs published since the mid-1990s that challenge or expand this consensus narrative by including sites, actors, and groups typically excluded from the popular narrative of the civil rights movement.

CONSENSUS MEMORY

When polled, my students often identify the US Supreme Court's *Brown v. Board of Education* decision of 1954 or the murder of Emmett Till in 1955 as the beginning of the movement, and the culmination as the passing of the Voting Rights Act of 1965 or the death of Martin Luther King three years later. When teaching graphic novels, or any novels, pertaining to the civil rights movement, I remind my students that the traditional temporal frame of the movement reduces to a handful of iconic flashpoints a decades-long, even centuries-long, struggle by committed African Americans and their allies for equality. I remind them that marches, lunch-counter protests, and other nonviolent strategies represented an urgent and critical element of the movement, one worthy of its lofty position of historical canonization—but they do not tell the whole story. Regardless, my students tacitly adhere to time frame of the civil rights movement as typically rendered, one that positions the teleology of the movement as both discernible and terminal, its goals accomplished by key legislative victories. In many ways, my students' assumptions regarding the civil rights movement—when and where it happened, what it set out to achieve—reflect a cultural consensus operating under the same narrative norms. The story is familiar: Martin Luther King Jr. and like-minded activists and college students began with a dream and a set of nonviolent principles, campaigned to integrate the South, and won. While students often seem nominally aware that this narrative is not apolitical, the version of events remains decidedly fixed in their awareness of the progress of US racial history. When explaining to my students our cultural fascination with this specific version of the trajectory of civil rights history, I often cite John Green's exceedingly useful *Crash Course* web series on US history. Green lucidly states: "Now, you might think the civil rights movement began with Rosa Parks and the Montgomery bus boycott or else *Brown v. Board of Education*, but it really started during World War II with efforts like those of A. Philip Randolph and the soldiers taking part in the Double V crusade. But even before that, black Americans had been fighting for civil rights. *It's just in the 1950s, they started to win*" (Green, "Civil Rights and the 1950s"; emphasis added). In many ways, the graphic narratives examined in this study operate within the boundaries of the classic civil rights temporal frame in order to celebrate these very victories and the iconic personalities associated with them. Even when illuminating histories and persons that the dominant narrative of civil rights has ignored, or when attempting to expand its borders, the narratives remain largely allegiant to the classic civil rights frame. As a result, *Graphic Memories* focuses predominantly on this stretch of civil rights history.

The field of civil rights study, however, has moved beyond this truncated frame and embraced what Jacquelyn Dowd Hall calls "the long civil rights movement," treating the victories of the 1950s and 1960s as part of a larger historical process reaching back into the early twentieth century. This elongated frame allows scholars to place the civil rights movement on a continuum stretching back to the social, political, and cultural debates on equality held in the immediate aftermath of World War II, moving through the Cold War period, and extending as far forward as the rise of the black, yellow, and Chicana/o liberation movements of the 1970s. Yet like my students, the graphic memoirs and novels under study here remain devoted to the "classical era" of the movement. Additionally, many of the titanic figures of our consensus memories tend to dominate the retelling of those memories, and so it not surprising that Martin Luther King Jr., Rosa Parks, and Emmett Till command much of the attention of many (but not all) of the narratives included in *Graphic Memories*. To address this tension, this project navigates the narrative terrain of civil rights consensus memory, a familiar version of the movement that has become solidified in American media and politics during the last fifty years and has reduced the movement's historical complexity to the pat historical narrative rejected by Hall and highlighted by Green. *Graphic*

Memoirs makes use of the concept of "consensus memory" as defined by Renee C. Romano and Leigh Raiford in *The Civil Rights Movement in American Memory*, an incredibly useful collection of essays to which my own work is largely indebted. In it, Romano and Raiford note, "There exists today what we might call a consensus memory, a dominant narrative of the movement's goals, practices, victories, and of course, it's most lasting legacies" (xiv). This consensus version of civil rights history maps directly onto the time frame of Hall's classic civil rights era and has, in many respects, overdetermined how its political priorities are remembered, as "a struggle that sought to change legal and social, rather than economic, barriers to equality" (xiv–xv). It is within these conceptual boundaries that *Graphic Memories* operates, even when they are not directly invoked.

Numerous civil rights short comics and longer graphic novels intended for a wide variety of audiences have emerged since 2000. Many of the most recent publications are intended for elementary-level or middle-grade audiences; for the most part, they reiterate (and reify) the version of civil rights history lodged in our consensus memory. For example, Capstone Press's Graphic Library series (2007) features a subset of graphic biographies of famed American icons, and its two civil rights entries feature, predictably perhaps, Martin Luther King Jr. (by Jennifer Fandel and Brian Bascle) and Rosa Parks (by Connie Colwell Miller and Dan Kalal). While both comics offer a glossary of key terms, as well as bibliographies and web links for further reading, the version of events contained therein uncritically adheres to a consensus-memory frame. In 2013, Gareth Stevens Publishing released the six-part Graphic History of the Civil Rights Movement series, which, to its credit, opens with short prose sections contextualizing the comic as part of a longer history.[1] But these comics focus primarily on key figures such as MLK, Rosa Parks, and Malcolm X, demonstrating a tendency toward "great-man history" in iterations of our consensus memories. Even their comics on the Little Rock Nine and Thurgood Marshall, figures that do not appear as frequently as MLK or Parks, focus primarily on the US Supreme Court's *Brown v. Board of Education* decision, which ruled legally mandated "separate but equal" schools unconstitutional and upended public school segregation—a touchstone of consensus memory. Only their comic on Medgar Evers, unmentioned in any other comic, is a standout. Likewise, Bentley Boyd's *The Civil Rights Freedom Train* (2005), published by Chester Comix, includes a profile on Jackie Robinson, the Los Angeles Dodger who broke Major League Baseball's color line.

Yet these comics typically treat their subjects in isolation, rather than as part of larger historical forces pushed forward by countless uncelebrated civil rights participants. In addition, *The Civil Rights Freedom Train* comic treats its readers with a surprisingly condescending attitude; the narrator, Chester the Crab, asks "Tamara" to stop listening to Lil' Bow Wow so he can tell her "a story of a rapper your grandparents listened to: MLK" (14). In all fairness, not all these educational comics are quite this reductive. Aladdin Paperbacks' comic *Little Rock Nine* (Poe and Linder, 2008), in the Turning Points series, uses the *Brown v. Board of Education* decision to frame a parable of white alliance. Like the Graphic History series, some attempt to situate the civil rights movement within a larger historical frame, such as Saddleback Educational Publishing's *The Civil Rights Movement and Vietnam* (Zubal-Ruggieri, 2009) or Sterling Publishing's *Still I Rise: A Graphic History of African Americans* (Laird et al., 2009). Yet even these close off the civil rights movement with the death of Martin Luther King Jr., tying the fate of the movement to this iconic leader. So while the deliberate pedagogical focus and intended young audiences of these comics warrant further study and focused scholarly attention, they nonetheless adhere so closely (and uncritically) to consensus memory that they fall out of this study's field of vision.

ON THE FRAGMENTS OF HISTORY

Noting that histories are built from fragments of the past, that teleologies are no more than assembled narratives more closely resembling fictive constructions than linear truth, feels blasé in light of our contemporary poststructuralist sensibilities. Yet as Michel Foucault predicted, we have left the era of linear history behind and embraced the fragmented nature of ineffable past. Foucault writes in "Of Other Spaces" (22): "The present epoch will perhaps be above all the epoch of space. We are in the epoch of simultaneity: we are in the epoch of juxtaposition, the epoch of the near and far, of the side-by-side, of the dispersed. We are at a moment, I believe, when our experience of the world is less that of a long life developing through time than that of a network that connects points and intersects with its own skein." It is admittedly unlikely that Foucault had comics specifically in mind when he made this observation, yet it is prophetically astute in its description of not only the way comics write history, but also of the way they generate meaning. As Will Eisner, Scott McCloud, Thierry Groensteen, and so many other theorists have taken pains to delineate, graphic narrative can function only through a vast array of narrative techniques built on juxtaposition, on fragments dispersed across the comic's page. As McCloud (*Understanding Comics*, 104) notes, these fragments reverberate through time, since "both past and future are real and visible and all around us," even creating a pocket epoch of "simultaneity" all its own. More importantly, on the comic's page, time is expressed through an arrangement of spaces, multiple temporalities existing "side-by-side," as Foucault mighty say. As Pascal Lefèvre notes, comics are a spatial medium, "with the different spatial relationships between elements in and across panels cueing readers to trace out the multiple time-lines at work in a given narrative" ("Some Medium-Specific Qualities," 26). In the hands of the brilliant author-artists whose work motivated this study, the medium-specific qualities of graphic narrative make it the ideal medium not only for representing history as a "sort of configuration," but also for revealing the process through which this configuration is produced (Foucault, "Of Other Spaces," 22).

As part of Foucault's "epoch of juxtaposition," the narratives studied here do more than simply teach history—they instruct us how to read it, enacting a metacritical pedagogy similar to that outlined in Michael Chaney's *Reading Lessons in Seeing: Mirrors, Masks, and Mazes in the Autobiographical Graphic Novel* (2017). Like Chaney, I believe that comics "teach their viewers how they ought to be read" (3) and, in the case of those analyzed in *Graphic Memories*, how history ought to be read as well. These comics foster in their readers a metacritical awareness of the consensus narrative of civil rights as a multimodal one comprising a familiar selection of iconic civil rights personas, photographs, and newsreel footage. In this vein, the authors' choice of the graphic narrative medium is a salient one, since it demands a metacritical engagement from its readers both visually and narratively. The formal elements of the comics page require readers to fuse disparate visual and textual elements into a cohesive whole via the concept of closure. As Barbara Postema puts it in *Narrative Structure in Comics: Making Sense of Fragments* (2013, xiv): "To create meaning all the various elements contain and produce gaps, creating a syntax and semiotics (what Roland Barthes would call a language), in which fragmentation and absence become operative throughout as signifying functions, while at the same time the gaps invite readers to fill in the blanks, making the reading of comics an active productive process." The graphic narrative's form forces the reader not only to work with disparate elements, but also to be aware of how those fragments and absences come together to generate a sense of narrative cohesion. Similarly, comics reveal how the writing of history follows comparable processes, a narrative strategy the average reader may not be acutely attuned to—evidenced, perhaps, by the very concept of consensus memory itself. Whether through the disorienting and destabilizing layouts of Ho Che Anderson, the enigmatic use of photography by Lila Quintero Weaver, or the subtle visual strategies of Nate Powell, each of the graphic narratives in this study do more than revise the content of our consensus memory. They engender a metacritical awareness of how those consensus memories were formed in the first place.

—

The graphic narrative medium's ability to cultivate new practices for the reading of mainstream, alternate, or counter-histories mirrors the manner in which this study engages with the concept of consensus memory itself. As Romano and Raiford make clear, the critical lens of consensus memory does more than provide a yardstick against which to measure historical accuracy: "In the dialectic between remembering and forgetting that is a central component of memory, such narratives beg us to ask what is at stake in these dominant representations of the past. What kind of civil rights movement is produced through this consensus memory and what vision of the present does it help legitimate, valorize, or condemn?" ("Struggle of Memory," xv). In this vein, *Graphic Memories* aims to explicate how the graphic novels and memoirs under study access this consensus narrative of the movement strategically and selectively in order to create a continuum that begins with our consensus memories but expands them beyond their arbitrary boundaries to remember something forgotten. Furthermore, *Graphic Memories* endeavors to map these graphic narratives' relationships with our consensus memories of the movement to elucidate how they undermine or reify this narrative. At times, these graphic novels and memoirs draw from the movement's lofty position of cultural authority, and at times they claim its power for contingencies, both past and present, not immediately associated with the civil rights drama—such as the contemporary LGBTQ struggle or the Black Lives Matter movement. Yet these narratives do not seek to reject this consensus memory. Rather, they attempt to expand its scope, augment its archive, and magnify the inconsistencies or elisions of consensus memory. Unavoidably, these narratives appropriate, implicitly or explicitly, the civil rights movement's innate cultural pathos, for sociopolitical ends. *Graphic Memories* aims to elucidate not only how these narratives of history and memory deploy the usable past of the civil rights movement, but also how they effectively make use of graphic narratives to write new histories and remembrances in the service of their individual sociopolitical projects.

In his foundational study *Comic Books as History: The Narrative Art of Jack Jackson, Art Spiegelman, and Harvey Pekar* (1987), Joseph Witek seems to anticipate the relationship between history and graphic narrative, writing that the increasing maturity of comics' forms, creators, and readers (as well as critical acceptance of the medium) would produce art of exceptional profundity: "It is clear that the comic book, a widely accessible and commercially available medium, is now being chosen as a form by serious writers whose themes have traditionally been expressed in the forms of verbal narratives (both literary and historiographical) and in films and other visual narratives, such as the photo essay" (5). Paul Buhle's oft-cited essay "History and Comics" extends this observation, noting scholars' growing fascination with "the treatment of comics and the vernacular graphic arts themselves *as a particular kind of history*" (319). Consideration of what "particular kind of history" the graphic narrative can uniquely accomplish is key to my project in *Graphic Memories*. Often called a populist medium, graphic narratives offer authors and artists modes for crafting new narratives of the civil rights movement's most celebrated characters and its forgotten actors. The concept of "graphic memories" intentionally invokes both the vividly brutal nature of the scenes of racial strife that compose our consensus memories, and the techniques and strategies made available by the graphic narrative for the composition of such memories on the page.

My book returns to celebrated comics such as Ho Che Anderson's biography *King* (2005), which offers a complex vision of Dr. King life that complicates the sanitary mythology of his martyrdom; Howard Cruse's *Stuck Rubber Baby* (1995), a fictionalized memoir of a gay man's coming of age, set against the backdrop of civil rights; and Congressman John Lewis's activist memoir *March* (2013), a *New York Times* best seller. I also draw attention to lesser-known works that narrate perspectives and sites of civil rights activism typically not included in the consensus narrative of the movement, including the Latina memoir *Darkroom* (2012), by Lila Quintero Weaver, and Mark Long and Jim Demonakos's memoir *The Silence of our Friends* (2012). I turn to more popular fare, too, closing the study with a personal exploration of Marvel Comics' superhero fantasy *X-Men* in order to elucidate the version of consensus memory that this civil rights allegory has promoted—and to examine my participation in consensus memory. Overall, I argue that these graphic novels and memoirs seek to augment the visual and narrative archives that underwrite our consensus memories of the movement. But even as these narratives seek to expand the movement's boundaries, the ingrained politics of this narrative remain largely in place, and nonviolence, integration, and martyrdom remain dominant themes. Hence, these stories are not counternarratives of the civil rights movement, but largely complementary ones.

"THIS BOOK IS ABOUT COMICS"

The study of the comics form is famously plastic. Scholarship in recent years has emerged from a richly diverse array of academic fields, including literary studies and cognitive science. As Charles Hatfield writes in his groundbreaking *Alternative Comics: An Emerging Literature* (2005): "Comics study encourages eclecticism, for comics urge the dissolution of professional boundaries and the mingling of theories and methods drawn from various fields. In this sense they

—

are antidisciplinary" (xiv). While I stop short of claiming an "antidisciplinary" approach in *Graphic Memories*, I nonetheless borrow liberally from an expansive list of academic traditions. My work draws heavily from contemporary scholarship on cultural memories of civil rights, in particular the work of Kate Capshaw Smith, Jacquelyn Dowd Hall, Edward P. Morgan, Renee C. Romano, and Leigh Raiford. Much of my work makes use of the rich history of photography studies, those by Susan Sontag, John Berger, and Dora Apel in particular. My work is likewise informed by the field of archival and cultural memory, especially the work of Nancy J. Peterson and Aleida Assmann. Sociological and political studies on representations of lynching by Harvey Young, Cassandra Jackson, and many others inform much of my work as well, particularly in chapter 5. These influences are supplemented by theoretical work on historiography by Michel de Certeau, Jacques Rancière, Pierre Nora, and, of course, Michel Foucault. Finally, *Graphic Memories* is bolstered by my own background in ethnic studies, the study of Latinx literary traditions in particular. Invariably, my work owes much to countless other scholars and traditions, evidence of the "antidisciplinary" nature of the graphic narrative field. In the study of consensus memory specifically, *Graphic Memories* will be the first of its kind, since no other scholars have devoted this level of critical attention specifically to graphic narratives of the civil rights movement.

Yet much like Hatfield's work, "this book is about comics" (*Alternative Comics*, 1). Thus, *Graphic Memories* finds its center of gravity in the emerging field of comics studies, in which I ultimately situate my work. There are many ways in which *Graphic Memories* contributes to a growing body of work that focuses on the writing of histories through the medium; scholars in this field include Martha J. Cutter, Cathy Schlund-Vials, Marianne Hirsch, Jared Gardner, and Ariel Dorfman. To date, only a few monographs focusing exclusively on graphic narrative and the writing of history have been published—although more appear every year. From this emerging body of scholarship, Joseph Witek's *Comics Books as History*, Jeet Heer and Kent Worcester's excellent collection *A Comics Studies Reader* (2009), and Hillary Chute's *Disaster Drawn* (2016) have had the strongest influence on my work. Like Witek's, my work is concerned with how the implicit truth claims of these narratives function either in concert with or against the ideologies embedded in any narrative of history. The wide variety of theoretical and methodological approaches represented in Heet and Worcester's collection mirrors my own. And much like Chute's, my work is committed to sustained and deep close readings of the prose, images, and narrative techniques on the page, with an eye to the historical, literary, and artistic traditions that inform them. In this regard, the oft-cited (and oft-debated) work of Scott McCloud in *Understanding Comics*

(1992), as well as Thierry Groensteen's *System of Comics* (1999), guides much of my interpretive work, supplemented by that of scholars such as Barbara Postema and Pascal Lefèvre. By focusing on a specific era from a variety of perspectives and a diverse array of writers and cultural positions, *Graphic Memories* adds to this rapidly expanding body of scholarship while simultaneously actualizing the rich potential for interdisciplinarity inherent in graphic narrative scholarship.

Graphic Memories contains five chapters, an introduction, an epilogue, and an appendix. The chapters work as conceptual pairs. The first two chapters engage with consensus memories of civil rights consciously and deliberately. The next two focus on memoirs concerned with expanding the narrative to include forgotten actors and places—the role of Latinos and Latinas in Selma in the 1960s, and stories of activist marches and judicial victories in the Third Ward of Houston, Texas. The final chapter and the epilogue focus on the use of civil rights history to discuss contemporary political challenges, from the LGBTQ rights movement of the 1990s to controversy surrounding the increasing militancy of the *X-Men* comics at the dawn of the Black Lives Matter movement. What draws them all together is their sociopolitical contestations of who is permitted to determine the contours of our memories of the civil rights movement, and how those memories are deployed to texture our understandings of contemporary political challenges.

Chapter 1, "Disrupting the Icon of the Once and Future *King*," examines Ho Che Anderson's comics biography of Martin Luther King Jr. and Anderson's attempt to break from the sanitized mythology of King as an idealistic dreamer and unthreatening integrationist. As Tavis Smiley notes in the introduction to his own recent biography of MLK, narratives of King's life that dramatize his fight for integration and his subsequent martyrdom render a vision of MLK that elides his political focus on the interplay of race, class, capitalism, and modern colonialism—instead representing "the Martin Luther King that the world wishes to remember" (Smiley, *Death of a King*, 4–5). I refer to this oversimplified version of King's life and politics as the "iconic King," a vision that Anderson's biography is eager to disrupt. I use the word "icon" specifically, as Scott McCloud does in *Understanding Comics*, to mean an image reduced and simplified into a symbolic abstraction. *Graphic Memories* contends that Anderson's use of a variety of visual art styles and motifs throughout *King*, which often jar the reader with their disruptive inconsistency and highly abstract forms, fractures and complicates the reductive vision of MLK offered up by the iconic nature of images of the man and the consensus memory of his life. By violating Groensteen's principle of iconic solidarity—which states that recognizable art styles and forms allow graphic-narrative sequencing to proceed—and focusing on more than iconic marches and boycotts, Anderson's biography offers a mythological rendering of King that aims to undermine the representation of his career in our consensus memory while revealing the inescapable media filters that amplify this simplified vision of MLK.

Chapter 2, "Bleeding Histories on the *March*," looks to John Lewis's three-volume graphic memoir, which memorializes a large cast of activists and actors involved in the classic civil rights movement by deliberately minimizing the role of Martin Luther King Jr. *March* can thus be read as an alternative to the "great man of history" tradition represented by Anderson's *King*. Lewis's memoir offers dual narrative tracks: his exploits as part of a large network of activists, and the inauguration of Barack Obama on 20 January 2009. This chapter examines how Lewis and Nate Powell (the artist on the book) bring all these concerns together through the use of images that are uncontained by their designated space and "bleed" into adjacent panels. This technique casts the dual narratives not as disparate historical moments, but as explicitly interwoven moments in US racial history that bleed into each other. The arrangements of images across all volumes of the memoir address a new consensus narrative of civil rights—that of a budding postracial US society—that begins with the career of King and ends with the election of the nation's first African American president. The narrative is propagated by numerous single-panel political cartoons that were widely published at the time of the inauguration of the forty-fourth president. As "Bleeding Histories on the *March*" demonstrates, Lewis's "bleeding history" of civil rights implicitly challenges the great-man theory of history underwriting a belief in a postracial society, instead narrating a vision of the movement as not having achieved teleological completion with the election of Barack Obama. Rather, Lewis argues strongly for a vision of history that extends beyond King and Obama and treats the civil rights movement as a force that will continue well into the future.

The second two chapters of *Graphic Memories* draw attention to actors and places of the movement that remain outside the scope of the consensus-memory narrative. Chapter 3, "On Photo-Graphic Narrative," focuses on Lila Quintero Weaver's *Darkroom: A Memoir in Black and White*, which centers on the often-invoked Selma marches of the 1960s. Written from the perspective of a fair-skinned Argentinean immigrant coming of age in the United States during the civil rights movement, *Darkroom* recalls the activist career of the pastor and photographer Nestor Quintero, father of the memoir's author. *Darkroom* accesses a traditional Latinx literary narrative of an immigrant's struggle with racial ambiguity and an inability to locate one's self on a strict racial hierarchy that recognizes only white and nonwhite as legitimate formations. Weaver employs this narrative to discuss her difficulty in locating herself along her school's racial battle lines, her unclear racial identity leaving her distrusted by her black friends and rejected by her white peers. In a larger sense, the novel functions as something of an allegory, prompting Latinx readers to consider their own position regarding racial injustice in the United States. Present throughout the memoir are hand-drawn reproductions of her father's photographs of the civil rights marches in Alabama, as well as some of the author's re-created memories likewise depicted as photographs—a motif I refer to as "photo-graphic narrative." Blurring the line between real and imagined photographs, *Darkroom* symbolically expands an extensive archive of civil rights photography to include Weaver's unique Latina perspective. In so doing, Weaver's work echoes concerns over the use of photography by such theorists as Susan Sontag, John Berger, and Roland Barthes. Weaver's memoir breaks from the presumed evidentiary function of photography, exposes the use of photography to construct historical narratives received as true, and challenges readers to reassess their potentially problematic reading practices of both race and history.

Chapter 4, "*The Silence of Our Friends* and Memories of Houston's Civil Rights' History," turns to Mark Long, Jim Demonakos, and Nate Powell's *The Silence of Our Friends: The Civil Rights Struggle Was Never Black and White*, and the artist's manipulation of diegetic and extradiegetic space on the page to mark sites of civil rights protest in and around Houston, Texas. *Silence of our Friends* narrates a sit-in and protest on Wheeler Avenue at historic black Texas Southern University in the predominantly African American neighborhood of Third Ward. The memoir closes with the trial and acquittal of five students accused of firing on police officers, killing one. The diegetic space of the comic, which Pascal Lefèvre designates as the fictive space in which the characters live and act, is marked by signals to the extradiegetic space (i.e., the world outside the comic) of Houston, Texas. *Graphic Memories* treats the consensus narrative of civil rights as its own form of extradiegetic space—a constructed historical backdrop against which the dramas of civil rights unfold. By contrast, the memoir remains a diegetic space removed from the dominant narrative of civil rights, an aspect denoted through a variety of motifs and chronotopes (configurations of time and space). By directing the reader to the historical extradiegetic space of Houston, Texas, *The Silence of our Friends* seeks to expand the boundaries of the civil rights drama beyond the neatly contained imagined space of the Dixie South.

Chapter 5, "Tropes, Transfer, Trauma," places Howard Cruse's fictionalized memoir of Toland Polk's coming-out during the civil rights movement in the context of political appropriations of the movement's legacies in the 1990s. *Stuck Rubber Baby* offers three distinct narrative tracks: Toland's early cognizance of racial difference and homosexual desire, his experiences in the civil rights movement as

—

a repressed gay white man, and a frame narrative of an openly gay Toland narrating from the 1990s. Cruse stitches these narratives together through the use of a set of civil rights tropes drawn from consensus memory. The most important, and troubling, of all these tropes involves a connective theme present in all five texts under study here: each climaxes with a symbolic, racially motivated murder that highlights the more mainstream elements of the movement's politics—the tragic sacrifices of African Americans and the imperative to achieve social integration. But Cruse's text ends with the murder of Sammy Noone, a gay white civil rights activist lynched by white supremacists. Cruse couples the use of these tropes with a paneling technique that breaks panels up into fragments in order to move into other scenes and moments in time. Paired with the fictionalized nature of the memoir, the technique allows Cruse to create a thematic unity between the racial-justice activism of the civil rights movement and the concerns of the gay rights movement of the 1990s, transferring the tragedies of the African Americans of Clayfield to the homosexual—and typically white—protagonists of *Stuck Rubber Baby*. Cruse's use of fragmented panels promotes a vision of the movement that inspired the gay rights movement of the 1990s. In many ways, *Stuck Rubber Baby* reflects a 1990s discourse that positions the LGBTQ struggle for marriage equality as the natural inheritor of civil rights legacies. While much of the narrative works to establish the parallels between the African American struggles and those of the LGBTQ community, the choice to culminate the narrative with the lynching of a gay white man at the hands of white supremacists is a problematic one. Yet this act of historical and traumatic appropriation has gone largely uncommented upon by popular and academic critics, who otherwise heap praise on Cruse's graphic complexity. To fill this void, *Graphic Memories* draws from the critical debate surrounding the depiction of lynching photography to frame an interrogation of the narrative choices, and their consequences, in Cruse's graphic novel. In a larger sense, *Stuck Rubber Baby* participates in a 1990s-era appropriation of the civil rights movement by groups on all sides of the political spectrum. It prompts us to consider who is allowed to lay claim to the movement's historical legacies in order to articulate contemporary political concerns over rights, representation, and the writing of history. In short, chapter 5 wonders, to whom does history belong?

The epilogue enters a more self-reflexive mode. I recount my participation in consensus memory through my enduring fandom of Marvel Comics' *X-Men*, a superhero-themed civil rights allegory in continuous publication since September 1963. "Cyclops Was Right: X-Lives Matter!" considers how internet fan culture participates in the writing of contemporary consensus memories, particularly in regard to the increasing militancy of the X-Men leader Scott Summers at the dawn of the Black Lives Matter movement. Since its 1960s debut, Stan Lee's comic has evolved from its original purpose as a civil rights allegory to become Marvel's catchall comic for the marginalized and oppressed while also showcasing the company's devotion to diversity and multiculturalism. In the early 2000s, however, the comic restored its allegorical status quo by once again moving to center stage the ongoing ideological conflict between Professor Xavier, mutant rights advocate and integrationist, and the militant mutant separatist Magneto. The epilogue considers the comic's return to its original conflict between a symbolic Martin Luther King Jr. (Professor Xavier) and a symbolic Malcolm X (Magneto), who is often (reductively) seen as a militant antagonist of the movement's nonviolent methodology and integrationist goals. This time, the battle is waged for the mind of Xavier's ideological heir, Scott Summers, aka "Cyclops," who becomes decidedly more militant after a human-supremacy (that is, white-supremacy) group bombs the X-Men mutant academy and kills many young students—which I read as an allusion to the infamous 1963 bombing of the 16th Street Baptist Church in Birmingham, Alabama. The story line ends with the death of Professor Xavier at the hands of Scott Summers after he embraces a violent separatist militancy in response to aggression from the American superteam the Avengers. Culminating only months before the protests in Ferguson, Missouri, this conflict not only reveals insights into how the civil rights movement is remembered, but also divulges cultural anxieties over the militancy potential of contemporary racial-justice campaigns such as Black Lives Matter. Marvel Comics decided to jail Cyclops and bring his past self into the future to witness his tragic, criminal descent into radicalization. This choice was met by an outcry from fans, many of whom sided with Cyclops over Professor Xavier. This started an online "Cyclops Was Right" movement that pressured Marvel into freeing the character and giving him a parallel team of X-Men as well as a new costume reflecting his Malcolm X–like militancy. *Graphic Memories* speculates on how current racial conflicts and racial-justice organizing made possible by social media are beginning to reshape our consensus memories of the civil rights movement. Further, I ponder how comics fandom and internet culture combine to give readers an avenue to participate in the writing of these memories—a dynamic that mirrors the active readership inherent in the enjoyment of graphic narratives.

Graphic novel author-artists use the medium to intervene in the collective process of consensus-memory-making to introduce either overlooked or erased elements of civil rights history and cultivate in their audiences new practices for the reading and consumption of history. By focusing on this growing corpus of literature—one might even consider it an emergent subgenre of history comics—*Graphic Memories of the Civil Rights Movement* lays bare the stakes involved in remembering and writing about the movement. On the ever-shifting terrain of civil rights memory, these narratives create space for readers not only to participate in the memory-making process, but also to realize that they already exercise the agency to shape this archive via their participation in a national culture that venerates a particular version of this history. Further, they remind us that our memories of politics are never apolitical; consensus memory always works toward the reification of particular truth claims and assertions of political or historical inheritance. These graphic narratives thereby ask us not only to reconsider the ways in which political, social, and popular cultures interact with history to form such narratives, but also to reconsider our roles in these processes.

CHAPTER 1

The Icon of the Once and Future *King*

*K*ing begins in shadow with a single step. The prologue opens with two large panels, the first showcasing a young boy's shadow draped over a descending staircase, the boy himself out of view (fig. 1.1). His feet enter the second panel—a first tentative step in a long journey that began, the panel states, in 1935. The following page offers the same layout as the boy steps partially into view, his face obscured by Anderson's shadowy inking. Cast against the wall, MLK's shadow is visible alongside him as it mirrors, doubles, and splits the boy. In the final panel, a voice enters from beyond the page. "ML? Is that you, boy?" it demands. "Yes, Daddy," the dutiful six-year-old Martin replies (2). The question implies an unrecognizable Martin Luther King Jr., one unfamiliar to readers. His father commands the young MLK to step out of the shadows, to "come where I can see you" (3). King's father, a pastor, begins referring to his son in ways the reader might find more familiar—as a troublemaker, and a young man of faith who should be "in the pews." Yet the protagonist of the American civil rights narrative who answered segregation and racism with faith and nonviolence does not step fully into view. And so, while Ho Che Anderson's vision of King often feels familiar as a racial rabble-rouser and a pioneer of peaceful protest, Anderson ultimately resists this iconic version of

—

1.1. Ho Che Anderson, *King*, 1:1–2

Martin Luther King Jr. Rather, *King*'s King remains essentially unknowable, even mythic. Anderson aims to complicate, via a variety of graphic narrative strategies, the version of MLK recalled by consensus memories and propagated by media and cultural narratives.

Anderson's *King: A Comics Biography* (1993), a biography of the eponymous civil rights martyr, was released in three volumes over the space of ten years.[1] Over the course of the volumes, Anderson sheds and takes on wildly different artistic approaches, seemingly at random, leaving the third volume radically dissimilar to the first. As Anderson told Dale Jacobs in an interview, he imagined "a book where the art style was fluid, where the technique could change with every panel if I wanted, a playground book, something that was pure sensation and experiment" (Anderson, interview, 376). Shifting easily between expressionism, photorealism, collage, painting, mixed media, and more traditional graphic narrative modes, Anderson's *King* presents a graphically unstable and sequentially chaotic vision of King's life, one that disrupts the more iconic vision of MLK recalled by consensus memory and propagated by media accounts. But unlike biographers who attempt to demystify King's life, Anderson embraces a "mythic" vision of MLK, blending fact and fiction indiscriminately. The result is a remarkable work of graphic biography that resists the iconic narrative of MLK's life without offering the reader a stable counternarrative, suspending the reader in the space between fiction and biography while constantly challenging and questioning the media filters through which this history is known. Anderson embraces the graphic narrative mode to disrupt, deconstruct, and disassemble the simplified historical narratives that accompany consensus memories of MLK. Rather than offer an alternative account, however, *King* forces readers into a set of reading practices that reframe their relationship to history, as opposed to simply replacing those narratives. Drawing on Scott McCloud's reading of the icon and his theory of "amplification by simplification," and buttressed by Thierry Groensteen's concept of "iconic solidarity," this chapter argues that images of Martin Luther King function as icons for the civil rights movement. I extend McCloud's and Groensteen's observations on iconicity to the life story of MLK, which, I posit, has been reduced to an oversimplified icon in popular cultural memory.

The story of Martin Luther King is inarguably the most familiar narrative of twentieth-century US racial politics—perhaps, even, of the entire US twentieth century—a story enshrined in national memory by the celebration of Martin Luther King Day. Every third Monday of January, the nation collectively commemorates the life and death of King, celebrated integrationist and civil rights martyr. The Deep South provides the venue, and familiar public spaces such as buses, lunch counters, and black churches provide the stage. Stoically victimized students led by saintly Baptist congregants are terrorized by belligerently brutal police officers, unconscionable Klan members, and bigoted bureaucrats, all of whom fill the chorus and the cast of this oft-retold historical drama. The star, of course, is Martin Luther King, the Black Gandhi and the American Jesus Christ—a dreamer, an integrationist, and (inescapably) the martyr of the movement. The script celebrates the victory of patiently urgent African Americans over the racial terrors of white supremacy and Jim Crow, culminating in key legislative victories and the martyrdom of King. "In this popular haloed myth," Kevin Bruyneel contends, "King stands as a figure of consensus deployed to 'impersonate' the idea that the U.S. is now a post-racial society in which collective and structural concerns about racial equality have been displaced" by the solutions proposed by neoliberalism ("King's Body," 76).[2] Today, King's career, his speeches, his nonviolent tactics—even his face—serve as icons of the movement in modern American memory, and these in turn are deployed to underwrite the story of American racial progress.

Of course, the truth about Martin Luther King the man is much more complicated, contradictory, and confounding than that of Martin Luther King the

—

icon. There are essentially two Kings with which any biographer must contend. The first is represented by the young boy called by his father to join him in his rectory, the prince destined to be the King in our consensus memories. We know him through the vast archive of media accounts (newsreels and photographs), national landmarks and celebrations, high school lectures during black history month, academic histories, and popular biographies in film, prose, or graphic narrative. "Bibliography: Sources for Martin Luther King Jr." (Zubal-Ruggieri, 2005), published by the Organization of American Historians, features nearly fifty book-length biographies of MLK from popular and academic presses. In addition, literally thousands of profiles, stories, articles, and memorials have been published yearly, online and in print, for decades. This is the King who spurred a dormant clergy into action with his "Letter from Birmingham Jail," who dramatized the plight of disenfranchised African Americans in the Deep South, who led the March on Washington in 1963, and who was killed for America's racial sins. This is the King who had a dream—the *iconic* King of the civil rights consensus memory.

SHADOWS AND MYTHS: THE ICONICITY OF MARTIN LUTHER KING

A second version of King haunts the iconic King of consensus memory—a shadow King who has inspired a cottage industry of biographies that attempt to bring him into full view—and I will return to this second King momentarily. First, however, I must delineate precisely what is meant by King as an "icon." When referring to the "iconic" King, I invoke the word "icon" in a particular sense. In *Understanding Comics* (1993), Scout McCloud uses the concept of the icon to build a critical and conceptual vocabulary for criticism of graphic narratives. At its most fundamental level, McCloud writes, the icon is defined as "any image used to represent a person, place, thing or idea" (27). He goes on to distinguish three broad categories of icons: "The sorts of images we usually call symbols are one category of icon, however. These are the images we use to represent concepts, ideas and philosophies. Then there are the icons of language, science and communication. Icons of the practical realm. And finally, the icons we call pictures: images designed to actually resemble their subjects. But as resemblance varies, so does the level of iconic content. Or to put it somewhat clumsily, some pictures are just more iconic than others" (27). McCloud further develops this third category, the pictorial icon, a picture that represents some "real life" counterpart (28). Using faces as his primary example, McCloud places a variety of iconic images on a spectrum (an "iconicity scale"), with "the photograph and the realistic picture," highly detailed and specific, on

—

one end of the scale, and the highly abstract, simplified "cartoon" at the opposite end. The cartoon, McCloud contends, offers the highest degree of abstraction and reader identification, since it eliminates all but the essential details of an image, allowing the reader to fill in details (36). The efficacy of the cartoon as an icon, McCloud insists, functions via the principle of "amplification through simplification": "When we abstract an image through cartooning, we're not so much eliminating details as we are focusing on specific details. By stripping down an image to its essential 'meaning,' an artist can amplify that meaning in a way that realistic art can't" (30). When I say that Martin Luther King functions as the icon of the civil rights movement, I mean it in this specifically McCloudian sense.

The more colloquial meaning of "icon," a cultural figure of exceptionality or acclaim, meaningfully overlaps with the semiotic logic outlined above. The name "Martin Luther King" functions iconically in much the same manner as the nonpictorial icons McCloud describes. His name has become synonymous with the "concepts, ideas and philosophies" of nonviolent political activism built on peaceful Christian principles and central to the American discourse on civil rights (as well as contemporary debates about the ethics of public protests).[3] As Edward P. Morgan contends: "The public memory that emerges elevates some aspects of the struggle to the level of iconic myth, attributes others to demonic forces that seem beyond comprehension, and obscures portions of the civil rights struggle that challenge hallowed beliefs about American traditions of tolerance and equality. The iconic figure of Martin Luther King towers over this public memory" (*What Really Happened*, 140).

Going further, the image of King's face has itself become a pictorial icon. Take, for example, the postage stamp released by the US Postal Service on 31 January 1979, commemorating King for its Black Heritage Stamp series. Rather than feature a photograph, the stamp bears a comics-style drawing of King towering over placard-wielding protesters. Emblazoned along the top of the stamp is MLK's full name, and the tableau below plays out in a microcosm of the narrative his name invokes. The top half of the stamp features a familiar image of King, his eyes kind and his shoulders clad in a black reverend's frock—itself iconic of his nonviolent Christian principles. Beneath him, a crowd of protesters, both black and white, march beneath his visage and under his tutelage. On the iconicity scale, MLK's face on the commemorative stamp falls near the center, a place for the somewhat abstract style of adventure and superhero comics (we might think of MLK as being treated "superheroically" in this regard).[4] The stamp, which bears a striking resemblance to a comics panel, makes use of the associations with MLK's face to amplify a simplified version of the civil rights drama, one that functions iconically.

—

It is in this final sense that the face of Martin Luther King is its most iconic. It is of course a pictorial icon—always meant to resemble its real-life subject. But it also functions nonpictorially, since it has come to represent the ideas of Christian nonviolence and the successes of American progressivism. Further, it brings with it an embedded narrative of civil rights that commemorates the successes of nonviolence and celebrates the victory of American inclusiveness and integration, a promised land to which Martin Luther King collectively led us. In many ways, the story of MLK is itself an icon—it simplifies the historical narrative of civil rights in order to amplify particular details, such as bus boycotts, freedom marches, voting rights, and the eventual redemption of US white society. As Morgan notes, the icon of MLK results in "representations of a political King who has virtually disappeared from mainstream mass media accounts. Public memory's Martin Luther King has been ideologically sanitized, detached from his own politics and their more radical, or system-critical, implications" (*What Really Happened*, 141). The resulting sanitized version of King functions not only to politically neuter MLK in a way that permits the lionizing of civil rights history, but also underwrites contemporary claims that America has, thanks largely to his good work, entered a postracial era.[5] And as Michael Chaney notes, Anderson challenges the media filters through which this narrative was built, since *King* "questions institutions of recollection, such as documentary photography and Hollywood cinema, upon whose premises any such thing as the past is produced for scrutiny in the first place" ("Drawing on History," 176). Hence, *King* interrogates how Martin Luther King, for many the face of the movement, has come to represent not the ideals of nonviolent civil rights protest, but the familiar, amplified, and simplified narrative of the movement embraced by popular media and constantly retold for contemporary political ends.[6]

Take, for example, the 1957 comic book *Martin Luther King and the Montgomery Story*, published by the Fellowship of Reconciliation. The composition of the cover is so strikingly similar to that of the 1979 US postage stamp that one must wonder whether the resemblance is intentional (fig. 1.2). Like the stamp, the cover features a stoic MLK in his reverend's frock with heavenly light cascading about his shoulders—we might think of this image as iconic in a traditionally religious sense. Beneath him play out familiar moments from the movement, specifically scenes from the 1955 Montgomery bus boycotts. The first page of the comic acknowledges that "50,000 negroes found a new way to work for freedom without violence and without hating" (5). Yet the narrative immediately moves to detailing the story of Martin Luther King, whose name "stood out among the hundreds" (2).[7] The comic features actors other than MLK, but they are typically

1.2. *Martin Luther King and the Montgomery Story* (1957), front cover

unnamed, with a few exceptions (for example, Ralph Abernathy is afforded three panels over the course of the comic, and Rosa Parks, two). Effectively, the story of King comes to represent the story of the movement itself, a truth reflected in the iconic imagery of the comic's cover.

The power of civil rights iconography was not lost on Anderson. In the first sentence of the supplemental materials in the ten-year anniversary collected edition of the comic, Anderson writes: "The first few years I worked on *King* I was constantly on the lookout for an iconic image to represent the comic" (*King*, 269). Although Anderson failed to find this iconic image, the first one in which the reader encounters Martin Luther King does resemble an icon of sorts. The boy is drawn with minimal features, resembling, to an extent, a cartoon as defined by McCloud. One can make out small white dots for eyes, a white line for a nose, and two thin white lines for a mouth. Lying at the far end of the iconicity scale, this minimalist approach allows for the maximum amount of abstraction—it functions iconically much like the cover of the 1957 *Montgomery Story* comic book or the 1979 commemorative stamp. Yet the inverted color palette, with white lines cutting across the inky shading of the page, implies a reversal. While the typical iconicity of Martin Luther King amplifies a particular (and simplified) narrative, Anderson's MLK remains ineffable, unrecognizable even to his own father. This image functions as a sort of anti-icon, abstracted to the point of indistinctness.

The second King looms over Anderson's biography, too. The boy's shadow represents the Other to the iconic King of consensus memory—a conflicted,

—

contradictory, and imperfect man. As in Anderson's epilogue, the presence of the iconic King invokes the shadow King—yet he remains elusive and indistinct. There have been a large number of attempts to capture the shadow King—including David Lewis's essential *King: A Critical Biography* (1970) and David J. Garrow's meticulously researched, Pulitzer Prize–winning *Bearing the Cross* (1986). Other books attempt to place MLK in the larger historical context of the civil rights movement's many actors, sites, and affiliates, such as Robert Penn Warren's *Who Speaks for the Negro?* (1965) or Taylor Branch's epic trilogy *America in the King Years* (1988, 1998, 2006). Some studies resist a narrow vision of King by specifically focusing on parts of his career edited out of his iconic narrative, such as Michael Eric Dyson's *I May Not Get There with You: The True Martin Luther King, Jr.* (2001) and Tavis Smiley's *Death of a King: The Real Story of Dr. Martin Luther King's Final Year* (2016). According to Clayborne Carson, there are also more than a thousand scholarly articles on King across academic disciplines: "King scholarship has paradoxically become more thematically ambitious and yet often more narrowly specialized" ("Paradoxes of King Historiography," 7).[8]

What brings these approaches together is the individual projects' relationship to the iconic King, since most approaches seek to expand, complicate, or disrupt the narrative of his life while attempting to bring the shadow King into clearer view. I sidestep such debates over historical accuracy or narrative authenticity. My work prefers to focus on how Anderson positions *King* outside the strictures of either consensus memory or the attempts to counter or deconstruct those memories. Rather, Anderson prefers to situate his biography in the space—or, perhaps, the gutter—between those opposing perspectives. In this sense, my work contends with the aesthetic choices Anderson made in creating his vision of MLK, as well as how those choices work to disrupt the reader's casual familiarity with this iconic civil rights leader. Besides destabilizing the reductive simplicity of consensus memory, Anderson avoids the pitfalls of the problematic truth claims of other ambitious but potentially pedantic counterhistories.

In regard to the narrative's depiction of King, Anderson initially portrays him as anything but a saintly or passive martyr, preferring a defiant King, one who is sardonic, sophomoric, and even salacious. For instance, early in volume 1, King and Ralph Abernathy, cofounder of the Southern Christian Leadership Conference, are walking down an Alabama street and discussing the murder of Emmett Till when a white police officer starts following them. Irritated, Abernathy scoffs, "You know how them crackers hate to see a black man hold his head up. He don't just hate it, he fears it. Probably thinks we stole the clothes on our backs from his mama"—to which King replies, "I got some advice for his mama. Next time, shut your legs" (*King*, 32). Such bawdy humor runs against the grain of the saintly figure portrayed in *Martin Luther King and the Montgomery Story* and similar versions of King—a contradiction that Anderson embraces by showing on the next page a warm domestic scene in which Coretta good-naturedly jokes about her husband's desire for twelve children (interestingly, the same number as the Apostles). King was both a womanizer and a family man, and Anderson does not shy away from the scandalous details of his affairs, peppering the biography with vignettes of his trysts. Even one of Anderson's recurring witnesses, who appears regularly to offer anecdotes from MLK's life, suggests that she had a sexual relationship with King: "I had such a crush on Dr. King. My girlfriends thought he was too dark, but I just *threw* myself at him, my God"—positioning King more as a sexual icon than a civic leader (9). Anderson embraces the contradictions of King through other personal relationships as well. We see many instances of King disagreeing fundamentally with not only his critics, but also his collaborators in the NAACP, the Congress of Racial Equality (CORE), and the Student Non-Violent Coordinating Committee (SNCC), whom Anderson often depicts as fearful and fractured. During a strategy session, Abernathy laments, "There are times I think we should have just settled for jobs on the cotton field. That life got to be simpler than this one," to which King quips, "They're still hiring, Abernathy, you want to do that so bad" (131). In other instances, these interactions take on a more sociopolitical bent, as during King's meeting with Floyd McKissick, national director of CORE, and Stokely Carmichael, chairman of SNCC, in preparation for King's Chicago Freedom Movement. Nor does Anderson shy away from the radical elements of King's politics. *King*'s third volume focuses heavily on his antiwar rhetoric and the friction that his unwavering anti-Vietnam stance caused between him and his associates.

But what differentiates Anderson's vision of MLK from many others is that he does not try to bring the shadow King into focus by offering a truer account of his life. Rather, Anderson's King is decidedly, perhaps paradoxically, both mythic in his grandeur as a spiritual leader, and exceedingly human in his fragility and imperfections. Rather than attempt to reconcile what can be known and what is imagined about the life of Martin Luther King, Anderson refuses to differentiate between the two and chooses to craft his vision of MLK in the space between. Essentially, Anderson offers a third version of MLK—a mythic King—that defies the iconic King of consensus memory while indicting the media and cultural apparatuses that propagate the easy narrative of racial healing that this version promotes. Rather than simplifying MLK's image, the mythic King builds on visual and narrative exaggeration, contradiction, and confounding multiplicity.

—

Anderson's mythic King resists offering a holistic or "true" counternarrative of his life, choosing to embrace the unknowability of America's presumed racial savior—like myth, it eschews the truth claims of traditional histories in favor of larger epistemological concerns. This is not to suggest that myth is somehow untied from or unconcerned with historical accuracy. Rather, Anderson's mythic King exposes the limitations of historical truth claims while calling attention to the manner in which such narratives are constructed, received, and reproduced. As a result, *King* is an unstable, disruptive reading experience, its narrative strategies seeking to capture a sense of who MLK was and might have been, a man rendered unknowable by the media celebrity bestowed on him in consensus memory. The solution to reductive, iconic consensus memories becomes not to counter their content, but to introduce a resistive reading practice firmly situated in an active reading of the graphic narrative mode that disrupts the ease with which such narratives are received.

Anderson signals *King*'s depiction of an essentially unknowable MLK on the first pages of volume 1. Following the prologue is a two-page sequence entitled "The Witnesses," which features nine unnamed characters offering competing visions of the life of Martin Luther King. The pages are arranged in even three-by-three rows in a nine-panel grid, drawn in stark black and white inks. The use of the nine-panel grid evokes midcentury US superhero comics, widely regarded as a uniquely American form of folklore and mythology. The grid signals to readers familiar with American comics forms a potential lionizing of Martin Luther King, one that likens him to costumed champions of comics lore. Yet unlike superhero comics, which are typically composed in a vibrant four-color palette and feature dynamic action sequences, Anderson's images are largely stagnant, featuring close-ups of interviewed witnesses and recalling the work of Harvey Pekar rather than Jack Kirby. Anderson opts for heavy black and white inks, which aim to capture a particular mood or sentiment rather than a crisp, clear vision of MLK. The interview subjects come across as wistful, pensive, skeptical, or hostile, the artwork highlighting the subjective state from which each recalls his or her account. The stark black-and-white artwork suggests that all knowledge of King emerges from the shadows of history and subjectivity, rendered by memory as much as (if not more than) by history. Tacitly, *King* asks readers to regard the man via this aesthetic sensibility rather than an easily discernible historical narrative.

The individual testimonies from the opening sequence heighten the instability in the biography's vision of King. Spread across two pages and eighteen panels, the witnesses function as a sort of contrapuntal chorus. Each recalls MLK differently, while the discrepancies achieve harmony through the visual balance provided by the nine-panel grid. MLK is regarded as both a troublemaker and an Uncle Tom, as a womanizing scoundrel and a lonely man in need of comfort, "a man devoted to peace" who nonetheless lives "a violent life" (9). Many of the voices use their recollections of MLK to reflect on their own experiences with segregation or class mobility. Some embrace integration and the improved social position it promises, while others angrily reject it. Anderson's vision of MLK, based on myth and rumor, arises from the shadows of the past, much as the testimony of the unnamed witnesses arises from the inky background of the individual panels. Perhaps the most revealing testimony comes from a weathered African American man (bearing a striking resemblance to James Bevel, the director of Direct Action and of Nonviolent Education of the SCLC):

> We weren't exactly friends. I'm not going to lie to you about that. You're in for a long wait, you expecting me to start singing his praises, 'cause Papa don't gild no lilies. Now—if perchance the *truth* is more to your liking—(8)

> He was just a man. Full stop. No better'n the rest of us. No worse'n the rest of us. Don't talk to me about myths and legends. I don't have no interest in that stuff. (9)

The man's first comment is interrupted by a speaker ruminating on the role of religion in shaping MLK's life: "That the church was what made him. It gave his whole world order, gave it balance" (9). The truth offered by the former—cut off from the rest of the text through a clever use of dashes—is rejected in favor of the mythic, religious language of the latter. Even the speaker's insistence that MLK "was just a man," while certainly true, is potentially lost in a chorus of competing voices. Implicitly, Anderson lays aside any claims to truth in his biography—not because of a lack of interest in truth, but because of the unknowability of the truth of MLK. If nothing else, Anderson leaves to the reader the choice of which and how many of these voices to believe.

The use of the witness accounts reveals how the graphic-narrative mode is perfectly suited to Anderson's disruptive tactics. "The Witnesses" visually echoes a documentary film in which a multiplicity of firsthand testimonials offer an air of veracity to the claims made by the individual project in which they appear. Anderson's images are both static and animate, and the reader's agency must work to give life to the still images within the panels as well as to navigate the multiplicity of simultaneous information offered by any single page. As Hillary Chute wonders, "Do more frames indicate more evidence? Comics, with its proliferation of frames, suggests plentitude" (*Disaster Drawn*, 16). The diversity of voices offered by "The Witnesses" seemingly suggests the sort of evidentiary plentitude on which Chute ruminates. Yet Anderson undermines even the veracity of the documentary trope of firsthand accounts. He confessed to Dale Jacobs that many of these conversations were drawn from Anderson's secondary research, with many of the more dazzling statements deliberately misattributed: "Of course the witnesses are every bit as unreliable in their role as narrators, affected by their experiences and their prejudices, right or wrong, same as the rest of us," adding, "I could use them to encapsulate a point of view, disseminate a specific bit of information, or if I came across a particularly moving quote I could assign it to one of them and the book felt all the richer for it" (Anderson, interview, 379). The witnesses, then, provide an aesthetic function more than an evidentiary role, much like *King* itself.[9]

THE HARLEM RENAISSANCE AND THE INFLUENCE OF "NEW NEGRO" SENSIBILITIES

While the narrative content of *King* pushes back against the icon of consensus memory, it is the artwork that drives the disruptive reading experience of the biography, particularly the wide range of art styles *King* employs. Anderson attributes this, in part, to the diverse array of artists who have influenced him: comics greats such as Frank Miller and the Hernandez brothers, the painters Norman Rockwell and Alphonse Mucha, and the filmmakers Spike Lee and Martin Scorsese (interview, 364).[10] In Anderson's pantheon of influences, it is perhaps the work of the Harlem Renaissance painter and commercial illustrator Aaron Douglas (whose work Anderson "loves") that provides the greatest insights into *King* (364). Born in 1899 in Topeka, Kansas, Douglas moved to Harlem in 1925 and immediately began illustrating issues of W. E. B. Du Bois's newspaper the *Crisis* and the National Urban League's *Opportunity*. He later studied under Winold Reiss, a German artist who had been hired by Alain Locke to illustrate *The New Negro* (1925). Reiss helped Douglas develop the modernist style of his early work, a style infused with African and Egyptian designs, in keeping with Du Bois's and Locke's calls for African American artists to express their cultural roots through their art. Douglas's art was so highly regarded and ubiquitous during the Harlem Renaissance, as his biographer Amy Helene Kirschke highlights, that he is regarded today as "the Father of African American art" (*Aaron Douglas*, xiv).

A close examination of Douglas's early work reveals thematic and graphic correspondences with Anderson's work in *King*. Compare, for example, Douglas's contributions to the November 1925 issue of the *Opportunity* (fig. 1.3). Like Anderson's work in *King*, Douglas's artwork is drawn in stark black and white with no shading, a style Kirschke refers to as Douglas's signature "cutout style" (*Aaron Douglas*, 80). Much like the young King in Anderson's prologue, the facial features in Douglas's pieces are drawn with thin white lines. Both pieces are heavily laden with religious imagery. In *Roll, Jordan, Roll*, a group of African Americans are cut off by four wavy lines from a radiating crown. The waves can be easily understood as representing both the Atlantic Ocean and the Jordan River, with the crown representing the kingdom of heaven (or perhaps Africa). The figures in the lower right look toward heaven with the lamentation and longing associated with the spiritual that inspired its title. *I couldn't hear nobody pray* features three weeping figures doubled over while one stands and cries out, mouth agape—frozen in a perpetual dirge. The figures stand in a plantation field before a cabin while God, drawn with the same flat black skin and white lines for facial features, attends to their pain. In *An' the stars began to fall*, Douglas employs familiar apocalyptic imagery: an angelic figure sounds a trumpet, which causes the dead to rise and

11. Douglas. *I couldn't hear nobody pray.* November 1925
© National Urban League

12. Douglas. *An' the stars began to fall.* November 1925
© National Urban League

10. Douglas. *Roll, Jordan, Roll.* November 1925
© National Urban League

1.3. Aaron Douglas's contributions to the November 1925 issue of the *Opportunity* (reprinted in Amy Helene Kirschke, *Aaron Douglas: Art, Race, and the Harlem Renaissance* [Jackson: University Press of Mississippi, 1995])

—

greet the black God from *I couldn't hear nobody pray*. As Kirschke notes, Douglas's contributions to the *Opportunity* "are meant to match the material reviewed, Negro songs and spirituals, and the style of drawing is accordingly simple and folklike, with an African influence" (73). In *King*, Anderson borrowed the cutout style to fuse historical, religious, and mournful themes.

Douglas's cutout, "folklike" style is reflected in Anderson's mythic (or folklike) depiction of the life of Martin Luther King, one that privileges aesthetic sensibility over historical commentary, without entirely eschewing either. More specifically, the wavy-line motif from *Roll, Jordan, Roll* appears in *King* immediately after the opening sequence with the witnesses (fig. 1.4). Over two pages, King dresses for his first date with Coretta Scott, whom he eventually marries. As in Douglas's piece, the scene is draped in heavy religious iconography: a cross that MLK uses as a jewelry stand, the pendant of the Virgin Mary that he wears around his neck. Wavy lines containing the lyrics of Nat King Cole's "Sweet Lorraine," playing on the radio, cut across the panels. The lines contain and transmit a hymn of sorts and unify the disparate images of MLK scattered across the pages, much as the wavy lines

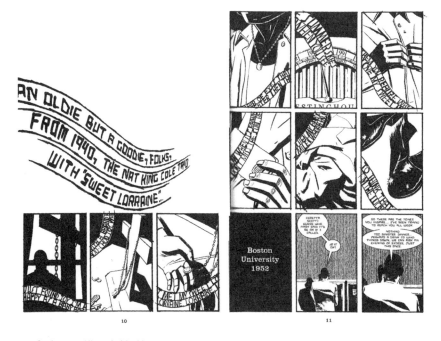

1.4. Anderson, *King*, 1:10–11

in Douglas's piece compositionally unify his work. In its religious thematics and modernist sensibilities, Douglas's work had an unmistakable influence on *King*.

The correspondence between Douglas and Anderson in fact runs much deeper. Anderson's use of a visual aesthetic closely matching Douglas's cutout style offers a window onto how Anderson approached the subject of MLK. Inspired by the cubist Georges Braque, Douglas eschewed "strong diagonals, foreshortening, and other perspectival devices that would give clear indications of depth in the traditional way of Western painting" (Kirschke, *Aaron Douglas*, 75). The lack of depth fundamental to Douglas's cutout style resonates nicely with the flat, two-dimensional image of the young King we see in Anderson's prologue. Like the cutout images in the *Opportunity*, the icon of MLK lacks depth or perspective, not by artistic choice but because of the simplification and amplification of MLK the icon in our consensus memories. Like Douglas's work, the MLK of consensus memory is two-dimensional, a reality that Anderson's use of a similar aesthetic both reflects and attempts to disrupt via the polyvocal and polyvisual nature of *King*. Finally, in depicting Martin Luther King through the lens of a Harlem Renaissance painter, Anderson creates a subtle bridge between the politics of the New Negro Movement and those of the civil rights movement, casting the latter as an extension or continuation of the former, rather than isolating the two events in discrete historical periods.[11]

POLYVISUAL NARRATIVE DISRUPTIONS

While Anderson's use of Douglas's cutout style helps him build a folklike and mythic vision of MLK, *King*'s polyvisual aesthetic suggests that even this frame might be too limited. Anderson's use of multiple styles may initially feel quite chaotic. But the artwork urges readers to embrace an unknowable vision of MLK, one that is alternately mythic, iconic, holistic, and contradictory—often at the same time. So although *King*'s primary visual mode renders MLK in a style reminiscent of Aaron Douglas's cutout aesthetic, Anderson regularly departs from this style, switching to paintings, series of distorted photographs, single panels in full color, entire sequences rendered in collage, or early twentieth-century cubism, to name only a few. Anderson attributes much of this eclecticism to his need to keep the book personally exciting. He feared burning out after a decade of working on *King*: "By that time I felt I'd put so much effort into the project that it was time to get some returns; if I was gonna do it, then it had to be fun to do. I'd always wanted to do a book where the art style was fluid, where the technique could change with every panel if that's what I wanted, a playground book, something that was pure

—

sensation and experiment, and this seemed like a good a place as any to take that approach" (Anderson, interview, 376).

Anderson's freewheeling, intuitive approach to *King*, one with no immediately evident method or pattern, both fascinates and intimidates. Often, these visual disruptions are limited to one panel, a small alteration that can nonetheless destabilize how the scene is to be read. For example, in an early scene, King mingles with the well-to-do of Boston's progressive elite, a group he considers little more than "white pseudo-liberals with their pet negroes" (*King*, 19). For the most part, the page is formally composed, employing a traditional nine-panel grid and eliminating the gutters from the top and bottom tiers. Placed over the top of the final panel is a distorted, highly contrasted photograph of a bus. The panel is out of sync with the grid, since it overlaps with the tier above it, eliminating the gutter between the second and third tiers and thereby disrupting the integrity of the grid. It is also offset, reaching all the way to the end of the page, "bleeding" off the page, as Scott McCloud puts it (McCloud, *Understanding Comics*, 103).[12] The distortion of the photograph blurs potential identifying information—the bus line, the city, and the date are all indiscernible. It seemingly exists outside the chronological time-space of the page. Given MLK's condemnation of what he views as white liberal hypocrisy represented by Bostonian elites, it can be read as invoking the racism of the city's busing crisis during its mid-1970s battles over school desegregation. Yet it is equally possible that this photograph evokes the Freedom Rides of 1961, which MLK publicly supported but did not participate in. Read in this manner, Anderson's imagery subtly undermines King's presumed moral superiority, highlighting his paternalistic relationship to grassroots movements such as CORE, which organized the Freedom Rides and often criticized MLK on similar grounds. Alternatively, it may have nothing to do with MLK whatsoever, since it can be read as a reference to Rosa Parks. However readers choose to interpret this panel, they must contend with how its presence and placement disrupt both the flow of the visual sequence and complicate its narrative content.

Altered photographs such as these are nearly omnipresent throughout *King*. Anderson visually refers to painful photographs of lynching, Emmett Till (including the infamous *Jet* magazine cover), and Rosa Parks, to name only a few. When asked about the presence of these images in *King*, Anderson contended that the choice was obvious: "Using the photos is so fundamental to how I approached the book that I don't even remember making the decision, it just always was. Looking back over the book I've come to realize that I wanted to remind people that these events actually happened to people, that they weren't just plot points in a story, and using photos and other elements seemed like a very direct, very blunt means of achieving this" (Anderson, interview, 379). Anderson's suggestion that the photographs point to a world outside the book, to the people and places that *King* depicts, echoes similar strategies from a variety of graphic novelists such Art Spiegelman, G. B. Tran, and Alison Bechdel.[13] But this stylistic choice does not explain why Anderson distorted or altered the photographs he chose to include. Since many of the images are iconic, their inclusion supports the spirit of the project in many ways. The majority of these iconic photographs represent the media filters (both photojournalism and network television news) through which the images continue to be disseminated and consumed. Since *King* is heavily invested in disrupting the iconic version of his life represented in media accounts and recalled in consensus memory, Anderson's choice to distort these photographs extends his aims. If indeed these altered photographs point to "events that actually happened," the distortion of them has the added effect of commenting on how these events are recalled and experienced by those who were not directly involved in the conflict. As Michael Chaney notes, "More than the sanctity of the life of King, it is rather the sanctity of photographic documentation and of the historical itself that this biography calls into question" ("Drawing on History," 180). Symbolically, Anderson does not distort the photographs so much as reveal their complicity in distorting the events of the civil rights movement by simplifying and amplifying them through such iconic images. In this way, Anderson highlights the dissonance between icons and the histories or lived experiences that those icons purport to represent.

Anderson's most disruptive technique may lie in how he depicts King himself. As in the prologue, Anderson prefers to ink King in deep shadow, hiding him from the viewer. When in clear view, King is often drawn without his iconic moustache or drawn to resemble Ralph Abernathy so closely that the two become nearly indistinguishable. The first "clear" vision of MLK comes well into volume 1. The witnesses return to detail the beginning of King's career as a minister at the Dexter Avenue Baptist Church (fig. 1.5). Once again, the reader encounters a standard nine-panel grid, each witness speaking from the confines of his or her panel (Anderson, *King*, 28). The two panels on the bottom left feature photographs of King, bathed in a luminous red wash, that literally interrupt the previous speaker. The first portrays King from a distance, placing the reader in the role of a congregant. The next photograph brings us close to King himself for the first time. Using a photograph here both draws us to King's familiar visage and distances us from it, placing us behind the lens of a camera. Since this is where *King* marks the beginning of MLK's career, it also suggests both a real version of the man (via the photograph) and the unavoidable distortion of the actual man

—

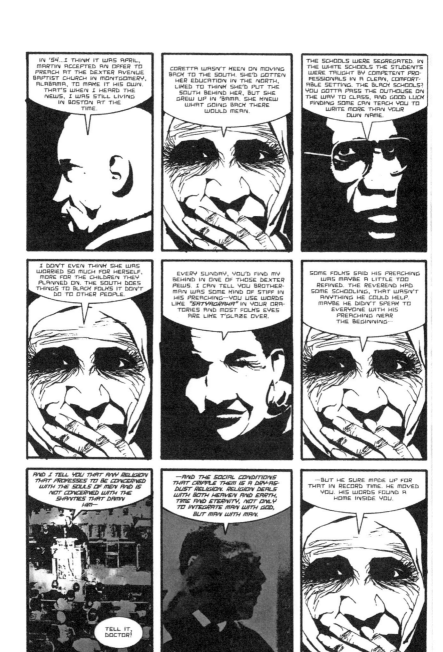

1.5. Anderson, *King*, 1:28–29

(via the alterations). The red wash predicts his untimely demise, and his death at the hands of a white supremacist is reinforced by the image of a lynching on the next page (29). Much like *King* as a whole, these panels force the reader to live in the ambiguous realm between fact and fiction.

Complicating matters further is the fact that this moment does not stabilize how Anderson depicts MLK. Rather, as the artwork of the biography grows increasingly complex, the reader is forced to constantly relocate and reidentify King on the page. In many ways, Anderson applies the multiperspectival nature of Douglas's Egyptian-influenced cutout style (an aesthetic largely abandoned in volume 3) to King on a macro level by offering many distinct and disjointed versions of its protagonist. In choosing to disrupt the iconicity of King's face in this manner, Anderson violates the principle of "iconic solidarity" outlined in Thierry Groensteen's study *The System of Comics* (1999). Groensteen contends that the foundational principle for the language of comics is iconic solidarity, defined as the use of "inter-dependent images that, participating in a series, present the double characteristic of being separated—this specification dismisses unique enclosed images within a profusion of patterns or anecdotes—and which are plastically and semantically over-determined by the fact of their coexistence *in praesentia*" (18). That otherwise disparate images can form a cohesive narrative experience because of a fundamental similarity to one another, a similarity that overdetermines all the following images in the sequence, may seem so intuitive as to warrant little comment. Yet it is precisely in the violation of this principle that *King* draws much of its disruptive force. By forcing the reader to constantly rediscover MLK throughout the book, Anderson resists the King of consensus memory. Images of King remain "disparate"—many of them represent different versions of the same subject, and others are distinct for no clear narrative purpose. These images of King and what they may (or fail to) represent force the reader to reconcile contradictions when possible and to accept others as impossibly fragmented.

DISRUPTING MEMORIES OF THE MARCH ON WASHINGTON

All of Anderson's disruptive storytelling techniques culminate in a grand and disorienting twelve-page sequence at the end of volume 2, made up of six splash pages (adjacent pages covered by one image or sequence) that depict King's iconic speech at the 1963 March on Washington. The sequence features a cornucopia of Anderson's signature modes, including traditional comics art, the stark black-and-white expressionism of Aaron Douglas, highly altered photographs, peculiar

—

panel layouts, and floating, highly stylized text. The sequence opens with a chorus of voices heralding King's arrival. Anderson begins the sequence by overlaying two "March on Washington: Jobs & Freedom 1963" buttons (*King*, 142). The buttons are translucent and slightly out of sync; one can be seen through the other. A black gutter behind the buttons dives down to the left third of the page, guiding the eyes to stark black-and-white illustrations of Mahalia Jackson belting out Harry Belafonte's "Buked and Scorned." The text of her song is unbounded by a word balloon, the grey text exiting Jackson's mouth directly and floating ethereally over the crowd and across the page. The technique recalls the wavy-line motif in the scenes of King getting dressed for a date (as well as its use by Aaron Douglas). The lyrics to "Buked and Scorned" stretch and warp as they leave the page behind, echoing, perhaps, beyond the history depicted on the page. Underneath sits a venerable Charlton Heston, who rebukes America's system of racial subjugation. Behind them both is a photograph of an immense crowd gathered at the foot of the Lincoln Memorial, altered to increase the contrast of the image, leaving only stark shades of black and white. On the opposite page stands A. Philip Randolph before a blurry, ominous visage of the sixteenth president as Randolph introduces "the moral leader of the nation" (143).

King enters the sequence on the top left of the second splash in three panels arranged down the left page, which Anderson places over two edited photographs of swelling crowds listening to King's speech, the photos cutting across both pages horizontally (144). These two pages can be read from top to bottom and left to right, a natural reading sequence that Anderson will soon disrupt. This disruption is hinted at via distortion: the top background photograph is so overexposed as to be nearly illegible, and the second is magnified in both contrast and proportion. King is introduced not in an image, but with text as the phrase ". . . Martin Luther King" hovers in the top-left corner. As in the opening sequence of the biography, we are introduced to King orally (as signaled by the quotation marks around his name) and textually (literally as text in a narrative) before we see him visually. This progression is reinforced by the text slightly overlaying the word balloon beneath, which contains the opening lines of King's speech, driving the reader to this iconic moment and the canonization it will bestow upon MLK. The first of the three panels in which Anderson presents his vision of King is the smallest, centered narrowly on an out-of-focus image of King's eyes closed in meditation as he gathers himself to speak. The next is larger, zooming out to a less distorted image of his eyes as King begins his oratory. The final panel brings King's face fully into view as we encounter the now-familiar cutout version to which Anderson often defaults. The sequence moves right, along the bottom of the page, placing us behind King as he addresses the marchers. We then follow the word balloons up to the top right, a disruption of the typical top-to-bottom reading orientation. The page is again disrupted by a high-contrast white-supremacist poster that offers both historical context and political stakes for the speech and the movement it represents.

The third splash is perhaps the most ordered of the set, since both the text and panels can be read left to right and top to bottom. In the center of the splash stands King, his black suit drawn with a few lines and largely devoid of shading, giving the impression of a minister's frock. His lectern serves as a pulpit. King's face and hands, by contrast, are pencil drawn and charcoal shaded, the increased detail suggesting that the public version of King, with which we are most familiar, is finally coming into view (146). Essentially, we have here a fully realized iconic King, based more on his public performances and media representations than on the man himself. The symbolic accoutrements of his position—the minister's frock and lectern—amplify the simplicity of this version of King, even as the increased detailing of his face implies a depth of character masked and left unexplored by the persona represented in consensus memory. Anderson places the Lincoln Memorial to King's left, dwarfed by the immense image of MLK in the center of the splash. To King's right are four orderly panels, vertically arranged, featuring photographs from the speech. The first, slightly skewed, features the crowd in the throes of vocal protest. The next is an easily recognizable photograph of King, fully realized as he delivers the most iconic line of the most iconic speech of the entire civil rights era, perhaps in all of American history. "I have a dream," King professes, over an undistorted image of the rapt audience. The final photograph returns to King, now surrounded by photographers as he shakes hands with supporters at the march. Whether this final, metatextual shot precedes the speech or follows it is left unclear.

MLK's delivery of the "I Have a Dream" speech is inarguably the most iconic moment of the civil rights era, so emblazoned in our consensus memories that it has come to represent both the spirit and the climax of the entire movement—evidenced perhaps by the memorial plaque placed at the spot where the speech was delivered. The integrationist tone of the sermon champions a vision of America where black and white children can play together, live together, and "be judged not by the color of their skin but by the content of their character" (Anderson, *King*, 148). The speech is iconic in a distinctly McCloudian sense—a minimalist image that represents a much grander and profound set of otherwise abstract and complex ideas. The speech is elegant and straightforward, and in this simplicity it finds its great beauty and power. Borrowing the resonance of that other iconic dream—the American dream—King's speech imagines a US society freed from what James Baldwin once called America's "racial nightmare," awakened to a postracial utopia (one we too often celebrate before achieving).[14] The ideas expressed in the speech—the urgent need for African American enfranchisement, its distinctly religious tenor, and the focus on, via the children of the movement, the future of American society—now encapsulate the movement in its entirety and casts King as its de facto leader and messianic martyr.

The relatively straightforward nature of the artwork, panel arrangement, and reading orientation of this sequence reiterates the simplicity of the iconic nature of the "I Have a Dream" speech. The problem is that this collapses the movement into an overly simplified and reductive narrative of integration and voter enfranchisement—eliding the more radical elements of King's politics as well as the reality that he was viewed as a troubling radical by white society during his career. The final panel of the sequence, showing King shaking hands to celebrate his newfound fame and acclaim in the midst of photographers recording the speech, underpins the notion that it is this speech that changed him from an indistinct figure to a prominent icon. Yet this panel quietly begins to disrupt the ease with which this narrative can proceed, since the panel cannot be integrated into the chronological sequence represented on the page.

With this subtle cue, Anderson leads the reader to the fourth splash page of the set—by far the most complicated and disorienting sequence in the biography (fig. 1.6). Gone is the orderly structure of the previous pages, replaced by a collage of photographs featuring distortions and alterations spilling across the first two-thirds of the splash. The top-left quarter of the page features overlaid and contrasting images of brutal lynchings, marches, and lunch-counter protests in tones of black and white. The words on the page, which contain the most oft-repeated and iconic lines from King's speech, are arranged circuitously. The speech bubbles move right to left, then top to bottom, and then back to the top, inverting the typical reading orientation of a graphic narrative sequence. Down the left side of the page, the images introduce color and text, and the sequence becomes increasingly chaotic and visually cacophonous. Beneath the image of a lynched woman at the top left, we pass through a glass window with "The Brotherhood of Sleeping Porters" etched in reverse. Through the window one can see a burning cross surrounded by the iconic white hoods of the Ku Klux Klan. The Klan members are skewed and distorted, and images of black protesters are projected onto the whiteness of the cloth. Moving right along the bottom edge, the images of the Klan members meld with a photograph of President John F. Kennedy Jr. and his brother Robert Kennedy. Half of JFK's photograph overlaps with a Klan robe, and the other half of his face is partially

—

1.6. Anderson, *King*, 1:144–145

burned away—suggesting both JFK's potential complicity in the KKK's racism as well as the Klan's culpability in the thirty-fifth president's assassination. Next to the Kennedy brothers are grainy black-and-white photographs of MLK and Malcolm X. The photograph appears cut out and photocopied from a photocopy, suggesting the image itself has become a sort of trope—constantly reiterated, out of focus, and distanced from the original moment. Taken together, the arrangement of the Kennedys, MLK, and Malcolm X echoes the arrangement of the presidents on Mount Rushmore, potentially lionizing the four men as assassinated pillars of the civil rights movement via the distortion of their media personas. This sentiment is echoed by three overlapping panels moving up from the Rushmore collage; they are bordered by black frames and arranged in a stack. The bottom two contain color-distorted photographs (one in negative, the other in sepia) of unnamed Americans listening to King's speech on television or on a car radio—iterating again how so much of what we know about King has been filtered through media sources. The altered photographs, the complexity of the collage, and the frenzied vibrancy of the sequence all express this deep ambivalence regarding such media sources of knowledge and history.

The collage not only disrupts the reading experience, but also violates Groensteen's principle of iconic solidarity on a large scale by removing all of the gutters that make individual panels distinguishable. As Barbara Postema posits, iconic solidarity cannot function without gutters and frames to create individual units for juxtaposition: "Comic panels exist together on the page *in praesentia* but differentiated from each other by empty space that becomes meaningful in its relation to the panels. Unlike the spaces between words, the space between panels does not always signify the same thing. We are faced with the necessity to *read* the spaces, as the space itself generates meaning" (*Narrative Structure in Comics*, 50). By removing the spaces that give pace and structure to a graphic layout, the sequence becomes, in some sense, unreadable—no intuitive meaning or clear narrative (as far as sequential art is concerned) arises immediately from the page. Of course, the page isn't literally unreadable. One can read the sequence without the guidance of gutters and panels to focus attention on juxtaposition, movement, and layout. Yet the reader must negotiate a historical landscape defined more by a proliferation of overwhelmingly multivalent (and often distorted) sources of information rather than simply accept the ease of narrative progression offered by the iconic history represented on the previous page. Since the collage is composed of media representations, Anderson suggests not only a distortion on the part of such mechanisms of historical documentation,

—

but a failure to legibly represent a discernible narrative of history as well. When Anderson switches back into a more traditional, sequential art mode, he implies that graphic narrative can somehow bring order and structure to historical narratives. In this instance, Anderson elevates graphic narrative above media accounts of King's life. *King* reveres the medium's ability to deconstruct historiography and demands reader participation in its reconstruction—a potential for veracity that Anderson later undermines.

In contrast with the left two-thirds of the page, the right third features a very traditional graphic layout, one large panel and four speech bubbles, showing Martin Luther King addressing the American flag (another icon) at his speech's crescendo. The move into a more typical comics mode suggests a corrective. Graphic narrative, it would seem, can order the chaos and reveal the distortion of the media filters represented in the collage on the left, as a traditional four-color panel featuring a brightly colored image of King giving the speech leads us to the right side of the page. The panel is in hues of blue and brown. As Chaney describes it, this version of King represents "one who has apparently found his public face in Anderson's painted world in three tones of opaque brown, not unlike a cartoon depiction" ("Drawing on History," 198). Chaney's invocation of the "cartoon" echoes McCloud. The image is simplified visually by its iconic aesthetic, standing out in contrast to the disordered pastiche on the left, and amplified compositionally by its location on the page as well as its relative size. According to McCloud, "The ability of the cartoons to focus our attention on an idea is, I think, an important part of their special power" (*Understanding Comics*, 31). But in this instance, the text of the speech highlighted in the panel is the most iconic element of the sequence. This lone word balloon, which overlaps with the final large panel on the right, contains a key passage from King's speech: "With this faith we will be able to work together, pray together, struggle together, go to jail together, stand up for freedom together, knowing that we will be free one day" (quoted in Anderson, *King*, 145). This line expresses many of the elements of King's career that are amplified in our consensus memories. It highlights the rhetoric of faith, integration, freedom, and American unity associated with the iconic King, who will lead American society to a postracial future. Yet as the biography (as well as the scholarship on MLK) reminds us, this version of King is remarkably and problematically limited, reduced as much as it may be amplified by such cartoonish depictions. The final image of the sequence portrays an imploring Martin Luther King building to the speech's oft-quoted climax. Drawn in the stony charcoal of the previous page, King here appears as if carved from the granite of memory, a graven image temporally frozen as both icon and memorial.

In the penultimate set of images in Anderson's "March on Washington" sequence, order is restored. Both pages feature identical three-tier layouts. The top image is a highly detailed painting of Martin Luther King in browns and blues similar to the hues used in the cartoonish panel of the previous page. Standing clearly in the foreground, King cries out his best-known prophecy: "Free at last! Free at last!" (Anderson, *King*, 146). Behind him are many obscured faces, depicted in photographic negative and in tones of sepia and blue, representing the long-forgotten victims of US racism lost to history. Appropriately, the panel bleeds off the page, evocatively suggesting that the history this panel speaks to continues well beyond the time-space of the comic. King remains clearly visible, as if rising to confront the margins of history and lead us, like an American Moses, to a promised land he will never see. This top panel also harks back to the work of Aaron Douglas, but not to the cutout style of his early years. Rather, it evokes the color palette of Douglas's series of murals for the 1936 Texas Centennial Exposition, hung in the segregated exhibition gallery called the Hall of Negro Life. For example, the mural entitled *Into Bondage* features the type of silhouetted forms found in Douglas's early work, here blended with abstracted forms and Egyptian painting to create a depth and resonance missing from his early cutout style. The images of chained slaves being driven to the auction block are painted in blue tones similar to those of the obscured faces in Anderson's "Free at Last" panel. The central figure, a tall powerful African soon to be forced across the Atlantic, does not lament his impending enslavement. Rather, he looks toward a shining star, a symbol of hope for a future beyond this terrible fate. The concentric circles radiating from the star suggest cycles and returns, the radiating light cutting through these patterns and offering the hope of escape—cutting through cycles of diasporic pain and bringing them to an end. In echoing this painting, Anderson bestows mythic prophethood on King—suggesting, for the moment, a fulfillment of the prophecy embedded in Douglas's painting.

Douglas's vision of the painting's sociopolitical purpose aligns with the goals of Anderson's work. As Renée Ater explains: "Aaron Douglas's murals stand at the intersection of the themes of the Texas Centennial Exposition: the intertwining of past, present, and future; the push toward progress and modernity; and the ideal of societal and economic transformation through industry. Although the murals were shown in a segregated space, they revealed to white and black audiences alike—almost half a million people—the epic struggle of slavery, the symbolic contributions of African American labor to the United States, and the

—

aspiration of an educated black community" ("Creating a 'Usable Past,'" 105). Douglas's murals and Anderson's "Free at Last" panel both seek to create a trajectory from past to future that offers hope to their audiences. Going further, Douglas's concerns with the acknowledgment of African American contributions, particularly to the vast outpouring of labor that built the United States, comes together with King's focus on labor and poverty, an element of his career explored fully in volume 3 of *King*. Finally, Douglas's connection with the New Negro arts movement of the Harlem Renaissance informs this scene. Central to the Harlem Renaissance was the development of a new sociohistorical sense of selfhood and peoplehood for African Americans, one that sought to reclaim the past and use it to build this new consciousness. In many ways, this sentiment reverberates throughout *King* in Anderson's efforts to liberate a central figure of African American history from the simplified and amplified narratives that have built the altogether too limited icon "Martin Luther King." In many ways, the graphic narrative's capacity for depicting multiple temporalities simultaneously, coupled by the medium's demand for active reader participation, offers the perfect mode for visually deconstructing and reconfiguring the past.

Yet Anderson refuses to grant the reader even this stability, by subtly undermining graphic narrative's propensity for creating a legible vision of King's life. After the "Free at Last" panel come the most traditional panel layouts of the "March on Washington" sequence. The splash features long panels across the top and bottom, with three vertical panels in between. I have suggested that Anderson's return to more legible layouts following the chaos of the collage suggests that graphic narrative can correctively order the media distortions that produce MLK's contemporary iconicity. Initially, these layouts suggest this dynamic, but Anderson's subverts this claim. The images beneath the "Free at Last" panel may be ordered, but the photographs in the panels, which depict cheering and adoring marchers and protesters, remain skewed—signifying that the page can reveal, arrange, and even contain media distortions, but not undo them. Slowly, Anderson removes photographs from the layout and returns to the stark black-and-white expressionism that opens the biography. This return to his previous style suggests a failure—that the narrative has returned to where it began, undermining the efficacy even of King's speech. The sequence ends on the next page, with all gutters, panels, and frames removed. Instead, volume 2 ends with a blood-splattered American flag with the words "Truth or Myth—None of that matters. All that matters is the legacy" emblazoned across it. Through the absence of any graphic narrative elements in this final image, Anderson seems to abandon this mode of storytelling—proposing its lack of efficacy. Yet the single line of narration dispenses with such fretting, imploring

—

the reader to realize that what matters is not how these histories are disseminated, but how King's legacy informs our future by calling us to put into action the lessons of the past. Graphic narrative, as much as any other medium, must be judged by how well it can serve these ends.

THE DEATH OF THE ICON

As if to disrupt even this easy platitude, *King's* third volume showcases Anderson "playground" sensibilities, switching up his style regularly. It focuses largely on elements of King's career elided by consensus memory—such as his adamant opposition to the Vietnam War, his clashes with Stokely Carmichael and the Black Power Movement, and his troubled Chicago Freedom Movement. These moments of King's life are afforded as much weight as his iconic speeches, which is shown simply by time and space allotted to King's final years. King's activist goals were met with resistance in the increasingly complicated political landscape of the late 1960s, and the artwork grows increasingly complex to reflect this reality. The biography ends, unavoidably, with the assassination of Martin Luther King on 3 April 1968 in Memphis, Tennessee, by a sniper's bullet. Anderson illustrates his death from two perspectives. The first, on a black page with two round panels, depicts King in the crosshairs of the sniper's scope, placing the reader in the perspective of James Earl Ray, King's assassin (Anderson, *King*, 225). The next page opens on a four-panel sequence spread across two pages, similar in layout to the prologue. Here, we see the world through the eyes of MLK, the first such instance in the biography. Across the four panels, we see a panicked Ralph Abernathy enter and exit the sequence, bleeding panels growing increasingly red as MLK bleeds to death on the second-floor balcony of the Lorraine Motel. The following two pages contain a single image, a red and purple abstract expressionist painting by Anderson. On it, in a small white font, are three pieces of text. The first repeats the opening lines of the Memphis police report of MLK's death. The next line, near the center of the painting, holds MLK's final thoughts ("Daddy . . . is this real? . . ."; 228). The image contains no panels, no borders, no gutters, reflecting the timeless nature of whatever may lie beyond. The floating text is the only element of sequential art present on the page.

The final piece of text on the painting begins on the bottom right, the corner a reader might grip while holding the page, and continues onto the next page. Here, Anderson returns to the Nat King Cole song that played while MLK dressed for his first date with Coretta. The ethereal text, drawn with the same wavy-line motif, implies the completion of a tragic cycle: "Once again folks . . ." On the following

—

pages, a splash features the shadow of a cross in black with a chain draped across its crossbeam, reiterating the themes of slavery and faith, as in Douglas's *Into Bondage*. To the right of the cross stands Martin Luther King, again a boy, as the lyrics to Nat King Cole's "Lorraine" drift across his body. The use of the song connects the first time we see Martin Luther King as an adult to the last time, a thematic element reiterated in the biography's final page. The top tier of the page features the same three panels as the first scene containing the lyrics to "Lorraine," their orders reversed. The first panel shows an open hand clutching a pendant of the Virgin Mary, followed by that same pendant draped on the cross that MLK used as a jewelry stand, and then, finally, the shadow of MLK underneath the same cross and the same chain from the previous page. Essentially, the biography ends as it began, in shadow. Anderson implies that King remains as unknowable in death as he did in life. The remaining two tiers, more than half the page, are blank, left as incomplete as the King's mission.

With this enigmatic ending, Anderson implies a cycle. By returning us to a moment before the iconic career of Martin Luther King began, Anderson displaces King from the limited chronology in our consensus memories. It also suggests that the struggle for civil rights is perpetual, and did not begin and end with King's career. King may have extended the scope of the struggle to include more actors, more agency, and more avenues toward justice, but he failed to break the cycle. Anderson denies the reader a traditional sense of narrative closure by breaking the expected linearity and teleology of a traditional biographic arc. Although the top tier of the final page positions the reader as the inheritor of this cycle, the blankness of the page suggests incompleteness—an unfinished project that the reader must symbolically complete. In this sense, Anderson offers the reader a different, graphic sense of closure. According to McCloud, closure describes the process by which a reader can take the disparate images of sequential art and "connect these moments and mentally construct a continuous, unified reality" (*Understanding Comics*, 67). In this sense, the ending of *King* offers readers a space within which to imagine the continuation of the civil rights movement into their contemporary political moment, the opportunity to participate in a new myth of MLK, one allegiant to the legacies of the movement rather than simplified narratives or historical authenticity.

This was not the original ending to *King*. The first version was a four-page vignette depicting scenes of contemporary, everyday racism. A young black boy fights with another young boy over a basketball, an Asian storeowner accuses a young black mother of shoplifting (who responds by mocking the former's broken, accented English), and police officers in squad cars follow a group of young men of color (echoing the similar scene in volume 1 with Abernathy and King). The following page is a vibrant painting of flames emanating from a burning cross with King's fiery words juxtaposed across the painting—"Thank God Almighty . . . We are free at last" (*King*, vol. 3, 84–85). This original ending undermines the entirety of King's career, suggesting abject failure rather than the ambiguity and incompleteness offered by the revised ending. As Anderson acknowledged, he found this ending excessively dark:

> Regarding the specific revision you mentioned, removing the scenes of contemporary racism, when I read the comic as a whole I just didn't feel those scenes fit. The whole book was about King and his immense struggle, and yet the original ending, which mirrored the opening's contemporary setting, seemed to be saying his struggle hadn't amounted to shit. And that just didn't seem like the right tone to end the story on. It seemed to betray their sacrifices somehow. I wanted a little bit more of a note of hope at the end so I replaced those scenes with the ending we have now. I don't know if it's a better ending, but it felt more like the right one. And once I'd made the decision to use an alternate ending suddenly the contemporary beginning didn't seem to fit either. (Anderson, interview, 377)

Anderson's concern and ambivalence in regard to how to end *King* reflects two of the biography's most glaring limitations. First, the focus on "King and his immense struggle" places the biography squarely in the tradition of "great-man" history—unintentionally isolating King from the larger movement he tacitly represents. While the biography pushes back against this tendency by highlighting King's personal conflicts with a wide cast of fellow activists, it nonetheless concerns itself with its primary and titular figure. Second, without its narrative frame of contemporary racism, *King* runs the risk of reiterating the logic of hope that too often underwrites claims that the United States has become a US postracial society, a vision proffered by many who appropriate the memory and politics of Martin Luther King to make such claims. The next chapter focuses on *March*, the three-volume autobiography of Congressman John Lewis, which seeks to avoid the pitfalls of great-man history while visually rejecting claims of a contemporary postracial United States.

—

CHAPTER 2

Bleeding Histories on the *March*

T he final pages of *March*, John Lewis's three-volume graphic memoir of his time as a civil rights activist, reflect solemnly on the inauguration of Barack Obama, forty-fourth US president, and its potential meaning for the legacies of the civil rights movement. What might occasion a celebration opens in mourning. The comic follows the congressman upstairs to his bedroom, where, in a silent panel at the bottom, he soberly and somberly contemplates the significance of the day's events (fig. 2.1). The panel's borders are hazy, and the encroaching inkiness of the black page adds a claustrophobic melancholy to his muted introspection. A blinking phone interrupts the congressman's thoughts, and a message from Senator Ted Kennedy plays on the following page: "I was thinking of you. I was thinking of you and Martin. I was thinking about the years of work, the bloodshed . . . the people who didn't live to see this day. I was thinking about Jack and Bobby . . ." (Lewis et al., *March: Book Three*, 245). The congressman, still silent, is visibly struck by the weight of these memories of loss and grief. As if to echo Kennedy's recollection of the blood spilled to reach this watershed moment in US racial history, the panel itself *bleeds*, spilling beyond the gutters to the edge of the page. The enigmatic ellipsis at the end of Kennedy's message suggests, paradoxically, both a perpetual mourning for those lost to

2.1. John Lewis, Andrew Aydin, and Nate Powell, *March: Book Three*, 244–245

racial violence and an incomplete process of recollection of those sacrificed for the nation's redemption. The memoir's epigraph, dedicated "to the past and future children of the movement," reminds us that to effectively anticipate the future, we must first grieve the past (*March: Book One*, 3).

The tone of this final scene may feel incongruous, given the presumed celebratory feelings brought about by the election of the nation's first African American president. Yet Lewis refuses to reflect long on the traumas of the US racial past, at least not while a new consensus narrative of an American future purportedly beyond the strictures of race was beginning to unfold. Accordingly, *March* does not linger on mourning. The bleeding edge of the final panel leads to the next page, where the scene is the congressman's DC office on the day after the inauguration. The darkness of the preceding black pages are replaced by bright white backgrounds, a clearly signaled shift in tone. Here, Lewis discusses next steps with his aide Andrew Aydin, cowriter of Lewis's memoir alongside the visual artist Nate Powell. "It's not going to be like yesterday," Aydin ruminates, to which Lewis responds, "There's no way it could be, Andrew—yesterday was something else" (Lewis et al., *March: Book Three*, 246). "Yesterday" is left deliberately ambiguous—it could refer to the previous day's ceremony or, more wistfully, to all the yesterdays of the past—yet what is certain is that Obama's election potentially signals the beginning of some new era, or at least the closing of a previous one. Certainly, the racial landscape of the United States shifted tectonically with the ascension of the nation's first African American president. The task at hand requires Lewis and Aydin to contend with the changes, to trace the contours of this apparent new stage in American history. It is in this context that Lewis returns to a seemingly whimsical notion. "We have to tell the story," Lewis urges. "People are gonna laugh at us. They're gonna say you've lost your mind," Aydin responds. "It won't be the first time, sonny boy," Lewis counters as he enters his office (246). That idea? A comic book.

Lewis's imperative "to tell the story" implies a tale untold.[1] Framed by the election of the forty-forth president, *March* details Lewis's memories of his time as a central figure in the civil rights activism of the 1950s and 1960s. His memoir recounts in painstaking detail and harrowing visuals Lewis's path from young farmhand to civil rights leader. *March* is Lewis's second such memoir; *Walking with the Wind: A Memoir of the Movement*, which covers much the same ground as *March*, was published 1999 to high praise. Given this fact, the notion that the story of the civil rights movement remains untold is, at least initially, a curious one. The narrative, or at least the popular version of it, can be quite a familiar one. Even the title of the memoir evokes one of the most familiar strategies of civil rights activism—a notion reinforced in the book's preface, which opens with the violence at the Selma marches. More curious still is the placement of this page at the end of the novel rather than the beginning, since it functions as a sort of preface to the project. Yet by the end of the memoir, the reader realizes that this is not the rosy, familiar narrative of civil rights found in our consensus memories. While *March* depicts many of the well-documented flashpoints of the movement, the narrative contextualizes these events through the experiences of actors perhaps unfamiliar to casual readers. The title evokes a sense of militancy, functioning as an imperative—*March*-ing orders perhaps—for the highly dedicated, well-trained, and disciplined army of nonviolent resistance whose story the memoir tells. In essence, *March* is more than the memoir of one great man—it is the biography of a movement.

In addition, the final page enigmatically calls into question the validity of the graphic narrative form to tell this story in the first place. Aydin's concern that "people are gonna laugh at us" reveals a potential insecurity. After all, aren't comic books for kids?[2] (No.) Aydin's concerns come across as surprisingly outdated, not to mention unfounded.[3] Yet it is impossible to deny that Lewis had young readers in mind when composing the memoir, as the epigraph to *March* makes clear. The frame narrative of Obama's inauguration reinforces this. *Book One* opens with

—

Lewis meeting with a pair of young African American boys and sharing stories of his time in the civil rights movement.[4] The children seem generally uninterested in Lewis's framed photograph of Martin Luther King's "I Have a Dream" speech, and much more curious about Lewis's collection of chicken-themed knickknacks. This disparity cues the memoir to move into its primary narrative. Although *March* was clearly written with children in mind, it is hardly child*ish*. The memoir is emotionally and psychically challenging, laying bare the violence faced by the civil rights movement. From hauntingly familiar martyrs such as Emmett Till, to lesser-known victims such as the murdered voter registration volunteers Mickey Schwerner, Andy Goodman, and James Chaney, *March*'s depiction of the violence faced by the movement is frank, visceral, and difficult to witness. Often, the memoir pauses on these visual depictions of violence via a bevy of graphic narrative techniques, asking the reader to reflect on the images' enduring effect on the American psyche. In this vein, Powell's layouts and panel work, particularly his use of bleeding panels, are integral to showing how memories of this violence linger in the present moment. Furthermore, Powell's use of the bleed functions as a key strategy in *March*'s attempt to reject a narrative of civil rights that culminates with the inauguration of Barack Obama and a new era of postracial prosperity. Make no mistake, the histories contained in *March bleed*.

Before delving directly into the visual and narrative strategies employed by Lewis, Aydin, and Powell, I first map *March*'s relationship to other examples of comic art that participate in similar discursive interventions. Of great significance not only for *March*'s narrative priorities but also for Lewis's activist and political career is the 1957 comic book *Martin Luther King and the Montgomery Story*. As a young man, Lewis read the comic book and told Grace Bello that it inspired him to answer the comic's call for nonviolence and social change:

> Lewis says of reading the comic back when he was a teenager, "It was part of learning the way of peace, the way of love, of nonviolence. Reading the Martin Luther King story, that little comic book, set me on the path that I'm on today." But *Martin Luther King and the Montgomery Story* was only the beginning of the story; much of the struggle was yet to happen: the student sit-ins, the March on Washington, Bloody Sunday, and the Selma to Montgomery marches. Lewis was a key figure in all of these events. (Bello, "Comic Book for Social Justice")

As Bello suggests, in many ways Lewis completes the history begun in the 1957 comic that inspired *March* by focusing on the contributions made by actors

—

other than MLK, thereby resisting the impulse to write great-man history. Before exploring how Powell uses subtle panel work, particularly the bleed, to resist this narrative, this chapter demonstrates how the single-panel political cartoon often functions in ways antithetical to *March*'s vision of the movement and its legacies. These single-panel cartoons propose a civil rights history that culminated with Obama's inauguration, framing America's racial sins as contained in a bygone past. *March*, on the other hand, identifies the graphic narrative mode not only as an ideal way to disseminate history (particularly to young people), but also as a site for correcting distortions and simplifications of that history.

THE GREAT-MAN HISTORY OF *MARTIN LUTHER KING* AND *THE MONTGOMERY STORY*

It was graphic narrative, *March* hints, that put Lewis on the path of antisegregation activism in the first place. In the first book of *March*, Lewis cites the 1957 comic *Martin Luther King and the Montgomery Story*, given to him by the pacifist and activist Jim Lawson, as a key inspiration: "Jim Lawson conveyed the urgency of developing our philosophy, our discipline, our understanding," Lewis writes, "His words liberated me. I thought, this is it . . . this is the way out" (77–78). Published by the Fellowship of Reconciliation (FOR), a group committed to nonviolent resistance, *The Montgomery Story* features two comics that left an indelible mark on John Lewis's career and his memoir.[5] The first details the budding career of a twenty-nine-year-old activist named Martin Luther King Jr., who by 1957 had risen to prominence as a nonviolent integrationist. The second story, narrated by MLK, offers pedagogy over biography, outlining MLK's "Montgomery Method," which serves as a handbook of sorts, detailing the philosophies of nonviolence, and offering a step-by-step guide for confronting racial discrimination in one's own community.

The influence of the Montgomery Method story on *March* is immediately evident. Immediately after mentioning the comic, the memoir depicts Lewis gathering a group of like-minded students and ministers to attend one of Lawson's nonviolence workshops. *March* shows Lewis and his compatriots practicing the fourth step of the Montgomery Method, which urges budding activists to "try and practice situations as we did in Montgomery" and to "make sure you can face any opposition without hitting back, or running away, or hating" (Lewis et al., *March: Book One*, 19). But what is limited to a single panel in the FOR comic is expanded in *March* to demonstrate what this process looks like in practice. The reader observes the black and white participants in Lawson's workshop abuse

—

each other with racial epithets, cigarette smoke, ice water, and even physical violence in preparation for the dehumanization they will face at the hands of violent segregationists. By dramatizing the Montgomery Method, *March* expands on, or even completes, the FOR comic's instructional goals.

The narrative of the emerging civil rights movement offered by the FOR's comic (published nearly a decade before the legislative victories of the 1964 Civil Rights Act and the 1965 Voting Rights Act) features a surprisingly optimistic tone—unlike that of *March* in many respects. The cover of *Martin Luther King and the Montgomery Story* purports to tell "How 50,000 Negroes Found a New Way to End Racial Discrimination." The comic's contents focus largely on the story of King himself rather than on a larger image of the movement. After all, he literally speaks for the entire movement in the second story included in the comic. The opening lines of the first story make this clear: "In Montgomery, Alabama, 50,000 Negros found a new way to work for freedom, without violence and without hating. Because they did, they put new hope in all men who seek brotherhood, and who know you don't build it with bullets. No one person made the Montgomery story, but one man's name stood out among the hundreds who worked so hard and unselfishly. That man was 29-year-old Martin Luther King, Jr., minister of the Dexter Avenue Baptist Church and President of the Montgomery Improvement Association" (Fellowship of Reconciliation, *Martin Luther King*, 5). While the book acknowledges that the Montgomery bus boycotts represented a shared victory for "the hundreds who worked so hard and unselfishly," it nonetheless participates in great-man history, which highlights the accomplishments of exemplary people (typically, men) who changed the course of their times. The hopeful tone, which suggests that readers will be able to "end racial discrimination," is mirrored in the comic's narrative. The story closes on a scene of two white detectives amid the wreckage of MLK's bombed-out home, declaring that acts of violence against African Americans must stop. "These bombings are giving Montgomery a bad name," the detectives lament, and since "the bus fight is over anyway," the integrationists had won (13). The task was to join the civil rights movement and stand on the right side of history. This easy path to racial enlightenment is echoed in the final panel: the story's smiling, unnamed narrator decides to cheerfully throw away his gun as he boards an integrated Montgomery bus.

Now, I do not mean to chastise a sixty-year-old comic for its historical or philosophical limitations. After all, at the time of the comic's publication, Martin Luther King and the Southern Christian Leadership Conference's victories in desegregating Montgomery's local bus lines certainly merited both recognition and emulation.[6] Yet in setting up MLK as the representative icon of the entire

—

movement, the comic inadvertently slights the contributions of countless actors whose sacrifices were invaluable to the civil rights movement's successes.[7] Furthermore, the comic's hopeful, even lighthearted tone masks the daunting amount of violence faced by civil rights activists at the time (and anticipated to come). Fifty years later, *March* expanded the narrow scope of *The Montgomery Story*'s vision to include less celebrated actors and reject a similar, postracial optimism.

Therefore, MLK's biography in the first half of *Martin Luther King and the Montgomery Story* bears the greater importance for *March*, since the memoir writes back against the comic's great-man history in significant ways. First, although *March* is the memoir of a specific man (John Lewis), its commitment to detailing the scope of a movement in which he participated avoids the trappings of the great-man approach to historical narrative. Lewis dedicates much of his memoir to less celebrated civil rights activists such Bob Moses, who organized voter registration in Mississippi, and Bayard Rustin, the principal organizer of the 1963 March on Washington, whose role in the narrative of the march has been minimized in large part because of his homosexuality.[8] Great-man history tends to be explicitly gendered, focusing on the contributions of heteronormative white male agents, but Lewis commits much of *March* to detailing the contributions of important female activists such as Diane Nash, a founder of SNCC; Fannie Lou Hamer, who represented the Freedom Democratic Party at the 1964 Democratic National Convention; and Margaret Moore, who inspired the Teacher's March of 1965.[9] Second, Lewis's memoir rejects the hopeful, even naive tone of FOR's comic, favoring a harrowing, often brutal retelling of the civil rights movement's key moments. Finally, in linking the movement to the inauguration of Barack Obama via the memoir's frame narrative, *March* comments on and ultimately rejects the narrative of a postracial United States—something of a great-man vision of the future.

Perhaps the most evident way that *March* resists telling yet another great-man version of the civil rights movement comes in its minimization of Martin Luther King—the great man himself. *March* positions MLK as a spokesman and spiritual adviser rather than as the messianic martyr of consensus memory. In the leadoff volume, MLK appears only once, when John Lewis meets him for the first time and is immediately starstruck (Lewis et al., *March: Book One*, 69). He reappears three times in the next book, first to urge Attorney General Robert Kennedy to send the National Guard to protect the Freedom Riders (Lewis et al., *March: Book Two*, 85), then to decline direct participation in the rides themselves (90), and again throughout the planning and execution on the March on Washington (146), which culminates with his oft-quoted "I Have a Dream" speech (173). The final volume likewise features MLK only thrice: once at the beginning, to eulogize the four young girls that fell victim to the 16th Street Baptist Church bombing (Lewis et al., *March: Book Three*, 17), toward the end of the narrative as part of the march to Selma (229), and, for the last time, at the signing of the Voting Rights Act (243). In fact, the memoir is heavily invested in recuperating the memory of Malcolm X, whom Lewis came to admire. Even this move can be read as a reaction to the great-man history represented by MLK hagiographies, since consensus memory often posits King and Malcolm X as diametrically opposed. I do not mean to suggest that Lewis somehow resents Martin Luther King or that the latter's minimization in *March* should be seen as dismissive or hypercritical, since he is generally treated with respect (although, in my opinion, not reverence). And while Lewis's memoir does not shy away from implicitly criticizing King in specific moments (as when he declines to participate in the Freedom Rides), what animates *March* is the desire to give a broader impression of the movement. Positioning MLK as simply one actor, albeit an important one, in the story is an extension of the memoir's larger goals.

RESISTING THE INAUGURATION OF A POSTRACIAL SOCIETY

Of greater interest is Barack Obama's role in *March*. The story of his inauguration frames the memoir, a narrative choice that evokes the specter of postracialism. As David P. Redlawsk writes in the introduction to *Political Psychology*'s special issue "The Obama Presidency," "Not long ago his election would have been improbable at best—only a little more than a generation has passed since the American civil rights act, and the gains made by racial minorities in the United States have come in fits and starts at best" (935). Flashes of the events of 20 January 2009 pepper the memoir, calling our attention to Obama's election at key moments of violence or racial strife, such as the beating of civil rights activists in Montgomery and Selma, or the bombing of the 16th Street Baptist Church. These instances are simultaneously celebratory and sorrowful; the memoir both lauds what the election of a black president means for the uplift and enfranchisement of the country's African American community and mourns the blood spilled to reach that pinnacle. The scenes often function contrapuntally, the celebratory nature of the inauguration scenes being undercut by depictions of the escalating violence against civil rights activists. Yet by employing this narrative frame in the first place, Lewis echoes an emerging discourse that sees Obama's election as evincing the dawn of a long-anticipated postracial age in the United States.

The notion of a postracial society did not begin with the election of Barack Obama, but that event provided a satisfyingly symbolic moment from which to write an accompanying historical narrative—one that has often evoked the civil rights movement as the moment's forebear. Obama's election prompted the nation to wonder what the event portended for race relations in the United States. Many looked to his ascent as marking the dawn of a postracial epoch. Gregory D. Smithers describes such claims as built on the belief "that nineteenth- and twentieth-century ideologies of racial essentialism are inconsistent with the multiracial contemporary American society" ("Obama and Race," 2). As the literary critic Jessica Wells Cantiello notes, others hoped the election of Obama signaled not a post*racial* society, but one that would be, at last, post*racism*, meaning that race would be only a neutral element of one's identity and no longer an organizing principle for politics or power (Cantiello, "Pre-Racial to Post-Racial," 168). For example, data from a Pew Research Center poll conducted within a week of the election revealed that 52 percent of Americans believed that Obama's victory signaled a significant improvement in race relations nationwide (Smithers, "Obama and Race," 2).[10]

Numerous editorials in print, on television, and on the Web contemplated, and even celebrated, the advent of this new age, each inflected with varying degrees of postracial sentiment, from naive exuberance to measured hopefulness. For example, in response to Obama's first State of the Union address, Chris Matthews, host of MSNBC's *Hardball*, stated ingenuously, "I was trying to think about who he was tonight. And, it's interesting, he is post-racial, by all appearances. You know, I forgot he was black tonight for an hour" (quoted in T. Lee, "Somewhere over the Rainbow?," 137). Tina Brown of the *Daily Beast* went as far as to connect Obama's election not only with America's troubled history of racism, but with the mounting challenges of international terrorism as well: "This was 9/11 in reverse. The last time I turned round and saw so many people behind me, it was that terrible day in New York when the twin towers burned and we poured out of our offices downtown and swarmed up Fifth Avenue. Then the faces were distraught. Now they were joyful. Then America had been assaulted by terror. Now it had been renewed by hope" ("9/11 in Reverse"). This outlandish sentiment was reiterated by Oliver Roy and Justin Vaisse of the *New York Times*, who believed Obama could use his status as the "first 'post-racial' president" to help the United States enter a "post-civilizational" age, when it would not treat Islam as a monolithic "source of the main problems on the planet" ("How to Win Islam Over").

Others took a more measured tone, such as Michael Eric Dyson, who struggled to assess the weight and significance of the moment in a *Los Angeles Times* editorial: "Contrary to many critics, his election does not, nor should it, herald a post-racial future. But it may help usher in a *post-racist* future. A post-racial outlook seeks to delete crucial strands of our identity; a post-racist outlook seeks to delete oppression that rests on hate and fear, that exploits cultural and political vulnerability" ("Race, Post Race"). Howard Kurtz of the *Washington Post* likewise tried to maintain a healthy skepticism, railing at the hopelessly positive responses to Obama's election, but nonetheless claiming that racial politics had definitely changed: "[Obama] didn't run as a black candidate. He ran as a politician who happened to be black. And so our journalism must be color-blind as well" ("The Clock Is Ticking"). Still, Matt Bai of the *New York Times* went as far as to openly consider whether the election meant the "end of black politics," since (according to the article) many young African Americans had begun "to embrace the idea that black politics might now be disappearing into American politics in the same way that the Irish and Italian machines long ago joined the political mainstream" ("End of Black Politics?"). Whatever the specifics of the editorialists' arguments, the theme remained largely the same: the long-anticipated era of America's racial redemption had finally (hopefully) arrived.

Many of these articles make explicit connections between Obama, Martin Luther King, and the civil rights movement, framing Obama's inauguration as the ultimate culmination of the struggle. In an op-ed for the *Los Angeles Times*, Shelby Steele wondered, "Does his victory mean that America is now officially beyond racism? Does it finally complete the work of the civil rights movement so that racism is at last dismissible as an explanation of black difficulty?" ("Obama's Post-Racial Promise"). Dyson pointed out a similar trajectory, reaching as far back as America's history of slavery: "Obama's historic win is the triumphant closing of a circle of possibility begun when former slaves boldly imagined that one of their offspring would one day lead the nation that enslaved their ancestors. In 1968, the Rev. Martin Luther King Jr. met a bullet in resistance to his dream of equality; 40 years later, Americans cast their ballots to make Obama president. The distance from King's assassination to Obama's inauguration is a quantum leap of racial progress whose timeline neither cynics nor boosters could predict" ("Race, Post Race"). Bai's article looks not to King but to his contemporaries, and he opens with anecdotes from Congressmen James Clyburn of South Carolina and John Lewis of Georgia. Both openly reminisced about King's legacy. While Bai sometimes questions the validity of a historical narrative that suggests the civil rights struggle ended with the election of Obama, his use of the framing anecdotes speaks to the civil rights movement's legibility in regard to the emerging discourse of postracialism.

The concept of a postracial era is not a recent phenomenon, as the field of critical race theory, a theoretical framework with a foundation in legal studies,

—

has made clear. Much of the logic and rhetoric of postracialism finds its underpinnings in the language of color-blind political philosophy—a logic that too often seeks to mask the realities of race rather than move past them. As David Theo Goldberg explains in *The Racial State* (242), this rhetoric works to blind society to the issues facing peoples of color, rendering "the structures of racist exclusion and derogation less visible." Derrick A. Bell, a foundational contributor to critical race theory, offers an even bleaker view: "Statistics on poverty, unemployment, and income support the growing concern that the slow racial advances of the 1960s and 1970s have ended, and retrogression is well under way" ("Who's Afraid," 2). I don't raise these issues in order to litigate the legitimacy of postracial fantasies or to insist on the reality of the racial problems facing the United States—such vital and urgent work continues to be done in a large number of academic and public venues. Rather, I highlight a troubling narrative myth of history built on our consensus memories of the civil rights era. We might think of this narrative as giving rise to a potential consensus present of assumed racial harmony. It is this narrative that *March* seeks to undermine through the power of Lewis's recollections and the subtlety of Powell's visual narrative techniques. As Derek Parker Royal has argued, "Such visual strategies are an essential component of multi-ethnic graphic narrative, writing that by its very nature relies upon themes of cultural context and contingency to create meaning" (introduction, 10–11). But even if the comics medium can stultify an emergent postracial consensus present by making the contexts and contingencies of such a simplified teleology visible, we must nonetheless contend with the ways in which the medium participated in the consensus-building process. I refer specifically to the multitude of newspaper comics published during Obama's presidential campaign that both reflected and produced the postracial myths *March* seeks to undermine.

HISTORY AS A CARTOON: TOWARD A THEORY OF SINGLE-PANEL TELEOLOGY

Dozens of politically charged single-panel cartoons appeared in major newspapers and Web outlets across the country on Election Day, 4 November 2008, and on 20 January 2009, the day of Obama's inauguration.[11] While not all of them were celebratory (many were satirical, divisive, or explicitly partisan), a great many were rife with what one might refer to as postracial imagery.[12] In particular, many of these cartoons feature Abraham Lincoln, crediting the sixteenth American president with the future ascension of the forty-fourth. For example, Dave Granlund of the website Political Cartoons depicted Obama with his hand on the Lincoln Bible, and Lincoln at Obama's shoulder, supporting the first African

—

American president. John Darkow of the *Columbia (MO) Daily Tribune* depicted Obama at the Lincoln Memorial sharing an enthusiastic thumbs-up with the statue of Lincoln. Jimmy Margulies of the *Hackensack (NJ) Record* produced an image of the Emancipation Proclamation, its text replaced by Obama's memorable campaign slogan "Yes We Can!" Other cartoons offered a wider historical, even prophetic scope. David Fitzsimmons of the *Arizona Star* depicted Obama being sworn in while standing on a "mountaintop" of red names listing important African American leaders, evoking both the stripes of the American Flag and a red-letter edition of the New Testament. Steve Greenberg of the *Ventura County (CA) Star* showed Obama bursting forth from the pages of a history book, which, interestingly, is drawn to strongly resemble a comic book (fig. 2.2). The photographs in Greenberg's cartoon function like panels in a sequence that tells the story of African Americans' struggle for civil rights. As an expression of consensus memory, the photographs capture those moments most ingrained in the American collective consciousness of the African American experience—slavery, lynchings, Jim Crow segregation. The final photos feature familiar figures of the civil rights movement such as the Little Rock Nine, Rosa Parks, and, of course, Martin Luther King. Obama enters the scene on the top right, bursting forth in full color, contrasting strongly with the black-and-white spread and suggesting

2.2. Steve Greenberg, *Ventura County (CA) Star*, 2008

an end to a world seen primarily in tones of black and white. Obama not only completes the history of the African American struggle for equality, but also, it seems, literally and even gleefully escapes from it.

Greenberg's use of the graphic narrative form implies both sequence and narrative: the images tell the story of the African American struggle for civil rights, which climaxes with the arrival of Barack Obama. Yet the single-panel cartoon has typically not been considered a fully formed iteration of the graphic narrative medium, since the comics form is built on multiple panels in sequence. McCloud makes this distinction when discussing single-panel comics such as *The Family Circus*: "There is a long-standing relationship between comics and cartoons— but they are not the same thing" (*Understanding Comics*, 21). As Groensteen's principle of iconic solidarity claims, a multiplicity of distinguishable images and frames in recognizable patterns that create sequence and narrative is essential to the comics form (Groensteen, *System of Comics*, 19). McCloud and Groensteen distinguish the cartoon from the comic on the grounds that narrative and time must be played out over the space of the page via the juxtaposition of multiple visual narrative units. Even McCloud's preferred term for graphic narratives, "sequential art," makes this clear. In short, the single panel may be related to the comics form, but without the ability to create sequence or chronology, it falls short of accomplishing the work of the medium.[13]

Yet, it is precisely because of these limitations that the single-panel cartoon warrants closer examination in the context of postracial sentiment. The results of such of an investigation offer insights into the narrative strategies employed by *March* to avoid the pitfalls of postracial sentiment. As McCloud and Groensteen make clear, temporality in the comics form is inextricably linked with the acts of closure made necessary by the gutters that join otherwise disparate images. And while Groensteen states that sequence does not necessarily overdetermine narrative, because of the reader's active participation, "it is between the panels that the pertinent contextual rapports establish themselves with respect to narration," "narration" being defined as the story's forward momentum through time in its arrangement across the page (*System of Comics*, 107). If the presence of multiple panels in juxtaposition drives the temporality of the medium, then we might consider the single-panel comic to function atemporally—devoid of chronological movement or momentum. This is not precisely true, however, since movement can exist within a single panel, and movement implies traversing space across time, a progression offering something of a microchronology. As Charles Forceville, who draws on cognitive theory and conceptual metaphors, notes: "The TIME IS SPACE metaphor is a very important one in the American action comics . . . Time and space, in turn, are crucial building

blocks in the image schema of CAUSE-EFFECT. After all, only an event A that has preceded an event B could have caused that event B, whereas the reverse is not true. . . .
Awareness of these two schemas helps comics readers understand sequences of
events, and their causal relationships—even if these events are depicted in a single
panel" ("Conceptual Metaphor Theory," 102; citations in the original deleted). So,
while sequence across juxtaposed panels remains essential to the magic of graphic
narratives, Forceville suggests that the arrangement of discrete panels is not the only
way to represent linear time across the space of the page. This notion is particularly
useful for unpacking Greenberg's Obama cartoon for the *Ventura County (CA) Star*.
The photographs within the single panel function almost like micropanels, offering
a microcosm of history. And, as Forceville notes, the reader can detect a distinct
cause-and-effect relationship. Placing the images in the cartoon's microsequence
implies such an effect, suggesting that the history of the African American struggle
for equality caused the Obama election. A dawning era of postracial harmony
would then be the long-term effect.

But Greenberg's cartoon is not sequential art, not exactly. It is still clearly
visible as a cartoon to any reader. In this sense, it functions as what Groensteen
describes in "Narration as Supplement," as "a single drawing [that] can synthesize
a complete anecdote, and exhaust the content of a micro-narrative" (167). Yet
Groensteen still sets these "micro-narratives" aside, contending that it is the
proliferation of a multiplicity of "figurative drawings" (in this case, panels) that
generates narrative sequences (167). In this sense, these single-panel cartoons
function as microhistorical narratives, neatly contained and without needing to
"proliferate" beyond the edges of their designated time-space. In regard to the
postracial sentiment of the cartoons described above, we might further imagine
these images as functioning not outside a sense of temporality, but within a completed one, as the expression of a terminal teleology. In other words, the single-
panel cartoon doesn't express a moment outside time, but one that completes it.
Furthermore, the single-panel cartoon eliminates the gutters that prompt a reader
to commit moments of closure, or "the act of 'filling in any connections which are
required,'" as Mario Saraceni describes it ("Relatedness," 123). The micronarrative
of the single-panel cartoon, then, eliminates the need for closure on emotional,
historical, and narrative levels. The single panel not only contains a particular history, but also symbolically closes off active reader engagement with that history.

As expressions of the culmination of America's racial past, these single-panel
cartoons should be read not as solitary images, but as symbolic final panels closing
off the narrative of the African American struggle for equality. They do not deny
history—they mark its end. It should therefore come as little surprise that of all the

historical references made by the multitude of political cartoons commemorating Obama's election, the most common by far was Martin Luther King. If Obama's election indeed provided closure (on emotional, narrative, and sequential levels), then the single-panel cartoons punctuated the termination of civil rights history. This reading would explain why so many of these comics are intentionally messianic and prophetic in tone, featuring MLK gazing approvingly down from the heavens. For example, another cartoon by Steve Greenberg, this one done while he was a freelancer, depicts MLK gazing at the White House from the clouds, admiring the Obama campaign poster hung from its rafters. Joe Heller of the *Green Bay (WI) Press-Gazette* draws MLK's offering a thumbs-up from the heavens, echoing Darkow's enthusiastic Lincoln Memorial cartoon. Other cartoons feature both Lincoln and King in a similar style, such as ones by Nate Beeler of the *Washington (DC) Examiner* or Peter Broelman, an Australia-based freelance cartoonist, who both illustrate Obama's swearing-in with the ghosts of Lincoln and King at his back. Even international outlets got into the act. The *Calgary (AB) Star* featured a boyish Barack Obama being helped up to the pedestal of history by a larger-than-life MLK, and David Lewis, another Australia-based freelance cartoonist, drew Obama as a child watching MLK deliver his "I Have a Dream" speech on television.[14] While the cartoons range from spiritual to humorous in tone, the theme remains the same. The invocation of MLK functions as form of iconic shorthand for the entirety of the African American struggle, and the arrival of Barack Obama signals an end to that history. These single-panel cartoons, then, offer a culmination of the civil rights movement, neatly contained in an atemporal frame and ready to be enshrined in our consensus memories, its project now complete.

By positioning Obama's election as the apotheosis of the movement's goals, this condensed narrative invariably frames the struggle for racial equality exclusively as a matter of voter enfranchisement and legislative representation—a central pillar of postracial logic. As Rodney E. Hero and Caroline J. Tolbert contend in their study on the reactions to Obama's reelection: "A common, and compelling, narrative in the public discourse is that America has become a 'post-racial' society as demonstrated in back-to-back elections of an African American president and seventy-three African American and Latino members of Congress, a record, serving in the U.S. Congress" ("Race and the 2012 Election," 628). While the election of these officials certainly represents an undeniable gain for their constituents, the suggestion that this achievement somehow signaled the end of racism as we know it feels helplessly naive in the face of the racial strife of the early twenty-first century.

Perhaps the most exemplary of these cartoons came from Dave Granlund, who draws side-by-side portraits of Martin Luther King Jr. and Barack Obama

2.3. Dave Granlund, PoliticalCartoons.com, 2009

(fig. 2.3). King is positioned on the lower left, his familiar visage looking left as if gazing toward the future. Granlund places 1963, the year of MLK's iconic speech at the March on Washington, on the far left, with the phrase "I have a dream . . ." hovering overhead. Level with MLK's eyeline is the presidential seal of inauguration. Obama is positioned to the right of the seal, slightly elevated above MLK, hinting at the upward trajectory from the events of 1963 to those of 2009. Beneath Obama, Granlund places the phrase ". . . come true," with the year of Obama's inauguration to the far right. The completed phrase, "I have a dream . . . come true," proffers the full realization of King's dream of a future America where children "will not be judged by the color of their skin but by the content of their character." By linking the realization of the dream with the election of the first African American president, Granlund defines civil rights activism as a movement motivated primarily by voter enfranchisement and political representation, which was a central concern of the movement, but hardly its only priority. Going further, the simplified, easily contained consensus narrative suggested by cartoons such as Granlund's elides the years of racial violence faced by the movement, in favor of a sanitized, and completed, version of this same history.

BLEEDING BEYOND TIME: *MARCH*'S REJECTION OF A POSTRACIAL CONSENSUS

Just as much of the work of postracial consensus memory happens within single-panel cartoons, much of *March*'s attempt to undermine this narrative likewise happens at the level of the single panel. Powell bleeds John Lewis's experiences in the civil rights movement into the election of the forty-fourth president of the United States in order to resist the postracial narrative that accompanied his inauguration. In "Time Frames," the fourth chapter of *Understanding Comics*, McCloud explores the techniques that comics artists employ to depict time and motion in what is essentially a static medium made up of juxtaposed images. Rather than assume that individual panels represent individual moments in time that are stitched together via gutters and layouts into linear time, McCloud insists that "time in comics is infinitely weirder than that" (94). The size of individual panels, the presence or absence of prose text within the panels (which can exist only in time, according to McCloud), and the arrangement of the panels affect the temporal structure and pace of both the individual comics page and the overall narrative. McCloud's description of panel bleeds bears the greatest significance for *March*: "When 'bleeds' are used—i.e., when a panel runs off the edge of the page . . . time is no longer contained by the familiar icon of the closed panel, but instead hemorrhages and escapes into timeless space. Such images can set the mood of a sense of place for whole scenes through their lingering timeless presence" (103). Panel bleeds, which defy or alter graphic temporality by breaking out of the temporal structures of the page's gutters and layout, offer Lewis and Powell a method to comment visually on the implied teleology leading from the civil rights movement to the presidency of Barack Obama. Unlike the succinct history of the single-panel cartoon, the histories held within the panels of *March* refuse to be contained and placed neatly into a presumptive postracial narrative.

Powell bleeds civil rights history into the twenty-first century from the very first pages of *March*. The story opens on a bleeding panel of a familiar scene— John Lewis and fellow activists marching from Selma to Montgomery, attempting to cross the Edmund Pettus Bridge (Lewis et al., *March: Book One*, 5). The top panel bleeds to the left and right edges, and down into the background as well. The bottom panel, neatly bordered, contains images of the state and local authorities who will soon brutalize the marchers. The bleed leads to blood as the following pages depict the infamous violence of the "Bloody Sunday" attacks of 7 March 1965. The last two pages of this opening sequence feature a variety of closed panels, skewed and overlapping, as protesters attempt to flee the violence contained within the panels (fig. 2.4). The scant dialogue on the pages is overwhelmed by the onomatopoeic cracks of the officers' batons and their hissing canisters of tear gas. The final page features three panels of varying size. The first shows an officer catching Lewis by the ankle. The next panel bleeds to the right of the page as the officer drags Lewis out of the frame, his arms blending into the white background of the page as the shadow of the officer, baton raised, looms fearsomely overhead.

2.4. Lewis, Aydin, and Powell, *March: Book One*, 8–9

The third panel is small and blacked out, contained by a faint white border. The whiteness of the background shifts to black along a ragged line, giving the impression of a panel at the bottom of the page. This panel bleeds to the bottom edges of the page and leads us to the memoir's title page: a shot of the Washington Memorial at sunrise with "MARCH" emblazoned across the sky like an order from the Lord for the marchers (and readers) to proceed.

Beneath the title at the bottom of the page, the Lincoln Memorial, draped in shadow, looks across the National Mall toward the Washington Memorial. In the distance sits the US Capitol, the sunrise behind it signaling new beginnings, new cycles—and, perhaps, new revolutions. All three sites bear enormous significance for America's racial history, from the founding of the nation to the emancipation of the slaves to the location of the inauguration of the first African American president. Placed together, these sites imply a teleology, the lines of the images drawing the eye from the Lincoln Memorial directly to the Capitol. Yet the time of the image is left unclear. The reader is left to decipher whether this is an image of the morning of the March on Washington (which preceded the march to Selma) or of Obama's inauguration (which came much later), or of another day entirely. This image, too, bleeds—no gutters are present on the page. Read in this manner, the image suggests not teleology but simultaneity, implying that the histories represented by each structure overlap and coexist in time rather than follow one another in any discernible temporal trajectory, not unlike the representation of time in a single-panel cartoon. What differentiates this title page from those cartoons is the bleed, which resists the containment of history and guides the reader beyond its bleeding edge. Turning the page, we encounter still another bleed. The top panel situates us firmly on the morning of 20 January 2009 in Lewis's DC home as he prepares to attend the inauguration. Placing the time stamp here and not on the title page ensures that the moment depicted on the title page remains ambiguous, suspended in the unbounded temporality of the bleed.

Powell employs these sorts of bleeding transitions throughout all three volumes of *March*. Perhaps the most powerful instances appear in a sequence near the middle of *Book Two*, which depicts the violence visited upon the Freedom Riders on two occasions (14 and 20 May 1961) in segregated Alabama. The Freedom Riders consisted of a group of thirteen civil rights activists (seven black, six white) that sought to challenge the nonenforcement of the US Supreme Court decisions in *Morgan v. Virginia* (1946) and *Boynton v. Virginia* (1960), which ruled segregated buses unconstitutional.[15] Arranged by James Farmer, director of the Congress of Racial Equality, the riders planned to travel from Washington, DC, to New Orleans, Louisiana, stopping in major segregated southern cities along the way—that is, until the riders ran afoul of the notorious Bull Connor and the Alabama chapter of the Ku Klux Klan. Designated riders rode in integrated pairs in the front of buses. Other members rode in the back in observance of local segregation laws; they would report back to CORE if the group met with resistance or arrest. The Freedom Riders met with resistance before they reached Alabama (John Lewis was assaulted in South Carolina), but it was in the "Heart of Dixie" that the violence reached its bloody zenith.

The first incident happened in Anniston en route to Birmingham on Sunday, 14 May 1961—Mother's Day. Connor, the elected commissioner of public safety of Birmingham, granted members of the local KKK chapter fifteen minutes of undeterred mayhem directed at the Greyhound bus carrying the Freedom Riders. The Klansmen attacked the bus not long after the riders left the terminal at Anniston, slashing its tires, firebombing the crippled vehicle, and barricading the doors in an attempt to incinerate the riders inside. Blessedly, no one was killed, due in large part to warning shots from responding highway patrolmen, who protected the riders from potential lynchings.

Lewis missed this leg of the journey; he was in Philadelphia interviewing for a volunteer program in India administered by the American Friends Service

Committee, a Quaker-run organization (Lewis et al, *March: Book Two*, 42). While he had planned to rejoin the riders on the day of the attack, his group "never made it to Birmingham" (43). The pages in which Lewis considers moving abroad are drawn on black paper; two long panels over the top third of the last page depict him contemplating his decision. As McCloud suggests, long panels often signal a pause in the perception of time (McCloud, *Understanding Comics*, 101), and here the length of the panel heightens the contemplative nature of Lewis's decision. Even more powerful is the space below this image, which Powell fills with billowing smoke from an unknown source. This image is unframed by panel borders, an unboundedness that, McCloud suggests, lends such images a "time-less quality" (103). In this instance, we might think of the moment as refusing to conform to linear time, since the smoke enters the layout from the following page, which shows the riders as seemingly out of time. The following two-page spread reveals the source of the smoke in one silent image: a Greyhound bus, ablaze in the midday Alabama sun after the KKK's attempted immolation of the Freedom Riders (fig. 2.5). Powell places the bus at the bottom center of the page, black smoke pouring out of broken windows. The Freedom Riders are foregrounded, desperately fleeing the blaze. In the background, armed Alabamans brandishing

2.5. Lewis, Aydin, and Powell, *March: Book Two*, 44–45

bats, rifles, and pipes charge the riders, seeking to inflict further harm. The black smoke darts up and to the left, as if fleeing the arsonists on the bottom right. The pages' composition balances tones of black and white, since the black smoke remains clearly divided from the negative white space of the page by thin black lines—a color scheme rich with metaphorical resonance.

The image of the burning bus functions as both a narrative and a visual preface to the assault on the riders in Birmingham on May 20. First, while the image might rightfully be considered a splash (one consistent image or sequence spread over two pages), it also functions like a lingering single panel. The image is wordless—no dialogue or narration—evoking a silent persistence. According to McCloud, "When the content of a silent panel offers no clues as to its duration, it can also produce a sense of timelessness. Because of its unresolved nature, such a panel may linger in the reader's mind. And its presence may be felt in the panels which follow it" (*Understanding Comics*, 102). The silence of this image certainly produces a sort of timelessness, as does the absence of any time markers such as gutters or overlaid panels, which would normally guide the reader past the image at a deliberate pace. Likewise, the violence depicted remains unresolved, since the reader enters and leaves the scene in media res. This single image echoes photographs of the burning bus taken by local photographers at the time, giving it a prominence that asks the reader to linger on its significance. Further, the echoing of photographs of this event implies distance in time and place between the viewer of the image and those depicted—a distance that slowly collapses as the memoir proceeds.[16] The image of the burning bus appears throughout *Book Two*, most prominently on the book's cover.

The image does more than simply hemorrhage and escape into timeless space, however, since smoke from the burning bus interrupts the previous page's layout. Besides asking us to symbolically linger on the page, the burning bus compels our attention, having drawn us in from the previous page. The splash skews the traditional forward (left-right) narrative orientation, demanding that the reader recontextualize the consecutive scenes in juxtaposition with each other. Like the single-panel cartoon, this image can be read as a micronarrative, since there is enough movement on the page to imply chronology. Yet the bleeding edges of the page refuse to close off this history, which reaches back to the past (on its left edge) while simultaneously driving us toward the future (on the following page). Going further, the absence of gutters offers no opportunity for closure but, rather, forestalls it, implying a moment of closure yet to arrive.

The subtlety of Powell's panel bleeds permeates the entire memoir, particularly in *Book Two*. Bleeds allow the artist both to access the notion that Obama's inauguration signaled the beginning of a postracial United States and to subtly reject that same claim. For example, the first page of Book Two features a mostly blank page showing a silent solitary bus driving away from the Montgomery city limits; on the following page, we are transported to 20 January 2009, to a close-up of Congressman Lewis shaking hands with a colleague. Both images, unbordered, are separated by a blank page, symbolizing the missing history that March fills in. In a sense, the lonely bus at the bottom of the first page traverses the blankness of the following page and figuratively drives the reader directly to the future inauguration of an African American president. This subtle arrangement cues the reader into reading these disparate moments in time in the context of each other, much in the same manner that time functions between bordered panels on a single page. Like the frame narrative itself, the arrangement of these moments implies a teleology—that the forward momentum of the Freedom Rides somehow culminated with the election of a black president, propelling the advent of a supposedly postracial society. Yet the absence of temporal structures suggests a narrative still in negotiation, a history still being written, and an indeterminate teleology still in flux.

The implied teleology of the frame narrative initially appears to reiterate a postracial sentiment. As the Freedom Riders face escalating violence, the temporal structure of the narrative continues to deteriorate, with moments in time haunting one another. In response to the violence at Anniston, James Farmer (at the behest of Attorney General Robert Kennedy) called off the Freedom Rides, fearing for the lives of the participants. Diane Nash, an activist with the Nashville Student Movement, urged Farmer to allow the Rides to continue, to which he responded, "You . . . you realize it may be suicide? You could be massacred" (Lewis et al., March: Book Two, 49). In a pair of panels, Nash responds, "We realize that—but we can't let them stop us with violence. If we do, the movement is dead" (50). The first panel is long, featuring Nash nervously peering out her window, suspicious of surveillance by the US government and fearful of the potentially violent end awaiting the Freedom Riders. The next panel moves us farther away, and we see Nash framed by the window to her home, the bricks of the building fading into the white background of the page, isolating her even further. The edges of the panel appear unfinished, suggestive of the continued work needed to bring the goals of the riders into view. The scene is interrupted by an unframed image of a loudspeaker peeking in from the lower right, blaring the words "Ladies and Gentlemen—" before continuing onto the next page, "The President-Elect of the United States, Barack H. Obama" (51). Nash's fears for the future of the movement are interrupted by the first appearance of Barack Obama, his presence symbolically reassuring her that the efforts and sacrifices of the riders will be validated. Placing them together in sequence frames Obama's inauguration as the culmination and validation of Lewis, Farmer, and Nash's student-led activism. To reinforce this notion, Obama's first words express gratitude to John Lewis for his efforts and then ask the congressman to pray for him (51).

After Obama's first appearance in *March: Book Two*, the memoir returns to the plight of the Freedom Riders and a history that does not rest, unwilling to be contained by the past. In a brutal nine-page sequence, Powell captures the overwhelming violence enacted upon the riders by the Alabama segregationists who ambushed them at a Montgomery bus station. The scene is both jarring and tragically familiar. The rioters accost riders of both races, journalists and cameramen, and even the federal agent John Seigenthaler—to whom *Book Two* is dedicated (77). The illustrations of this scene are appropriately disturbing and chaotic, featuring multiple skewed panels, floating unbordered images, and bleeds. A particularly unsettling moment features a young boy gleefully clawing at the eyes of a rider as his father cheers him on: "Git him! Them eyes—git them eyes" (75). Drawn facing the reader, the young boy menaces the page; the perspective puts the reader in the place of the rider and symbolically subjects the reader to the same violence. As if to heighten the tragic absurdity of this exhilarated young boy's viciousness, an African American cab driver refuses to help the riders escape unless the white passengers exit the vehicle, in observance of an Alabama law that forbids integrated cab rides. The white passengers stay behind with Lewis and are severely beaten until Floyd Mann, a public safety officer, fires a warning shot into the air, demanding that the rioters disperse before someone is killed (78). The sequence closes on a quiet shot of the Greyhound station in the aftermath of the mob's violence: bodies, blood, and automobiles lie strewn across the pavement. The panel bleeds to both edges of the page, with a lone word balloon waving, like a flag, across the tragic tableau, the lyrics to "America," rolling ironically across the scene.

The word balloon bleeds, too, stretching across the entirety of the page from left to right, simultaneously swaying back into the past and lurching toward the future. The next two pages, a splash, feature an unbordered image of Aretha Franklin belting out "America" at Obama's inauguration (fig. 2.6). The celebratory tone of Franklin's rendition is undercut by overlaid images of the aftermath of the Montgomery bus attacks. The lyrics to "America" curve around the images as if to both avoid these memories and accommodate them. The memories are boxed in discrete panels, dispersed in three diagonally adjacent pairs. The panels feature victims and perpetrators alike: elated segregationists, their bloodied victims,

U.S. CAPITOL, WASHINGTON, D.C.--
11:41 AM, JANUARY 20, 2009
SWEET LAND OF LIBERTY, OF THEE I SING;
LAND WHERE MY FATHERS DIED, LAND OF THE PILGRIMS' PRIDE FROM EV'RY MOUNTAINSIDE
LET FREEDOM RING!

2.6. Lewis, Aydin, and Powell, *March: Book Two*, 80–81

and indifferent police officers. The young boy from the previous page stares in dismay at the blood on his hands as his father places a conciliatory hand on his shoulder to reassure him of the righteousness of their violence. The panels are silent, contrasting mightily with the exuberance of Franklin's singing. Further, the panels feature no gutters or intuitive arrangement and feature no clear chronological structure. Rather, the panels and the memories they contain haunt the celebration, a racial trauma that lingers despite the potential for (post-)racial reconciliation represented by the inauguration.

These individual images function narratively like single-panel cartoons. All are neatly contained by the borders of their panels, implying fixity, even completion. As individual micronarratives, however, they offer little in terms of meaning or chronological content, since they contain little or no movement. And although they proliferate, as Groensteen puts it, across the page, they do not offer any clear narrative sequence and resist the cause-effect relationship outlined by Forceville. This layout destabilizes any narrative claims that event A (the civil rights movement) led directly to event B (the inauguration of Obama and the postracial era) by visually disrupting this teleology. Overlaying these small panels on the larger image of the inauguration celebration eliminated any gutters, forbidding acts of emotional or narrative closure that a more traditional arrangement might promote. The word balloon that contains Franklin's singing bleeds to the edge of the page, as if to push past the discomfort of this layout, as if hoping to flee these memories, but it fails to avoid the darkness and dangers of the dire past. The next page switches from a white background to deep black. The words "Oh Let Freedom Ring" arc over the top of the page, partially obscured by the smoke pouring forth from the mouth of a Molotov cocktail. A lone hand hurls the homemade explosive toward the next page, striking Montgomery's First Baptist Church, where the reeling Freedom Riders sought sanctuary and refuge, its blast ringing through its rafters (Lewis et al., *March: Book Two*, 83). While Obama's first appearance in the memoir imbues the scene with the potential for hope and change, the persistence of the memories of America's racial past reverberate into its idyllic future. In *March*, the past bleeds into the present, staining the future with its inescapable traumas.

The climax of *Book Two* draws all these threads together and weaves them into the volume's most powerful rejection of a postracial sentiment that would consign America's past racial sins to oblivion. *Book Two* closes with MLK's iconic speech at the March on Washington, followed directly by Barack Obama approaching the inauguration lectern where he delivered his own iconic speech at the Capitol (176). The parallelism *March* establishes between MLK's "I Have a Dream"

—

speech and Obama's inauguration speech mirrors the postracial logic found in the single-panel cartoons that appeared nationwide on 20 January 2009. This logic is reiterated by the graphic composition of the page: Obama is placed on a lone white page featuring one long panel that strongly resembles a single-panel cartoon. Facing to the right of the page, as if looking toward the future, Obama begins his speech. The word balloons enter from the top of the panel's frame, as if drawn into the panel itself, contained by the moment and ready to be pasted into our scrapbook of iconic consensus memories and then placed on the shelf. But on the far left, the word balloon bleeds, and Obama's words carry us not to the future, but to the past—specifically, to Sunday, 15 September 1963—to an unnamed man in a phone booth preparing to make a call. The open phone booth resembles an uncontained bleeding panel. The phone call represents a gesture to orality, of an open correspondence between the past, the present, and the future. The reader turns to the final page to a sequence of bleeds that fail to contain the explosion at Birmingham's 16th Street Baptist Church, carried out by four KKK terrorists, which claimed the lives of four young choir girls practicing hymns (178).[17] One panel depicts the man in the phone booth being blown clear of the page, the phone he holds severed from the line. Subtly, *March* suggests, the tempting reconciliatory tone of postracial sentiment does little more than sever a dialogue with the past, potentially erasing "the sacrifices borne by our ancestors," sacrifices that Obama's speech sought to honor, not forget. Rather, Powell's visuals maintain, the inauguration did not heal America's racial traumas, but rather reopened the wounds to bleed this history into the present.

As McCloud suggests, bleeding panels give the reader a sense of something unresolved, much as the issue of race in the United States remains largely unsettled. In these moments, *March* reveals a tension at its heart. The ascension of the nation's first African American president only a generation after the Freedom Rides represented an astounding validation of their good work. In many instances, *March* celebrates this watershed moment in the centuries-long struggle for African American enfranchisement and uplift. Yet in doing so, the memoir risks engaging, even unintentionally, in the postracial discourse that casts Obama's presidency as marking the end of racism, thereby not only commemorating the struggle for African American rights, but celebrating its end as well. If *March* wanted to imply that Obama's presidency marked the end of racial strife in the United States, it could have arranged its story chronologically. But the disruptive chronological sequencing on both macro and micro levels, made legible by graphic narrative composition, allows the memoir to resist such naiveté. Rather, Lewis and Powell frame Obama's inauguration not as a

—

culmination of the fight for civil rights, but as its continuation from a higher standpoint. In this vein, *March* functions as important connective tissue, linking the hopefulness of the Fellowship of Reconciliation comic of the past, which inspired readers such as Lewis, to readers facing contemporary challenges in the present. *March*, much like the bleeding panels that permeate its pages, refuses to allow the history of the African American struggle for equality to rest within the designated boundaries of the past.

Ultimately, *March* frames postracial sentiment not as naiveté, but as temptation, an enticing salve that is ultimately cosmetic rather than truly therapeutic. Yet the memoir is not devoid of instances of postracial logic. *March* largely succeeds in complicating claims of postracialism built on simplified historical frames culminating in Obama's inauguration. It nonetheless falls into the trap of framing increased governmental representation as the primary goal of the movement. For example, *Book Three* focuses largely on voter-registration initiatives, the controversy surrounding the 1964 Democratic National Committee,[18] and the 1965 Voting Rights Act. The memoir closes with the signing of the act and Lewis claiming, "It was the last day of the movement as I knew it," without elaboration (243). Ultimately, *March* becomes the story of African American political enfranchisement, a narrative that minimizes or elides concomitant movements focused on poverty (such as Martin Luther King's Poor People's Campaign), black liberation movements spearheaded by Malcolm X or Stokely Carmichael, or the antiwar movements that overlapped with them all. And while it is often critical of the great men of civil rights history, either subtly, as in its minimization of MLK, or directly, as in its condemnation of Lyndon B. Johnson, it does not extend this treatment to Barack Obama. By the book's publication in 2013, concerns over the Obama administration's racialized implementation of drone warfare in the Middle East and the expulsion of record numbers of undocumented immigrants, a large majority of whom were of Latin American or Hispanic descent—factors that further undermine claims of a postracial United States—were being widely discussed, but *March* does not comment on them. And for all its symbolic reclamation of the civil rights past in order to inform the future of US race relations, the book fails to gesture to contemporary racial inequities such as the plight of the children facing deportation (known colloquially as Dreamers, after the DREAM Act) or to movements such as Black Lives Matter, which emerged at the time of the book's initial release. These issues fall outside the narrative and chronological scope of *March*, but not outside the purview of its readers in 2013. These issues inescapably bleed back into readers' participation in the construction of *March*'s vision of the past and the present.

—

Furthermore, the memoir frames the civil rights conflict as primarily a black-white struggle. And though this was largely the case, contributions by Latinx or Asian American groups active at the time go without mention. A focus on increased representation by African Americans in federal arenas of power under-cuts the book's desire to celebrate the contributions of women, since all three branches of the government remain disproportionately male. Even the 115th Congress, sworn in in 2017 and hailed as the most racially diverse one to date, features thirty-one male African American congressmen to only eighteen female. Unavoidably, perhaps, *March* privileges the ascension to the status of political insider of some of those previously marginalized, rather than focusing on the net gains of the movement's many actors and their constituents. It is in this context that we turn to Lila Quintero Weaver's *Darkroom: A Memoir in Black and White* (2012), a memoir that hopes to expand the scope of our consensus memories to include perspectives and experiences that tend to fall out of the narrative vision of otherwise impressive counterhistories such as *March*.

CHAPTER 3

On Photo-Graphic Narrative

"TO LOOK—REALLY LOOK" INTO THE *DARKROOM*

E arly in Lila Quintero Weaver's *Darkroom: A Memoir in Black and White* (2012), the author-artist stands in her father's darkroom as he develops a photograph. In a scene rich with metaphorical resonances, the first panel covers two-thirds of the two-page spread, the scarcely lit darkroom's red safelight glowing softly white in the memoir's grayscale tones. In the center of the image stands a young Weaver, dutifully heeding her father's lessons as he instructs her on how to develop photographs. Weaver writes, "Once developed, the negatives were ready for the enlarger. Clear patches in the negatives let a blaze of light pass through, invisibly transferring the image onto the paper" (15). Many of the images in this scene preface the memoir's historical interventions.

Weaver sets out to narrate an iconic civil rights story—the death of the activist Jimmie Lee Jackson, which sparked the highly documented Selma marches of 1965. What differentiates Weaver's account from the one recalled in our consensus memories, or in other graphic memoirs such as John Lewis's *March*, is Weaver's commitment to speaking from a perspective unheard in most civil rights accounts—that of a Latina immigrant. In this sense, Weaver "enlarges" the narrative to include such previously elided voices, symbolically rendered as her father "transfers" his own narrative authority as the family documentarian to his

—

daughter. Given her father's photojournalistic contributions to these histories, his lessons prepare his young daughter to be not only an active agent of history, but its author as well. Simultaneously, *Darkroom* reveals the constructed nature of such histories by revealing the "clear patches in the negatives" where the light of Weaver's account can shine through. The panels to the right of the page, small at first and slowly increasing in size, reflect the importance of process in the creation of narratives of history. By calling attention to process itself, Weaver reminds the reader of the indebtedness of civil rights history to material forms of documentation such as the photograph, which is as susceptible to elision and editorializing as all other forms of media. These elements of *Darkroom* are heightened by Weaver's rejection of the implicit authenticity of the photographic archive in favor of her graphic art to fill the gaps in a civil rights narrative that has excluded Latinx contributions and experiences.[1]

Darkroom: A Memoir in Black and White chronicles the arrival of Weaver's Argentinean immigrant family in Marion, Alabama, at the height of the 1960s US civil rights movement. The narrative's subtitle highlights the ambiguous "sliver of gray" that Weaver feels her family occupied in Alabama society—neither black nor white, yet somehow, even paradoxically, defined by a juxtaposition between the two (19). The tenuous position of her family in a black-white society troubled Weaver's budding political consciousness, and her light skin often barred her from participation in the civil rights activism of her African American friends and classmates. The title of the memoir indicates its debt to an extensive, often black-and-white photographic archive of the civil rights movement. In particular, photographs taken by her father, a pastor and photojournalist, are re-created in Weaver's realistic aesthetic throughout the narrative. Initially, these re-created photographs chronicle the family's journey from Argentina to Alabama. They then corroborate her family's presence at civil rights demonstrations—in particular those that led to the iconic Selma marches of 1965. By reproducing the documentary contributions of her father, Weaver brings to the fore often unheard and unseen Latinx contributions to the civil rights movement, made outside of a strict black-white positionality.[2]

Without deliberately differentiating between the two, Weaver blurs the line between photographs and graphic narrative as potential sources for articulating family history. *Darkroom* does more than borrow the implicit authority of photographs to document her family's immigration to the United States or to authenticate her narrative of civil rights activism. After all, if Weaver had just wanted to detail her family's journey or substantiate her presence at these marches, she could have produced the actual photographs rather than generate

—

pencil drawings. Instead, her drawings of photographs pull together the personal and social themes the graphic memoir pursues. Photographs taken on school picture day frame Weaver's struggle to locate herself in a stark black-white dichotomy, bringing her work in line with Latinx literary traditions that explore the midcentury US racial binary.[3] Furthermore, Weaver's drawings of photographs pull from real images (that exist outside the narrative) and imagined ones. Drawn photographs allow her to augment an expansive civil rights photographic archive by highlighting gaps in the historical record, particularly in regard to the Marion marches, which resulted in the unseen death of Jimmie Lee Jackson. I refer to Weaver's aesthetics as "photo-graphic narrative," a style that blends re-created photography with original drawings (also often depicted as photographs) to blur the line between photography and graphic narrative as methods for writing history.[4]

As signaled in the scene in her father's darkroom, Weaver's concerns are ultimately pedagogical, and the didactic nature of her memoir is only thinly veiled. In an early section entitled "The Lesson," Weaver recounts taking art classes, as a child, in which she began to learn how to properly draw human bodies. Despite recounting a personal memory, the section is narrated in the second person, and coaches the reader to draw a human figure as an instruction manual might. She learned an important lesson from these classes: "As you learned to look—to *really* look—you began to see the wishful thinking behind the formula" (Weaver, *Darkroom*, 57). By using the second-person point of view, Weaver's imperative to the reader becomes clear. The symbolic representation of a human being through art, particularly in such idealized modalities, amounts to little more than empty artifice that constricts possibilities, much as race constricted the possible identity formations available to Weaver in Marion. For Weaver, the photograph came to represent how these idealized visions of race and history conspired to elide her potential contributions to the national narrative of civil rights, largely because of her ambiguous position within a stark midcentury US racial dichotomy. Consequently, Weaver's interrogation of the photograph simultaneously invokes the potential complicity of the viewer of the image in assigning racialized meanings to such representations. Weaver ultimately challenges her readers to "really look"—a signal to develop a self-awareness concerning their own interpretations of race and history. She hopes to train her readers to see the necessarily constructed nature of race in the United States and to consider how race's accompanying historical narratives are likewise constructed (57).

—

WEAVER'S METHODOLOGY, *ON PHOTOGRAPHY*, AND AN ETHICS OF SEEING

To elucidate how Weaver constructs her photo-graphic narrative, I draw from Susan Sontag's landmark essays collected in *On Photography* (1977). Like Weaver, Sontag frets over the fact that the photograph is "treated as a narrowly selective transparency," masking its artistic origins and political choices (6). Sontag reminds us that while photographs may function as "experience captured," they are also a product of artistic endeavor—that photographs are as much artifice as artifact. She argues that while the industrialization of the camera promises to "democratize all experiences by translating them into images," the making of photographs still occurs in the context of power, privilege, and access (7). To create a photographic record "means putting oneself into a certain relation to the world that feels like knowledge—and, therefore, like power" (4). Photographs, then, do not reveal the world as it is, but rather construct it according to the epistemology of the photographer. While Hillary Chute argues in *Disaster Drawn* that the comics form is "conspicuously drawn by hand and this inherently reject[s] transparency" (198), Weaver sidesteps this potential pitfall by consistently making us aware of both process and creator. By including metamoments that highlight *Darkroom*'s constructedness, Weaver exemplifies Chute's insistence that "nonfiction comics call crucial attention to the fact that in any medium or genre, 'accuracy' is always an effect" (199). These insights, which align well with Weaver's narrative goals, texture this reading of *Darkroom*. Drawn photographs cannot disguise their artistic origins and can therefore address Sontag's concerns over transparency. The juxtaposition of Sontag and Weaver reveals representational strategies at play throughout *Darkroom*'s interrogation of the photograph.

Furthermore, both Weaver and Sontag are ultimately invested in the ethics of what the art historian John Berger refers to as "ways of seeing" in a collection of essays. "In Plato's cave," Sontag writes, "in teaching us a new visual code, photographs alter and enlarge our notions of what is worth looking at and what we have a right to observe. They are a grammar and, even more importantly, *an ethics of seeing*" (*On Photography*, 3; emphasis added). Sontag's ethical concerns over what the viewer has a right to observe are grounded in her interrogation of the power dynamics associated with being a photographer: "A photograph is not just the result of an encounter between an event and a photographer; picture-taking is an event in itself, and one with ever more peremptory rights—to interfere with, to invade, or to ignore whatever is going on" (11). Weaver's memoir shares similar concerns; it climaxes with the death of the activist Jimmie Lee Jackson at the hands of an Alabama state trooper, a murder that went unphotographed.

THE FAMILY PHOTO ALBUM AS HISTORICAL NARRATIVE

By shifting between art styles that often juxtapose a photorealistic aesthetic with flat, two-dimensional outlines, Weaver sketches a vision of the 1960s that illustrates the role of the photograph in crafting her immigrant memoir. Repeatedly, *Darkroom* acknowledges the project's indebtedness to photography; the book's epilogue confesses, "Every image I have of Argentina is faded, borrowed, outdated, or imagined" (246). That line is superimposed on the family photo album, which contains a series of overlapping and presumably re-created family photographs. Like the photo album, *Darkroom* seeks to arrange images into a narrative that documents her family's history of immigration to the United States. The comic functions as a sort of meta-family-album in this respect, one that tacitly acknowledges its own construction. For Weaver, the visual motif of the family photo album underscores how the photograph interacts with other images to create an arranged and constructed narrative of personal and political histories, much like the graphic narrative form. The family album first appears when Weaver recounts her father's life from his growing up in Argentina to his departure for the United States. The page that summarizes his journey features nine images arranged in three rows of three (fig. 3.1). The snapshots are drawn with white borders and shadowed on two sides to evoke a sense of tangibility—the images appear as photographs placed on a page rather than as drawn panels. The cartoonish nature of the snapshots attests to their fictional nature, as does the final panel—showing Nestor's first camera—which suggests that the preceding eight images, all from Argentina, were imagined. The organization of the snapshots into neat rows simultaneously evokes the graphic narrative form, since the arrangement of the images strongly recalls that of panels on the page of a comic (which, of course, this is). Weaver thus employs the photo-graphic narrative as a form of family history that augments an existing record by filling in for Nestor's unavailable camera.

The image of the family photo album can be read also as a visual commentary on the relationship between photography, documentation, and narrative. Sontag insists that while we might "know the world if we accept it as the camera records it," photography ultimately atomizes the world, denies interconnectedness, and obscures possible continuities, actions that amount to "the opposing of understanding" (*On Photography*, 23). Weaver, then, must contend with the limitations of the photograph if her narrative is to proceed. On the page after the nine drawn snapshots, we encounter a full-page image of a closet with boxes upon boxes of photographs, followed on the next page by multiple overlapping photorealistic re-creations of family photographs (fig. 3.2). Weaver writes, "The camera didn't miss much," and indeed the page seems overwhelmed by the images. Gone is the neat

—

UP TO 1961, WHEN MY WHOLE FAMILY CAME TO AMERICA, MY FATHER'S LIFE CAN BE SUMMARIZED IN A SERIES OF SNAPSHOTS:

BORN IN ARGENTINA AT THE FOOT OF THE ANDES

ORPHANED AT AGE NINE

LEFT HOMELESS ALONG WITH HIS BROTHER

RESCUED BY AMERICAN MISSIONARIES

TAUGHT HIMSELF TO READ

CALLED TO PREACH

WED TO MY MOTHER

IMMIGRATED TO AMERICA

ACQUIRED THE FIRST OF MANY CAMERAS DESTINED TO RECORD MUCH OF OUR LIVES

3.1. Lila Qunitero Weaver, *Darkroom: A Memoir in Black and White*, 21

3.2. Weaver, *Darkroom*, 22–23

THE CAMERA DIDN'T MISS MUCH.

three-by-three panel arrangement of the previous page, exchanged for a visual cacophony of snapshots practically demanding to be arranged—to be narrativized. As if responding to an implicit plea for structure, the following page begins to organize the images, placed over a pencil drawing of a globe, into a narrative of her family's arrival in the United States. The reader's eye moves across the family's history as the Quinteros move across continents—a move that places their story into a transnational context of arrivals and departures. The accompanying narration explains that despite her family's extensive photographic record, gaps in the narrative remain and that certain key moments "exist only in my mind's eye," reminding the reader of the limitations of photographic documentation (Weaver, *Darkroom*, 24). Sontag contends that "only that which narrates can make us understand" (*On Photography*, 23). For Weaver, photo-graphic narrative not only augments the family's photographs of their journey but arranges, revises, contextualizes, and narrativizes them as well.

In narrating her family's story, Weaver claims the role of family documentarian, a position previously filled by her photojournalist father. In using the graphic narrative form to link her family's history with the larger national narrative of the civil rights movement, Weaver deconstructs the archive of our consensus memories in order to reconstruct them to include her own. In this sense, Weaver enacts the role of the counterarchivist—a role often filled by women writers of color—as outlined by Nancy J. Peterson in *Against Amnesia*: "Such texts attempt to intervene in official versions of American history and identity by bringing to consciousness counterhistories that trouble the conventional narrative. But it is also significant that literature is an unofficial, unauthorized site for writing history. As unofficial histories, literary texts can address issues and events that are marginalized or ignored by the rules of safe politics and clear evidence that underlie official historical accounts" (5). Although *Darkroom* is not a work of literary fiction in the sense that Peterson outlines, Weaver's graphic memoir nonetheless functions in much the same spirit. Weaver's *Darkroom* employs "a postmodern poetics of absence and silence to emphasize the limits of recovery efforts" and to "mark the spaces, gaps, aporias that cannot be filled" by traditional historical accounts of the civil rights movement (Peterson, *Against Amnesia*, 9). The graphic narrative form, which is built on spaces, gaps, and aporias, is perhaps uniquely suited for these purposes, since it reconciles such gaps in its own fragmented narrative aesthetics. By drawing our attention to the necessarily constructed nature of the photograph, of history, and of her memoir itself, Weaver ultimately can, in Peterson's words, "compel a reader to investigate further" the interplay between history, fiction, and the photographic archive, as well as the role that race plays in the construction of each (17). And as Jared Gardner argues, graphic narrative is uniquely capable of fulfilling this deconstructive-reconstructive mode, since the comics form "depends on an active and imaginative reader capable of filling in the gaps in time" (*Projections*, xi). While Gardner refers more specifically to the formalistic elements of graphic narrative, such as closure, the form's compatibility with Peterson's call to action should, at this point, be immediately evident.

Darkroom's prologue immediately signals the memoir's interrogation of the relationship between photographs, narrative, and history. Entitled "Home Movies," the prologue reflects on the family's home-movie nights and explains that Weaver's favorite moments came at the end, when her father would rewind the films and let the children watch them in reverse (fig. 3.3). Much like her father, Weaver manipulates the home movie, this time by converting it into the visual grammar of graphic narrative, drawing film frames as separate panels in a filmstrip. In doing so, Weaver reminds us that a film is essentially a series of photographs manipulated to give the appearance of narrative progression. The page is arranged in four rows: the first two contain one panel each, and the bottom border of the second is interrupted by an overlaid drawing of a strip of film winding across the page. The linear arrangement of the shots in the third and fourth rows invokes the strip moving the reader through the frames one image at a time. By drawing these panels as film frames, Weaver is able to depict the temporality evoked by film in the atemporal medium of graphic narrative. Rearranging the panels to reverse this temporality disrupts the teleology inherent in film, namely, that one moment leads directly to another from a known starting point to a predetermined destination. The motif continues on the following pages as the narrative shifts its attention to African American protesters in Marion. This teleological disruption reminds the reader that "progress," whether it involves the assimilation of the Quintero family into suburban domesticity or the African American struggle for the same social mobility, does not proceed evenly. If at all.

The motif of the strip of film implies a reading practice, too—the page aims to evoke the rhythm of film by mimicking its appearance—at a pace Weaver determines. This allows Weaver to slow the pace of her history to distill her family's home movies down to their essence—a series of photographs arranged and constructed to give the appearance of a holistic narrative. Thierry Groensteen refers to the arrangement of panels to evoke a sense of time as the "rhythmic function," and he compares the use of panels to frames in cinema. Groensteen argues that the content of panels is subordinated to the pace established by their arrangement: "The 'text' of comics obeys a rhythm that is imposed on it by the succession of frames—a basic heartbeat that, as is seen in music, can be developed, nuanced,

HOME-MOVIE NIGHT
HAD ME IN ITS THRALL.

MY FAVORITE
PART CAME AT
THE END.

AT THAT POINT, DADDY REWOUND
THE FILM, AND WE SAW IT ALL IN REVERSE.

THE BACKWARDS FLIGHT OF A SNOWBALL

3.3. Weaver, *Darkroom*, 2

and recovered by more elaborate rhythmic effects stressed by other 'instruments' (parameters), like those of the distribution of word balloons, the opposition of colors, or even the play of graphic forms" (*System of Comics*, 45). Groensteen is commenting on how panel work and frame arrangement influence the pace and rhythm at which a reader can engage with a graphic novel, which is similar to film in this regard. More importantly, the graphic narrative form allows Weaver to make the distillation of her family's home movies visible to her reader. Symbolically, these initial pages serve as a microcosm of Weaver's entire project to reveal the constructedness of civil rights narratives, which owe a great deal to photography and film. She does this not simply to counter them, but to expand their scope.[5]

Furthermore, these panels call our attention to the role of film in recording personal and national histories. The following page re-creates family recordings of African American protests in Marion at the height of the civil rights movement. It contains a single full-page panel portraying a gathering of Marion protesters marching on the local courthouse. The subsequent pages again reverse the flow of the action as Weaver comments that her family would play the film in reverse over and over, and that "the march took them around the courthouse I don't know how many times" (*Darkroom*, 7). Weaver's narration slyly notes the cyclical nature of African Americans' struggle for civil rights, hinting at the potentially Sisyphean nature of their endeavors. These pages replace the film motif with traditional comics panels while still slowing the rhythm for readers, inviting them to dwell on their significance. Her comment on the following page that "the movie doesn't show how white people reacted" to the Marion marchers highlights the medium's limitations—film and photography may evoke an evidentiary air of fact or truth, yet they cannot portray the entirety of the civil rights movement. Weaver's decision not to complete the picture implicitly argues that her photo-graphic memoir can highlight the incompleteness of even such well-documented eras in US history. Photo-graphic narrative offers Weaver a form that can uniquely complement and complicate popular recollections of the civil rights movement and introduce, as she puts it, the "sliver of gray" that represents her Latina perspective (57).

RACIAL IDENTITY IN TWO DIMENSIONS

Weaver's memoir maintains a deeply complicated relationship to the photograph. Rather than simply borrowing its implicit authority or offering her photo-graphic narrative as a corrective, supplement, or alternative, Weaver uses the photograph to carry multivalent possibilities in the text. It functions not only as an artifact or a point of reference but also as an object of scrutiny and a racial signifier. This multivalence is perhaps best represented in the interplay between the memoir's narrative content and its photorealistic aesthetic. Weaver casts her father, Nestor, a part-time pastor, teacher, and photojournalist, as both a mentor and the source of the family's political history. Returning to the opening sequence of the first chapter, "In the Dark" features Weaver dutifully following her father's instructions for developing photographs (*Darkroom*, 14–15). Weaver's narration draws the reader's attention to her highly symbolic use of the idea of a photograph; for example, she says that in her father's darkroom, "much came down to the interplay of light and dark" (14). In this vein, *Darkroom* details the author's developing racial consciousness; "the interplay of light and dark" signals how her budding cognizance of the differences between black and white Americans—both in appearance and in social standing—frames her perception of Latina identity. Consequently, Weaver's desire to create space for her Latina identity within the larger narrative of the civil rights movement forces her to reconcile her position outside the racial dichotomy of Alabama society. In doing so, Weaver interrogates the role of photography in shaping her vision of the United States and her place within it.

Weaver's anxieties over how to articulate an identity in a black-white dichotomy into which she does not neatly fit are ultimately emblematized in the act of taking a photograph. Her struggle is confronted directly in chapter 5, "Ancestral Lines," which outlines her inability to articulate a Latina subjectivity in a society that cannot recognize such an identity formation. The title of the chapter signals the racial battle lines being drawn in her recently desegregated high school as well as the liminal space that she, as a Latinx subject, occupies between those lines. In one particularly revealing moment, Weaver struggles to mark her racial identity on a grade school form in which only "White" and "Negro" are options. Weaver comments in the accompanying text, "I'm certainly not a Negro. That only leaves one choice. But I don't really *feel* white" (*Darkroom*, 86). Weaver casts racial identity not only as a legal or phenotypical distinction but also as a formation residing somewhere at the intersection of privilege and consciousness. The text, depicted in small round bubbles that represent thought rather than speech, is not completely contained by the frame. These bubbles mirror Weaver's budding recognition of her place outside the stark American racial dichotomy, represented by the form. This symbolic placelessness is prefaced when a white female student dismissively wonders, "Argentina. Hmm . . . Oh! Is that in South Alabama?" More succinctly, an exasperated white male student demands to know, "WHAT are you?" (86). These are only two of many such moments in which Weaver is displaced socially, visually, and racially. Such moments of misidentification are not limited to the perceptions of white students. Her older sister, Lissy, is mistaken for "Eye-talian" by the young African American men in her high school (216). That these boys take Lissy's non-Anglo appearance as an indication that "she didn't seem to be off-limits" adds a distinctly gendered quality to Lissy's racial experiences. Weaver also includes an anecdote of a black classmate asking to feel her hair, inverting a trope typical of African American female experience in order to accentuate both her proximity to and distance from any steady racial identification (216).

In the context of Lissy's ambiguous position within the US racial hierarchy, photographs frame the narrative's discussion of the development and construction of subsequent potential identities. For example, the chapter "Passage" (a clever double entendre indicating both traveling to the United States and the desire to be viewed as white) highlights how photography influences narratives of Americanness. As Weaver recalls how women's magazines such as *McCall's* influenced her perceptions of whiteness and beauty, an American flag waves proudly in a large panel overhead that dwarfs the figure of Weaver beneath (*Darkroom*, 38). This scene is filled with images of a scantily clad woman, suburban houses, jewelry, and fancy automobiles—the expected consumerist trappings of midcentury America. The images are scattered about the page without panels or borders, an atomized arrangement that mirrors Weaver's own scattered sense of self. This scene implicitly indicts photography-based popular magazines that obscure as much as they highlight; for example, the Quintero children are surprised to encounter African Americans in the United States. Weaver recalls wondering, "Where did all the black people come from? The magazines had never shown them" (42). Later, the photograph's ability to either highlight or obscure race drives Lissy's anxiety about being seen in school as the "girl with nigger lips," leading her to tuck her lips back in order to approximate an "'Anglo' grin" for her school picture (81). Lissy's anxieties about race are emblematized in the act of taking a photograph, since she fears how she is seen, will be seen, or, perhaps, will not be seen by viewers who gaze upon her image.

Weaver's concerns over how the viewer's gaze works to construct race is not limited to the photograph or to those who view Weaver through the problematic lens of race. Flat, unshaded, two-dimensional line drawings present throughout the memoir stand in stark contrast with the dominant photorealistic aesthetic. Typically, Weaver deploys the simplified style to mark individuals with shallow perceptions of race, showing their "two-dimensional" racial consciousness that considers only white and black as available options and typically reduces those of other races to simplistic, typically racist caricatures. For example, Weaver draws the classmates that wonder about her racial identity in this style, which mirrors their simplistic racial perspective. Weaver also uses this style when Lissy is accused of having "nigger lips" (*Darkroom*, 80). By using simple line drawings to depict people with a two-dimensional view of race, Weaver reduces them to their worldviews. Stated simply, she has us see them as they might see others.

Weaver's most damning use of these two-dimensional drawings indicts not only the racist whites of Alabama, but herself and her readers as well. When Weaver recounts the moment she received her first pair of glasses as a young schoolgirl, she says that her corrected vision was still imperfect in one very important sense (fig. 3.4): "*What a discovery.* The visual world was a thing of wonder. I hadn't suspected its breadth and richness. But now I saw. Still, my eyeglasses didn't correct a particular blindspot: the faces of black people looked interchangeable to me. I knew only one black person those days—Mrs. Jackson, the lady that helped out with ironing now and then. She refused invitations to join the family at lunch, which left me asking, *why?* I couldn't bear to see her eating alone, so I sat with her. But neither of us spoke" (*Darkroom*, 74). The narration is scattered about the page, some words in text boxes or circles, others borderless, as if the text is struggling to be placed on the page as much as Weaver struggles to interpret the "blindspots" in her improved vision. The prominent central image features a group of four African Americans walking down the street. The figures are drawn two-dimensionally, in the same flat style typically reserved for the white racists of Marion. The panel is placed beneath the image of Weaver trying on her new glasses for the first time, indicating to the reader that this represents Weaver's perception of these four figures, who are depicted in the kind of simple line drawings that usually represent someone with a shallow perception of race. By placing the image in sequence after the one of Weaver trying on her new glasses, Weaver indicts her own reductive, juvenile view of race. The four African Americans are not two-dimensional, but only perceived as such by the younger Weaver. Weaver acknowledges her own limited perceptions of race and thereby recognizes her need "to look—really look." This scene is rife with implications for the reader as well, since in the opening panel glasses face toward the reader. Symbolically, readers see the world through Weaver's eyes in this moment, and it prompts them to consider their own potentially problematic ways of seeing.

Weaver's story indicts her younger self not only for how she sees African Americans but also for how she regards herself as an activist in their cause, as well as for how her efforts are perceived. These insights prove particularly resonant in the book's discussion of the politics of participation in civil rights activism, even

WHAT A DISCOVERY.

THE VISUAL WORLD WAS A THING OF WONDER. I HADN'T SUSPECTED ITS BREADTH AND RICHNESS. BUT NOW I SAW.

STILL, MY EYEGLASSES DIDN'T CORRECT A PARTICULAR BLINDSPOT:

THE FACES OF BLACK PEOPLE LOOKED INTERCHANGEABLE TO ME.

I KNEW ONLY ONE BLACK PERSON IN THOSE DAYS—MRS. JACKSON, THE LADY THAT HELPED OUT WITH IRONING NOW AND THEN.

SHE REFUSED INVITATIONS TO JOIN THE FAMILY AT LUNCH, WHICH LEFT ME ASKING, WHY?

I COULDN'T BEAR TO SEE HER EATING ALONE, SO I SAT WITH HER.

BUT NEITHER OF US SPOKE.

3.4. Weaver, *Darkroom*, 26–27

on the relatively small scale represented by Weaver's high school. Inspired by her father's activism, Weaver begins to flout cultural mores that insist on the cultural segregation of African American students from white ones—in outright defiance of the integrationist mandates of *Brown v. Board of Education* (1954). At school, she begins to befriend her black classmates, despite calls home from concerned (white) parents in the neighborhood who are worried that fraternizing with African American males, and the implied sexual threat they represent, would ruin her future before she reached it (*Darkroom*, 222). Rejecting her school's demands that she "restrict [her]self to bona fide academic activities," Weaver begins to pride herself on standing on her activist bona fides instead. Yet the indeterminate nature of Weaver's racial identity—particularly her light skin—disrupts her newfound progressive politics, since her African American friends still regard her with guarded skepticism. In one particularly tense high school scene, Weaver attempts to break up a fight between two African American girls, both of whom she considers her friends. One of the girls shouts angrily that Weaver should mind her own business, calls her a "cracker," and demands that she "go back to her own kind" (227). Taken aback, Weaver defends herself by claiming, "I've taken a stand for equality, and I've lost most of my white friends because of it!" The phrase "white friends" is perhaps the most telling, since it both implies a sacrifice for which her African American friend should be grateful, and insists that Weaver is in fact not white (which is true).

Yet the design of the central panel of this scene, showing Weaver's high school identification card, disrupts any potential earnestness we might bestow on Weaver's beleaguered younger self (fig. 3.5). On the card, Weaver's photograph voices her demand that her social sacrifices be acknowledged. The photograph explains how Weaver insisted on being seen. The background of the ID is emblazoned with Weaver dressed as a sort of civil rights Joan of Arc bearing the banner of progress ("Down with Racism"), with her personal martyrdom etched haphazardly across her image: "Standing up! Hostility! Solidarity! Principles! Rejection! Lost reputation!" In stark contrast with her shaded photo, the image of Weaver as a civil rights martyr is drawn two-dimensionally, casting this vision of herself as little more than a shallow self-perception that subtly challenges the claims of her photograph. Further undercutting her assertion is Weaver's accompanying narration—"Blah blah blah!"—to the right of the photograph. On the following page, the reader is greeted by an angry set of eyes challenging Weaver's claims to civil rights martyrdom. "We don't like you neither, cracker," her angry classmate yells. "You are not one of us! You got that? You are not one of us!" It is in this moment that Weaver faces a stark realization: she is seemingly relegated to an unstable proximity to whiteness that she can neither fully claim nor truly inhabit.

The inclusion of this anecdote allows Weaver to underscore the tensions between Latinx and African American communities in the midcentury United States, which often prevented cross-ethnic alliances. Brian D. Behnken notes that although "cultural dissimilarities, class tensions, organizational and tactical differences, and geographic distance reduced the cooperative ventures" between Latinx and African American communities, racial identification remained the most prevalent challenge to such cooperation (*Fighting Their Own Battles*, 11). And while Behnken's work focuses specifically on tensions between Mexican Americans and African Americans in Texas, *Darkroom* depicts these insights more broadly, linking Weaver's work to writers such as Piri Thomas, Edward Rivera, Julia Alvarez, Rudolfo Anaya, and Nash Candelaria, who explore the racial ambiguity of Latinx communities. Weaver's exploration of the significance of the racial imagery associated with photography and phenotype through the photo-graphic narrative mode allows the reader to "really look" at the double bind that young Weaver found herself in. On the one hand, she was unwilling (perhaps incapable) of claiming a white identity, but her relative proximity to whiteness nonetheless frustrated her desire to participate in the civil rights struggle. Much like her father, who in his home movies of civil rights protests was relegated to the role of documentarian and witness, Weaver is sidelined, her participation in a black-white civil rights struggle hindered by her inability to locate herself at either pole of this dichotomy.

Weaver's memoir makes it clear that rejection by one side of the struggle did not guarantee inclusion in the other. Predictably, perhaps, her attempt to participate in her classmates' struggle for equality is met with hostility by her white peers; for instance, a group of young boys threatens her brother with violence after he defends her reputation. Here, the reader encounters Weaver's younger brother, Johnny, directly for the only time in the narrative. She describes her brother's eyes as distant, containing the sort of "strange detachment" she had only seen in the eyes of desperate African American men (*Darkroom*, 233). Johnny is drawn like a typical Latino boy—full lips (like Lissy's), thick black hair, with skin shaded slightly darker than that of the white boys around him. The implication is clear: Weaver and her siblings may not be black, but they certainly are not white either. It is only after the fight is broken up that Johnny confesses to his sister that he was defending her against the accusation that she was a "nigger lover" (235). The reader is left to decide to what extent, if any, Johnny's reactions

IT GOT RATHER IMPASSIONED.

to this comment are charged with the same racial anxieties that beset his sister Lissy, who fears being seen as anything other than white. Weaver's recollections of her time in high school close on a now-familiar motif, with a two-page layout of Weaver reimagining the entire scene in reverse. The reader again witnesses the scene play out backward as the individual panels take Weaver back to the school-yard to confront her accuser (236–237). In this imagined confrontation, Weaver responds to the accusation with a guffaw and dismissively calls her accuser an "idiot"—a cathartic fantasy made both possible and visible by photo-graphic narration. And while the photograph on Weaver's high school ID may represent an officially sanctioned identity (issued by a governing body—the high school), anxieties about how the image is interpreted by the viewer remain a crucial thematic. Weaver's failure to have her high school activism acknowledged, naive as it might have been to expect that, in many ways motivates the memoir. She may not have been seen as an ally of the movement at the time, but photo-graphic narrative makes her contributions (and their incumbent angst) visible to her readers in the present.

All these scenes preface one of the memoir's chief interventions by reminding the reader that to look upon a photograph is not a passive act. Weaver enacts Jacques Rancière's notion of the "emancipated spectator." Rancière claims that activist theatre attempts to convert audiences from passive voyeurs to active participants in order to awaken some form of new political, social, or intellectual consciousness. Since Weaver hopes to awaken some latent political consciousness regarding the reader's gaze, comparisons resonate between Rancière and Weaver. Rancière's activist theatre uses human bodies as signifiers for the sake of storytelling and narrative. Conversely, it might be said that graphic narratives use signifiers to represent human bodies, in this case ones forgotten or disavowed by particular historical narratives. Rancière warns his readers that the dichotomy of the active versus passive spectator presumes that viewing is innately passive, denying its inherent potential for change. Rather, Rancière claims, the emancipation of the spectator "begins when we understand that viewing is also an action that confirms or transforms" (*Emancipated Spectator*, 13). Weaver's photo-graphic narrative functions in much the same vein. As Lissy's previous anxieties about race highlight, to gaze upon a photograph is an interpretive act—a reality often lost upon the viewer, in part because of the photograph's presumed evidentiary nature. One does not so much see a photograph as read it—the viewer implicitly interprets and constructs the image's meaning as opposed to simply receiving it. Weaver does not so much emancipate her spectators as remind them of their already potentially emancipated state.

—

DARKROOM'S ETHICS OF SEEING: WITNESSING AND TESTIMONY

Of course, how one "sees" is of equal concern to Weaver as what is seen. As Sontag insists, the photograph is not simply an artifact to be seen; it concurrently induces an ethics of seeing, one linked to the performance of witnessing, documenting, and testifying. We might say that Weaver's ethics of viewing are grounded not in the "right to observe," but in an obligation to bear witness. In this regard, Weaver's ethics echo Berger's basic assertion: "We only see what we look at. To look is an act of choice" (*Ways of Seeing*, 8). Weaver's emancipation of the reader draws our attention to this deliberate process of seeing—to a conscious, willful, and ethical process of interpretive viewership. To illustrate this, Weaver's memoir features recurrent images of eyes, ubiquitous throughout the text—a motif present even on the front cover. When Weaver discusses her father's history of activism, the reader encounters a splash page of repeating images drawing our eyes to her father's (fig. 3.6). The image of her father's eyes witnessing the brutal beatings at Marion foreshadow the riots of 18 February 1965, which resulted in the death of the unarmed African American activist Jimmie Lee Jackson and inspired the iconic Selma marches, which catapulted the movement toward key civil rights legislative victories in the mid-1960s. The accompanying narration sets the scene on that night: "Mayhem ruled. No streetlights, no flashbulbs. Cameras smashed, film exposed. Neither journalists nor amateur photographers like daddy salvaged a single frame from that night. It was Marion's darkest hour" (*Darkroom*, 26–27). Nestor watches, aghast, the brutality unfolding before his eyes; the violence is captured in a series of small panels scattered about the page. These small panels are overlaid on top of the repeating image of Nestor's face, disrupting the flow of the panels underneath, in defiance of Groensteen's principle of rhythmic function. The repeating images of the beating suggest a trauma for Nestor—a disruptive memory that cannot be assimilated.

The pace of the sequence signals a narrative trauma that the memoir reveals rather than heals. Besides skewing images of the beating spread across the page, Weaver skews the pace of the sequence by eliminating nearly all the gutters between the repeating images of Nestor's eyes. While comics can employ gutters and layouts to influence how long a reader lingers on a certain moment or sequence, the splash page of Nestor's reaction to the beatings contains no such transitions, and the lack of gutters compresses the temporal rhythm of the scene. The lack of gutter space and the consistency of the image suggest a moment frozen in a repetitious cycle. McCloud describes the incremental, even if only infinitesimal, amount of time that passes in a frame-to-frame panel arrangement as "moment to moment," an arrangement that seeks to mimic the movement of

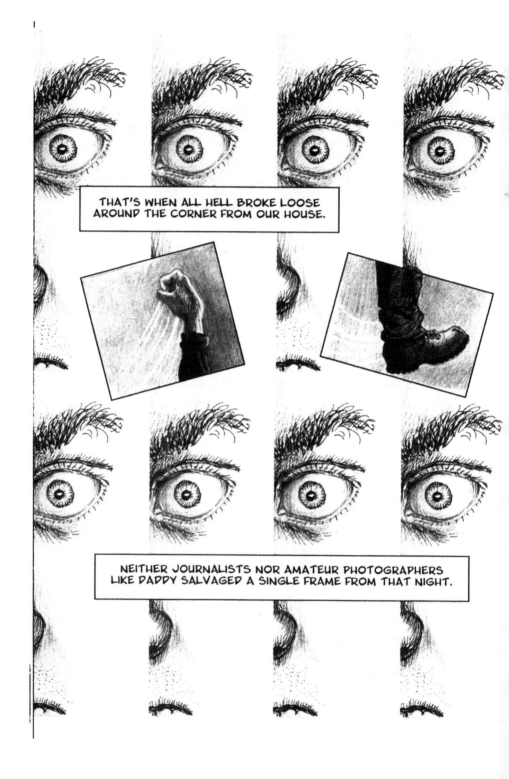

THAT'S WHEN ALL HELL BROKE LOOSE AROUND THE CORNER FROM OUR HOUSE.

NEITHER JOURNALISTS NOR AMATEUR PHOTOGRAPHERS LIKE DADDY SALVAGED A SINGLE FRAME FROM THAT NIGHT.

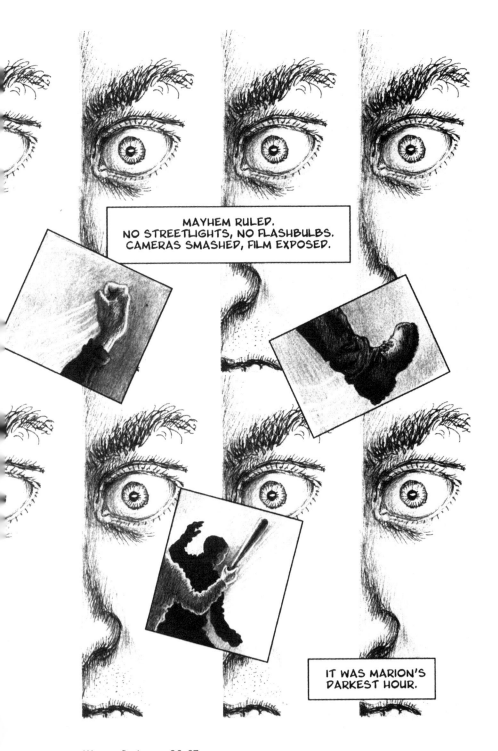

time as much as possible (*Understanding Comics*, 70). The fragmented images of the violence, depicted as photographs, defy easy placement on the page or in the narrative. In fact, without the accompanying narration by Weaver to contextualize the image, the reader might be put in the same position as Nestor—witness to an event that defies immediate comprehension.

Yet these photographs invoke a sense of immediacy for the viewer. Superimposed over Nestor's eyes, these snapshots depict acts of violence captured only in her father's memory, a documentary silence created not by the limitations of the photograph, but by an Alabama society unwilling to allow itself to be seen—Weaver later reveals that Nestor's camera was destroyed in the riot by white supremacists. Weaver's deliberate pacing (or even lack thereof) echoes the work of the comics journalist Joe Sacco, whose drawings are described by Hillary Chute as "slowing readers down and asking them to grapple with producing meaning as a deliberate technique positioned against the unremitting speeding up of information that characterizes" other forms of documentary media, such as film (*Disaster Drawn*, 37). These scenes also share Sontag's concerns about what the camera is permitted to purposely elide from the historical record. The recurrent images of eyes in this scene and throughout the memoir remind us that observation is a form of documentation, one that compels us to witness—and to testify. Weaver's symbolic testimony takes the form of the photo-graphic narrative and fills gaps in the history of the civil rights movement by making "Marion's darkest hour" visible to her readers.

Through the use of photo-graphic narrative, *Darkroom* addresses the brutal suppression of journalists and photographers at the hands of white supremacists at the Perry County courthouse in response to a church-organized protest of the incarceration of the civil rights worker James Orange (fig. 3.7). Unlike the predominantly white backgrounds of most of the memoir's pages, the scenes at the Perry County courthouse are drawn on black paper, highlighting "Marion's darkest hour" (*Darkroom*, 162–163). Here, that description takes on additional meanings. The scenes open with white supremacists cutting the power to the streetlights illuminating the protest and smashing any cameras or flashbulbs that might document the ensuing one-sided attack on the protesters and journalists. In this sense, "Marion's darkest hour" refers both to the malicious nature of this event as well as the lack of corroborating physical documentation because of the darkness of the unlit street. The text marks this moment both as missing from the photographic record presented in the memoir and as an unavoidable stain on that very history. This scene even marks the physical book: the pages are left unnumbered yet are easily identified, since the black pages stand out in stark relief, even when the book is shut.

The first page of this scene returns the reader to a shot of Nestor's eyes, who "witnessed the madness" but was unable to record it. Weaver again employs snapshots to imagine the violence, which defy easy arrangement on the page—another visual signal of the difficulty of incorporating this violence into her narrative, and an echo of the effect seen in figure 3.6. Weaver chooses to leave some of these imagined snapshots completely blank—a tacit admission of the limitations of even her photo-graphic narrative to recall or document these scenes of racial violence—again evoking Chute's and Sontag's call for transparency.[6] Initially, one might read these photographs as depicting the result of the film in the broken cameras being exposed and ruined. They also represent a sort of failure to expose, since they would have been the sole corroborating evidence of the identities of the perpetrators of these crimes. Since these are not actual photos but re-creations, readers know to interpret both the blacked-out images and the black frames and borders as deliberate aesthetic choices that replace the absence of evidence with evidence of the absence. In a manner of speaking, Weaver's memoir documents the darkness itself.

Nonetheless, these pages still enact Weaver's imperative to bear a continual form of present witness to the violence the camera missed in the past. The onomatopoeic text at the bottom of the scene—WHACKWHACKWHACKWHACK-WHACK—suggests continuous violence against African Americans that began before this scene and continues beyond, violence that cannot be contained by the page. The following pages of this section move between more traditional graphic narrative panel arrangements and a single image of a man with a can of black spray paint pointed evocatively at readers (*Darkroom*, 165)—suggesting our own potential silencing. Eventually, Weaver's artwork returns a scattering of photographs from the initial layout (166–167), each representing a failed attempt to document the madness of this racist rampage. At its climax, this section settles on two full-page images of Alabama state troopers chasing the unarmed Jimmie Lee Jackson and his parents into a diner where Jackson will be murdered. Both these full-page images are bordered in white, offsetting them from the black background, metaphorically dramatizing the manner in which Jackson is surrounded as well as giving the appearance of still photographs. The first of these images is hazy, blurry, barely lit, showing Jackson shuffling his family into the diner, spotlighted by the oncoming headlights of a police cruiser. The moment appears frozen in time, a dark memorial for the last time the reader sees Jimmie Lee alive (168).

The next image, also resembling a photograph, moves closer to the action, but does not enter the diner. Taken together, the two images offer something of

MY FATHER WITNESSED THE MADNESS.

EEEEEEEK!

WHACK

WHACK

WHACK

WHACKWHACKWHA

3.7. Weaver, *Darkroom*, 162–163

a microsequence, with the page fold operating as a gutter. The images appear to begin a narrative sequence leading to the moment of Jackson's murder, but Weaver stops short, excluding us (and herself) from witnessing the moment the sword falls. A final piece of enigmatic narration marks the inevitable: the phrase "a shot in the dark" adorns the bottom of the page, placed (like the reader) outside the gutter, looking in. This final phrase offers three possible meanings (169). The first is literal, referring to the bullet that claims Jackson's life. The second is figurative, referring to any photography that might have captured the murder as an evidentiary gap that keeps this moment in history perpetually "in the dark." Finally, we might consider *Darkroom* itself to be "a shot in the dark," a self-reflexive gesture that acknowledges its own limited, even ill-fated, attempt to fill this gap in history. As the reader is left to grapple with this aporia, the final image closes on a climactic and fatal BOOM to mark an all-too-familiar and predictably tragic conclusion, to which Weaver's readers can bear only distant witness: "Jimmie Lee Jackson, dead at 26" (173).

Choosing not to depict the death of Jimmie Lee Jackson is an admission of the limitations of testifying to a murder unseen. Yet Weaver does not release herself or her readers from their obligation, and Nestor's eyes return to insist we bear symbolic witness to Jackson's tragic demise. Through Weaver's photo-graphic memoir, photography and graphic narrative function in concert as contrapuntal modes of documentation and expression that do more than verify events for readers. They challenge readers to be witnesses as well, offering a call to action emblematized by the woman on the lower right of the splash page, shown in figure 3.7, who makes eye contact with readers and begs for their "help" (163). This imperative reminds us that witnessing must be an active process, a skeptical act that acknowledges the limitations of documentation and representation.

Weaver's return to the protests of Marion prompts her readers to consider what the writing of political histories might elide or suppress. Joseph Witek claims that historical graphic novels and comic books, which vary widely in perspective and point of view, do not exist primarily to counter dominant historical narratives. Rather, Witek argues, historical comics reveal the innate ideological construct-edness of dominant historical narratives, and their authors must contend with the retelling of "an event that is 'already told,' already so weighted with cultural significance that any telling risks the loss of its individual rhetorical force in the face of previously established readings and individual associations" (*Comic Books as History*, 17). Witek's concerns over "an event already told" echo similar sentiments expressed in Michael de Certeau's analysis of the historical event as a concept. Rather than taking events as facts, Certeau insists that events, even singular moments, are smaller narratives woven together into the tapestries of history. He claims that so-called events do not explain history or delimit its ruptures, but rather foster the intelligibility of historical narratives by providing the building blocks of teleology (*Writing of History*, 96). For Certeau, events represent historical moments imbued with meaning and arranged and contextualized into particular cultural narratives. And as Sontag claims, photographs might be thought of as such narrative events, since "picture-taking is an event in itself" (*On Photography*, 11). In returning to the series of events on the night of 18 February 1965, Weaver retells a story already told in order to ensure that those events survive to *be* retold, since the suppression of journalists at the protests meant that there was little corroborating evidence that this "event," Jimmie Lee Jackson's death, ever occurred.

In reflecting on the power dynamics implicit in photography, Sontag makes an interesting observation: "People robbed of their past seem to make the most fervent picture takers, at home and abroad" (*On Photography*, 10). In Weaver's case, we might say that she was not robbed of her past per se, but that her ambiguous position as a Latina subject excluded her from participation in a larger national history. Relegated to the role of witness to the civil rights movement, rather than participant, Weaver nonetheless writes (or, perhaps, *draws*) her own history of activism in the movement. Through the concomitant narratives of her father's activism and her own difficulties in joining her classmates' struggle, Weaver implicitly argues that bearing witness can be a form of participation.[7] Weaver's photo-graphic narrative allows readers "to really look" at her subjective experience of a politicized Latinx childhood, one invisible to her peers at the time and absent in popular accounts of the movement. The graphic form allows her contribution to be seen, not as a counter to popular narratives, but as a contribution, while revealing the innately racialized frameworks of such histories. Rather than deny or indict these realities, Weaver's work documents them and, in so doing, prevents us from losing sight of the histories themselves as constructed and interpreted narratives. Ultimately, Weaver charges not only the authors of history but also their readers with the need to develop an ethics of seeing. She reminds us that to look is to interpret, to imagine is to witness, and, finally, that *how* we see matters just as much as what we *choose* to see. Or cannot.

Moreover, by speaking from a Latina perspective, Weaver challenges any presumed concerns over who is allowed to testify, just as she refuses to be relegated to the racial sidelines in her youth. Her family's presence at civil rights flashpoints throughout Alabama complicates the presumed black-white dichotomy foundational to our consensus memories, just as her narrative breaks down the presumed distance between witnessing and active participation. Furthermore, *Darkroom* highlights the importance of positionality to narratives of civil rights participation and to the legibility of civil rights narratives. While *Darkroom* explores the sociocultural importance of positionality along the vectors of race, ethnicity, and gender, place also plays a prominent part. In many ways, *Darkroom* is able to make itself visible as a legitimate civil rights narrative because of the Quintero family's physical presence at a site loaded with civil rights legacies and cultural memories—namely, the state of Alabama. In many ways, the geography of *Darkroom* offers the narrative legibility, even credibility, to a degree that no single photograph ever could.

CHAPTER 4

The Silence of Our Friends and Memories of Houston's Civil Rights History

R eaders of Mark Long's *The Silence of Our Friends* first encounter a single image in his civil rights memoir before they encounter a single phrase: "Houston, TX. 1968" (1). Beneath this text, an expansive Texas sky billows above the small Gulf Coast suburb it dwarfs. Houston's downtown skyline appears minuscule on the horizon, recognizable only (one presumes) to residents of Texas's most diverse and populous city. This aerial establishing shot places readers at a distance while simultaneously grounding them temporally and geographically. The opening shot signals the importance of distance, in both time and space, for the events of this narrative. On the next page, the memoir closes the distance, moving down into a suburban backyard on "Tejas Street, Sharpstown" (2). In the bottom panel, a young Mark Long plays army with his sister Michelle as they stalk "VC"—or Vietcong. Safe in the security of their suburban space, the children mimic the outside world, their game functioning as a form of play—both as a child's game and as a staged and scripted performance.

The performative and jovial nature of these opening scenes is immediately undercut, however, when Mark and Michelle enter their home and join their mother, Patricia Long, to watch that evening's newscast (fig. 4.1). In a silent sequence, the family's domestic bliss is interrupted by the airing of the infamous

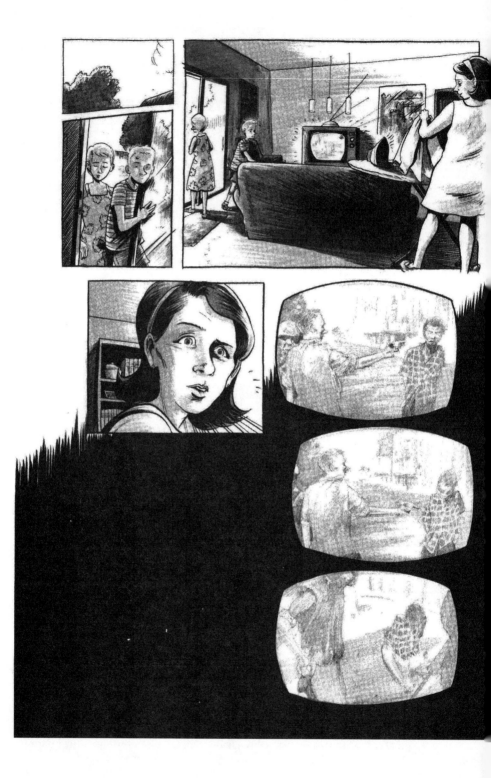

4.1. Mark Long, Jim Demonakos, and Nate Powell, *The Silence of Our Friends*, 6–7

execution of Nguyễn Văn Lém by General Nguyễn Ngọc Loan during the Tet Offensive. This grotesquely iconic scene is depicted in parallel panels running down the right side of the page, panels shaped like antique cathode-ray television screens, artifacts of a predigital world. The shocked stillness of the scene is broken by Patricia's shaken tears and her daughter's attempts to console her. The silence of the moment suggests a trauma that cannot be articulated in prose— only represented visually.[1] Framing these horrific images as television-shaped panels suggests both a paradoxical nearness to and an impossible distance from the world outside suburban America, which intrudes via its increased televised visibility. This sentiment is reinforced by the second page's final two panels, the first depicting a silent Mark contending with his access to a global reality he is unprepared to comprehend. The second panel returns to a view of Sharpstown similar to the one that opened the sequence, a panel that holds the reader's gaze, suggesting a desire to elude a terrifying world by staying within the presumed safety of this domestic space. The opening page of *Silence of Our Friends* introduces a proximal tension exacerbated by televisual access to world events, which only further entrenches the viewer's distance from them. These paradoxes lead the reader to yet another conundrum. Despite the silent power of this opening sequence, an unvoiced question looms over the entire scene: isn't *The Silence of Our Friends* supposed to be about the civil rights movement?

Cowritten by Jim Demonakos and illustrated by Nate Powell (the artist for John Lewis's *March* trilogy), Mark Long's *The Silence of Our Friends: The Civil Rights Struggle Was Never Black and White*, focuses on his father's friendship with a local African American community organizer. The central conflict details the case of the TSU Five, students at Texas Southern University who were accused, and eventually acquitted, of murdering a police officer at a 1967 student-led sit-in. The book's title comes from Martin Luther King Jr.'s 1967 speech "Nonviolence and Social Change," given as part of the Canadian Broadcasting Corporation's Massey Lectures: "In the end, we will remember not the words of our enemies but the silence of our friends." The quoted phrase signals many of the prevalent themes of the narrative. First, by focusing on the friendship between John Long, a local white television reporter, and Larry Thompson, a black TSU professor and civil rights activist, the memoir enacts the spirit of MLK's remark by urging potential allies to speak out against the injustices and inequalities suffered by the marginalized.[2] Ostensibly, then, *The Silence of Our Friends* offers a narrative of white political redemption, a drama that tries to position its white characters as contributors rather than protagonists. The memoir addresses another form of silence, too, that of the historical elision of Texas Southern University's civil rights

———

drama from the master narrative of the movement. In this context, Long, Demonakos, and Powell reveal a tension by choosing such an iconic MLK quotation for the memoir's title. Ostensibly, as the memoir's subtitle makes clear, *The Silence of Our Friends* asks readers to read it in the context of the civil rights struggle. Yet given its focus on Houston in 1967, the narrative falls out of the traditional temporal and geographic sites typically associated with our consensus memories of where and when the civil rights struggle took place. Even the time of the first image—1968—does not cohere with the primary content of the memoir, since the events it recounts take place largely in the prior year, adding a certain instability to its time frame.

The memoir's multiple conflicts—between domestic and public spaces, its elision from the master narrative of the movement, and its temporal instability—all represent, in one form or another, a larger tension between memory and history. In this sense, *The Silence of Our Friends* struggles with the exclusion of individual remembrances from the larger constructions of national histories—a conflict lucidly delineated in Pierre Nora's classic essay "Between History and Memory: Les Lieux de Mémoire." Nora positions memory and history as "far from being synonymous" but in fact as being "in fundamental opposition" (8). Nora describes memory as an eternal dialectic between "remembering and forgetting," vulnerable and unstable, an active process susceptible to recovery and appropriation, forever bonded to the perpetual present. Memory, Nora insists, "is life" (8). In contrast, histories are always reconstructions, distant and cold curations of the past, unavoidably (or deliberately) edited and incomplete (8). Memory, for Nora, is paradoxically both plural and individualized, embracing multiplicity and contradiction—which makes it antithetical to the project of history, which embraces teleology and stability. For this reason, Nora believes, "history is perpetually suspicious of memory, and its true mission is to suppress and destroy it" (9).

In this vein, Long's memories must necessarily fight to position themselves alongside a legible narrative of the civil rights movement whose official history, crafted in our consensus memories, would, in Nora's words, "annihilate what has in reality taken place" ("Between History and Memory," 9). Rather than attempt to solve this conflict, *The Silence of Our Friends* chooses to represent it through a series of visual codes that express these literal and symbolic historical silences. The memoir accomplishes this task via a dialogue between what Pascal Lefèvre has termed the narrative's diegetic space (i.e., the fictive space within the narrative) and the extradiegetic space of the memoir's historical landscape (i.e., the world outside the narrative). Given the memoir's temporal and geographic location, *The Silence of Our Friends* must also contend with a late-1960s America whose media culture and national politics had lost interest in a civil rights movement largely understood as having accomplished its goals in 1964–1965, and then having given way to black power militancy. *The Silence of Our Friends* works to expand our consensus civil rights memories to include the drama of the TSU Five while chastising the complicit media apparatuses at least partly to blame for its erasure. Essentially, Long's memoir addresses a historical erasure based not only on elision, but also on distancing and forgetting—a process that threatens to annihilate his memories of the movement.

DISTANT MEMORIES AND THE "ACCELERATION OF HISTORY"

The Silence of Our Friends refracts the story of the TSU Five through the friendship between the African American community organizer Larry Thompson and the white journalist John Long, who covers racial issues for Houston television station KRCC. The relationship between the two men prefaces many of the themes that *The Silence of Our Friends* pursues, a narrative agenda established succinctly during the first interaction between its protagonists. Thompson and Long's relationship is introduced when the latter covers the initial sit-ins held in response to the firing of Mack Jones (who isn't actually named in the memoir) and the banning of SNCC from campus by the dean of TSU, a historically black college near the center of the city. Thompson rescues Long and his television camera from a group of angry protesters who accuse Long of simply being "another liar with a camera" and threaten to destroy his equipment (29). Long thanks Thompson for his assistance, and quips, "I'm sure there's lots of razors in those shoes," suggesting that the SNCC demonstrators had a propensity for violence, an implication that perturbs Thompson. Long apologizes for his poor choice of words, reassures Thompson that he doesn't actually believe the protesters are armed, and offers an excuse for his crude characterization: "That's something my mother used to say" (30). The following silent panel depicts Long taking an awkward pull from a pocket flask as Thompson stares at him suspiciously from the right of the panel. The terse conversation ends with Thompson telling Long, "You're the only reporter I trust. You wouldn't be much good to me in the hospital" (31). The scene ends with another silent panel, in which the two men no longer face each other, a stifling disquiet hanging in the air.

The tense exchange between Thompson and Long points to issues that the memoir wishes to address. First, the fact that Long is the lone reporter at such an event echoes the opening sequence's muted lament of US media and political culture losing interest in the civil rights movement as it moved on to issues of communist containment and the imperialist US intervention in Vietnam.[3] Further, the protesters' initial distrust of Long signals the memoir's distrust of media accounts of the civil rights movement that elide such lower-profile venues and events as the protests on Wheeler Avenue—the street that bisects the TSU campus. Worse still, the protesters' distrust stems from media and political narratives that distorted the goals of their activism to suit the needs of a white-supremacist narrative linking black militancy with presumptions of criminality. Long's ill-advised joke about razor-blade-wielding activists inadvertently reifies a political narrative that validated the brutal repression of civil rights activists because of their alleged propensity for violence. Long's clumsy apology suggests something of a temporal trajectory, of racial prejudices that reproduce themselves unreflexively and without self-awareness from one generation to the next. The racial overtones of the quip go unspoken, and so the context of the moment offers the only clue to its racialized meaning. The lack of spoken explanation suggests a deafening silence regarding such matters, one that the memoir hopes to break. Additionally, Thompson's choice to refrain from commenting on Long's joke signals a strategic use of silence. After all, Long is the only reporter whom Thompson trusts, and he needs him in order to gain access to the very media apparatuses his fellow activists thoroughly distrust. Finally, the uncomfortable silence between the two friends in the final panel, and the disquiet of the racial gulf between them, signals the silence of the movement's white allies, the breaking of which is a priority signaled by the title of the memoir.

The Silence of Our Friends focuses largely on Jim Long, a reporter who covers the growing racial tension in "the bottoms"—a nickname for the racially segregated Fifth Ward of inner-city Houston. When Bubba, a neighborhood boy, mocks Mark's father, telling Mark, "He was just talkin' about some nigger. Who cares anything about niggers," Mark hesitates, managing only a meek "I dunno" in response (fig. 4.2). His little sister steps forward, insisting that at least her father does, to which Bubba responds, "Yeah, well, no one else gives a shit" (62). Resigned to silence, the children retreat to their home, where a NASA rocket launch is airing live on television. Though unspecified, the particular flight must be Apollo 4 (9 November), the only launch of a Saturn V in 1967. Since the 1960s was an auspicious decade in American spaceflight—featuring the first time humans left low-Earth orbit, the successful testing of the Saturn rockets, and, eventually, the first moon landing—the image resonates with US cultural significance. The children watch in silence as the rocket proceeds through its preflight diagnostic routine, their troubling exchange with Bubba still lingering quietly in their young minds. Symbolically, the children's viewing of the launch sequence enacts the

4.2. Long, Demonakos, and Powell, *The Silence of Our Friends,* 62–63

problem of the "acceleration of history," which, Nora maintains, eradicates "real memory" with constructions of history—"which is how our hopelessly forgetful modern societies, propelled by change, organize the past" ("Between Memory and History," 8). While the realities of racism and the uneven progress of the civil rights movement were still shaping the lived experiences of the residents of Sharpstown and the Fifth Ward alike, history continued its amnesiac ambulation forward. Houston, it seems, would be relegated to an emergent past still very present to its citizens.

As with the execution shown in the opening sequence, the contradiction between the iconic image of spaceflight on live television and the recent struggles with racial strife of the Long family signals a media culture propelled away from the ongoing civil rights drama at the rocket speed of history. Given both the shape of the panels and the content within them, the juxtaposition of these two sets of panels functions, figuratively speaking, as a sort of non sequitur transition. This is the rarest form of transition, defined by McCloud as an arrangement that "offers no logical relationship between the panels whatsoever" (*Understanding Comics*, 72). McCloud then undermines this assertion, suggesting that the process of closure forbids the presence of any actual non sequiturs. Likewise, I do not mean to suggest these images are wholly unrelated to one another. Rather, the stark juxtaposition between the lived experiences of the Long family and a US society rapidly losing interest in those experiences disrupts, in McCloud's words, the "alchemy at work in the space between panels which can help us find meaning or resonance in even the most jarring of combinations" (73). In other words, this panel arrangement suggests an incomprehensibility for the Long children, who struggle to reconcile the racial tensions in their neighborhood with the hopeful optimism represented by the space rocket.[4] The silence that this contradiction entails troubles *The Silence of Our Friends*.

The visual motif of the 1960s cathode-ray television functions as sort of Bakhtinian chronotope, a marker that anchors a narrative in a specific set of time-space coordinates. Typically, chronotopes are used in fiction and creative nonfiction to establish a narrative firmly within particular temporal and geographic coordinates. As M. M. Bakhtin, the theorist who defined the term, writes: "We will give the name chronotope (literally, "time space") to the intrinsic connectedness of temporal and spatial relationships that are artistically expressed in literature. [. . .] In the literary artistic chronotope, spatial and temporal indicators are fused into one carefully thought-out, concrete whole. Time, as it were, thickens, takes on flesh, becomes artistically visible; likewise, space becomes charged and responsive to the movements of time, plot, and history. This intersection of axes and fusion of indicators characterizes the [. . .] chronotope" (*Dialogic Imagination*, 84). My reading is narrower than Bakhtin's, since I am primarily interested in the unity of time and space as a reminder that material conditions are not abstractly historical or geographic and, thus, that artistic works do not exist outside their historical conditions.[5] Here, these chronotopes function primarily to mark the memories contained in *The Silence of Our Friends* as materially excluded from this history. It is through the motif of the cathode-ray television set that the memoir acknowledges its place outside the typical geographic and temporal parameters of our civil rights consensus memories as it despairs over that exclusion.

The television set motif is present throughout the narrative, beginning with the opening scene. By beginning *The Silence of Our Friends* with recognizably iconic images from the Vietnam War, Long suggests that the national conversation has moved beyond the concerns of the civil rights movement. Going further, beginning the story in "Houston, TX., 1968" likewise places the narrative outside the typical temporal and geographic locations typically associated with the heyday of the movement. As Jacquelyn Dowd Hall notes: "Centering on what Bayard Rustin in 1965 called the 'classical' phase of the struggle, the dominant narrative chronicles a short civil rights movement that begins with the 1954 *Brown v. Board of Education* decision, proceeds through public protests, and culminates with the passage of the Civil Rights Act of 1964 and the Voting Rights Act of 1965" ("Long Civil Rights Movement," 1234). Even John Lewis's *March*, which pushes back against a postracial narrative that sees the work of the civil rights movement as having culminated with the election of Barack Obama, closes with the signing of the Voting Rights Act, claiming that "the movement was never the same" after the legislation passed.[6] Additionally, as Hall's description suggests, the dominant narrative of the "classical" civil rights movement functions within a specific, even if arbitrary, temporal frame, a frame that contains associated spaces accompanied by an archive of iconic imagery. Namely, the drama of the civil rights narrative as typically recalled plays out in schoolrooms, courthouses, lunch counters, and bus depots across the heart of Dixie—particularly in Mississippi, Alabama, and Georgia. Of course, the narrative landscape of the classical civil rights account is hardly a stable one, since contentious debates surrounding monuments and memorials continue to permeate the discourse surrounding its legacies—after all, Nora reminds us, memory is rooted in spaces ("Between Memory and History," 9).[7] Yet the shape and the scope of the consensus narrative of the civil rights movement invoke a particular set of familiar time-spaces, and "Houston, TX, 1968" does not number among them. But it is precisely through the use of the television set motif and the depictions of Văn Lém's execution and the launching of the Saturn rocket that Long marks the story of the TSU Five as lying outside the typical parameters of the classical civil rights narrative, despite the contemporaneous nature of Long's memories and the acceleration of US history.

Long's roster of chronotopes includes many others, which appear throughout the memoir, all with their own multivalent possibilities. Initially, these chronotopes fix the reader in the specific time-space of Houston in the late 1960s. While the chronotopes that Bakhtin discusses are typically, even exclusively, based in prose, the graphic narrative medium allows for the use of visual signifiers for specific time-spaces. As McCloud argues (and as numerous other scholars have noted), "In learning to read comics we all learned to perceive spatially, for in the world of comics, time and space are one and the same" (*Understanding Comics*, 100). From broad spaces such as the TSU campus and expansive Texan landscapes to more specific signifiers such as street signs or highway markers in Houston-area communities such as Sharpstown, Freeport, and Huntsville, these visual cues situate the reader firmly within the boundaries of the Gulf Coast's most populous city and its environs. Similarly, references to popular music, such as Sam and Dave's "Soul Man" or Otis Redding's "Sittin' on the Dock of the Bay" (released in 1967 and 1968, respectively), remind the reader of the memoir's specific time. Casual references to local television stations, news reports, and trials reinforce this effect.

Yet it is also through the use of such visual cues that Powell builds in a sense of distance from the time-space the memoir works to establish. Take for example, the street signs for Freeport Beach in the establishing shot of a scene in which Larry Thompson takes his son crabbing. The opening shot depicts the Thompsons' car driving toward the beach, the street sign to the lower right of the panel telling the reader that the pair still have eleven miles to go until they reach Freeport—a local beach roughly an hour south of Houston. The map that Danny, Larry Thompson's son, holds in his lap establishes both the geographic distance the pair travels as well as the social distance between them and the Long family they have befriended (Long et al., *Silence of Our Friends*, 68). The map places the Thompsons in a specific set of time-space coordinates while simultaneously hinting at a sociopolitical resonance for that signifier. This social distance is laid bare when Thompson and his son are verbally accosted by a racist patron at a local bait shop. Predictably perhaps, the shop owner sides with the white customer and refuses to sell to Thompson, directing him toward "a colored store down by the bridge," lamenting the days when it "used to be we had a sign up, no coloreds" (69). Following the encounter, Thompson storms out. He takes out his frustration on his son, smacking him for talking back to his father. Eventually, Thompson and his son reach the shore, where in a series of largely silent panels, the pair proceed with their plans, their tense experiences hanging like a quiet but palpable pall over the afternoon. "Sittin' on the Dock of the Bay" spills out of Thompson's car radio, perfuming the air with Otis Redding's lamentations.

By employing visual cues that function like chronotopes to evoke a specific time-space and yet echo emergent histories and spaces that lie outside it, *The Silence of Our Friends* positions itself within a civil rights narrative that has ended and yet not ended. Essentially, Powell activates Michel Foucault's notion of the "epoch of juxtaposition" and suggests a conflict between perceiving a recent US racial past as passed and experiencing it as still very much present in Houston in 1967. In his discussion of history, the nineteenth century's "great obsession," Foucault suggests that we begin to think of history as moving into the "epoch of space," when history will be understood less by linearity than by juxtaposition, of the side-by-side copresence of the near and far, of the included and the dispersed: "Structuralism, or at least that which is grouped under this slightly too general name, is the effort to establish, between elements that could have been connected on a temporal axis, an ensemble of relations that makes them appear as juxtaposed, set off against one another, implicated by each other—that makes them appear, in short, as a sort of configuration" (22). Nora's observations regarding the violent clash between memory and history might make us think about this battle being joined over a series of adjacent spaces, both figurative and literal (or, perhaps, literary). In this sense, the visual cues at play in these scenes serve multiple functions, both establishing and disrupting the time-space of the sequence, placing Houston's memories of the civil rights movement parallel to the history written in consensus memory, without integrating them (so to speak).

The street sign for Freeport and the map on the boy's lap suggest not only place but also distance, a symbolic indication of the distance the pair must travel socially in order to be treated as equal to white Texans. The largely silent nature of the sequence emphasizes these visual cues, which are interrupted only to remind the reader of the racial stakes at play in what should have been a relatively mundane interaction with a shopkeeper. The shopkeeper laments that the "no coloreds" sign that used to hang in his store—an unfortunate chronotope—forestalled uncomfortable interactions of the sort he had with Thompson. Although the visually absent but textually present signifier of the "no coloreds" sign potentially intimates a shift away from the era of legal segregation, which such a sign would signal, the result of the shopkeeper's interaction with Thompson dashes that hope, since de facto segregation replaced its legislated, Jim Crow form. The Otis Redding lyrics quoted in the scene's finale—"Look like nothing's gonna change / Everything still remains the same / I can't do what ten people tell me to do / So I guess I'll remain the same"—heighten this sense of stagnation and reaffirms the distance still remaining between African Americans and white US society. According to McCloud, graphic narrative, unlike other mediums, allows multiple temporalities to simultaneously exist on the page: "Both past and future are real and visible and all around us" (*Understanding Comics*, 104). The juxtaposition of the lived experiences of the Thompsons and the silent nature of these emergent memories, set off against the accelerating national history from which these memories are being excluded, indicates the sort of eradication that Nora fears at the hands of consensus memory. The memoir employs these visual strategies to remind readers that progress does not proceed evenly, and to draw our attention to those places ignored both then and now.

Many of the visual cues employed throughout *The Silence of Our Friends* manage, paradoxically, to situate the reader in Houston in 1967 while also displacing the narrative into a not-so-bygone era of US segregation. The memoir chides Texas for lagging behind the times, but also highlights a nation that moved on from the national narrative of the civil rights movement, and left places like inner-city Houston behind altogether. For example, in an early scene, the Longs' young daughter, Julie, returns home from school. In the silent five-panel sequence, Julie finds a flyer tied to her front door, a flyer she unceremoniously drops on the living-room coffee table next to her lunchbox (23). The crumpled, unrolled flyer appears in a single panel on the following page, announcing a Ku Klux Klan rally taking place later that week (fig. 4.3). The visual cues assume the reader's familiarity with the easily recognizable image of the hooded, torch-wielding rider before a stand of burning crosses—neither "Ku Klux Klan" nor "KKK" is stated on the flyer. They also locate the reader in the specific time-space of Gessner Boulevard, a major street in the heart of Harris County, where Houston is situated. The panel bleeds at the top and to the left, unbound by traditional panel frames, suggesting a continuation of the Klan's presence beyond the temporal frame of this single panel.[8] Yet the presence of a Klan rally so near the Longs' home goes uncommented upon. Instead, in a word balloon interrupting the panel, Mrs. Long discusses the televised execution of Nguyễn Văn Lém with her bigoted neighbor. Mrs. Long's irruption into the top panel redirects the reader's attention away from the Klan handout and toward the Vietnam War, and treats the flyer as an ordinary, unnoteworthy piece of paper.

—

4.3. Long, Demonakos, and Powell, *The Silence of Our Friends*, 24

PARALLEL DIEGESIS WITHIN AN EXTRADIEGETIC SPACE

The Long family's seeming lack of interest in discussing, or even acknowledging, the presence of a Klan rally in their community mirrors the attitude of a US media culture that by 1967 had lost interest in domestic racial conflict in favor of the international intrigue of the Vietnam War and the space race. Powell's television motif silently signals this shift, an exceedingly clever use of the narrative capabilities of the comics form. More importantly, the motif takes on additional significance when deployed in graphic narrative, since both the motif and graphic narrative as a medium are intrinsically linked with the narrative construction of time and space. Powell uses such visual cues in a fashion that echoes the construction of diegetic and extradiegetic space. Pascal Lefèvre defines "diegetic" space as "the fictive space in which the characters live and act," which is constructed by "elements that appear inside the frame of a panel and by elements that remain unseen" ("Construction of Space," 157). Lefèvre continues that a reader anticipates a coherent construction of this space, one that proceeds at a "consistent pace, because he tries on the basis of cues (given in the panels) to form a global image of the complete space" (159). Moreover, the world implied by and crafted through those images, as Lefèvre suggests, forces readers to create a coherent universe from a series of otherwise isolated images. In contrast with diegetic space, Lefèvre writes, readers are keenly aware of a comic's extradiegetic space, which exists beyond the boundaries of the physical page: "In addition to the diegetic space every comic has also an extradiegetic space, namely the space outside the fictive world of the comic. The extradiegetic space is the material space that surrounds the individual panels: not only the whites between the panels, but all the real space in which the reader is located" (160). Lefèvre's distinction between these spaces is, of course, based on materiality. In short, diegetic space refers to images on the page, while extradiegetic space highlights the outside world, which contains both the reader and the book. In a figurative manipulation of a multiplicity of such spaces, *The Silence of Our Friends* constructs the narrative, sociopolitical, and historical distances between the story of the TSU Five and civil rights consensus memory, and then attempts to collapse that distance.

As mentioned, *The Silence of Our Friends* functions on two parallel time-spaces: the memoir's primary narrative and the emerging historical narrative of Vietnam and the space race, projected into homes via television. And while the memoir technically classifies as a work of creative nonfiction, we can still describe its (re)construction of Houston as fictive in the sense that like traditional fiction, it is both recalled and reimagined. We might think of these distinct time-spaces as parallel diegetic spaces, each replete with geographic and temporal markers.

Often, these diegetic spaces are literally parallel, arranged side by side on the page, as with the opening sequence, with little or no overlap or intersection in their panel structures. Yet the memoir's concerns about the overarching historical narrative of consensus memory essentially treats the latter as a figurative extradiegetic space, as a world that exists beyond the boundaries of the memoir's primary narrative. Lefèvre notes that diegetic narratives typically do not signal or acknowledge the extradiegetic reading space in which they operate, with the obvious exception of comics that visually break the fourth wall ("Construction of Space," 161). But by constantly pointing to the dominant historical narrative, from which it has been excluded, *The Silence of Our Friends* collapses the distance between its parallel diegetic spaces. It not only treats consensus memory as an extradiegetic space, but also pulls it into its own diegetic space via the television motif. So, as Lefèvre contends, readers are "conscious of the unseen but virtual space outside the panel borders, and to link the fragments together, the reader is looking for overlaps" that allow the construction of such a space to proceed in the first place (159). By pulling the extradiegetic narrative space of consensus memory into the memoir, *The Silence of Our Friends* asks its readers to find the overlaps between the fragments of history presented therein, thereby linking the story of the TSU Five to the greater narrative of the civil rights movement. In this way, the memoir seeks to address history's consumption of memory, as Nora puts it, by collapsing these parallel visions of the past into each other.

But before making such narrative linkages possible, *The Silence of Our Friends* must contend with the reluctance of potential white allies of the civil rights movement to speak out against the continued oppression of African Americans. The political redemption of the Long family in general, and of John Long (the author's journalist father) specifically, anchors the memoir and forms its central thematic concern. Given that Long is a television journalist and therefore linked with the television motif, he not only represents the need for vocal allyship, but also links those alliances with the media apparatuses that created the need for the memoir in the first place. Through the narrative of John Long's political redemption, *The Silence of Our Friends* highlights the power of media culture to both spur contemporary change and rescue individual memory from the jaws of consensus history—a truth recognized by the civil rights movement, particularly by the ever media-savvy Martin Luther King. Culminating with Long's testimony at the trial of the TSU Five, where his videotaped coverage of the riot is presented as evidence against the accused students, the memoir contends that such media narratives can be commandeered for either good or ill if one exercises the agency and the will to do so.

The principal event that concerns *The Silence of Our Friends* occurred at about midnight on 16 May 1967, when Houston police chief Herman Short unleashed six hundred police officers on a student-led protest at Texas State University, a historically black university founded in 1927. As described by the historian Brian D. Behnken, the officers attacked dormitories filled with students, and in the ensuing riot, the Houston Police Department (HPD) shot nearly five thousand rounds of ammunition into buildings filled with African American students—it is nothing short of a miracle that no students were killed (*Fighting Their Own Battles*, 159). At the end of the chaos, two officers received minor gunshot wounds and five hundred students were arrested. Tragically, Officer Louis Kuba was struck in the head and killed, and HPD arrested five students in connection with the shooting, all of whom were later acquitted when it was ascertained that Officer Kuba died from a ricocheted bullet fired from a fellow officer's gun.

Hostilities between the African American community and both the mayor's office and the HPD had been escalating for quite some time before the chaos of 16 May. Tensions in the city began to run high in 1964 when Mayor Louie Welch replaced Police Chief Carl Shuptrine, a man largely respected by white and black communities, with Herman Short, a man whom Behnken refers to as the "'Bull' Connor of Houston" (*Fighting Their Own Battles*, 156). A year prior, an HPD officer shot an unarmed African American man for allegedly stealing a loaf of bread, which prompted an increase of black power activism and more "mainstream" nonviolent activism at Texas Southern. The university fired the respected professor Mack Jones for inviting the Student Non-Violent Coordinating Committee to the campus. In response, student-led protests and sit-ins demanded the reinstatement of Professor Jones and the closing of Wheeler Street, which bisected the campus. In the appendix to the memoir, Long notes that Wheeler Street has since been beautified, particularly near the TSU campus. But things were different in the late 1960s: "At the height of the civil rights struggle in Houston, racist whites would cruise down Wheeler in cars, hurling obscenities at students, and often doing violence. TSU was at one end of the street. At the other was Wheeler Avenue Baptist Church, Houston's 'Ebenezer' and the spiritual seat of Houston's Third Ward. It was said you could go from terror to joy in a city block on Wheeler" (Long et al., *Silence of Our Friends*, 196).

Finally, a local tragedy ignited the powder keg of racial animosity building in Houston since the appointment of Police Chief Short. On 8 May, a week before the TSU riot, eleven-year-old Victor George fell into a garbage-filled pond in an African American neighborhood and drowned—a stark reminder that most of the city's landfills were located in black neighborhoods. Eventually, the protests targeting all these events culminated on Wheeler Avenue on 16 May with the police-led riot that would claim the life of Officer Kuba.

As the memoir's opening scene conveys, deliberation of these issues is framed by the tension between the domestic space of the Longs' suburban Sharpstown home and the public arenas that stage Houston's civil rights dramas. Within the safety of this domestic space, the Long children begin to form interethnic friendships with local African American children—in particular the children of Larry Thompson (Long et al., *Silence of Our Friends*, 106). The first interaction between these children happens in the Longs' home, and begins, perhaps expectedly, with awkward silence, one breached by Cecilia "CC" Thompson's innocent curiosity about why the Longs' house smells funny ("It doesn't smell BAD. Just funny.") (106). Julie notices the bandage on CC's head, a visual reminder of the violence she has experienced on Wheeler Avenue—which she insists "don't hurt." CC's assurances signal a form of agency, one that permits her to have some power over the trauma of her assault at the hands of white supremacists. Unperturbed, Julie sheepishly asks CC, "Can—Can I see what y'all look like?" (107) before placing her hands on CC's face—a reminder that Julie, who is blind, has been learning Braille in school. From here, Julie notices that CC's hair "feels funny"—a particularly irritating microaggression in most contexts. But the Thompson children take the comment in stride, and Danny reaches out and touches Mark's spiky blond hair, noting that "it's like a brush, how it sticks up like that" (107). The equivalency of experience suggested by this racially egalitarian exchange is heightened by Julie's initial request to "see" CC's face through tactile physical features rather than via phenotypical markers such as skin color. Julie represents a sort of praxis, one that implies the deliberate adoption of a color-"blind" outlook as a path to a postracial era wherein children can be judged by something other than "the color of their skin" (or, in this instance, the texture of their hair). These scenes work to redeem John Long's previous assertion that his razor blade joke revealed more about the attitudes of his parents than his own, an element of the narrative reinforced by the Long children's budding racial consciousness.[9]

The Long family's home functions as something of a symbolic diegetic space where their family and friends are free to construct a microcosm of racial harmony sheltered from the outside world. Within this domestic-diegetic space, the Long family articulates the significance of images such as Mark's spiky blond hair, which "stands up like a brush," or the bandage on CC's forehead. In essence, the children in these scenes function as the authors of the central fiction constructed in this diegetic space: racial harmony can be articulated through such simple gestures as touching each other's hair. Furthermore, Julie's colorblind approach to the

Thompson children authorizes the Long children to ignore racialized meanings inherited through time (handed down through the generations) and space (like the attitudes of their bigoted neighbors). These scenes represent the sort of lived memory highlighted by Nora, protected from the consuming nature of official histories. The children remain keenly aware of the extradiegetic space outside their home, a space where they have no agency to construct or challenge racist attitudes, but within their own diegetic space, they can proceed as they see fit.

The final panel of this racially utopian scene subtly undercuts its unavoidable, charming naiveté. On the following page, while the kids move on from their fascination with the texture of each other's hair to singing along with Sam and Dave's hit "Soul Man," the final panel zooms out to a now-familiar shot of the Longs' suburban backyard. This shot reminds the reader of the safety of the domestic-diegetic space within which this exchange takes place. Implicitly, the Long children risk reproducing the silent sins of their parents, engaging in racial inclusivity within the safety of their home but tacitly permitting the politics of racial exclusion to continue in the public sphere. After all, after their playdate with the Long children, Mark and CC Thompson will have to return to their home near Wheeler Avenue and all the racial terror contained therein—serving as a stark reminder not only of who constructs these sorts of colorblind fictions, but also for whom they are constructed. In this context, CC's insistence that her forehead wound "don't hurt" reads less like an exercise of political agency than a willful self-silencing, a demoralizing sacrifice she makes in order not to disrupt the tableau of racial harmony unfolding before her. This final panel subtly signals the extradiegetic distance between their worlds, both physically (roughly thirteen miles separates TSU and Wheeler Avenue from Sharpstown) and figuratively, and the distance between their social spheres and experiences with race. So while these scenes function as a sort of racial disclaimer, reassuring readers that the Long family does not share the racist attitudes prevalent in their suburban community, their progressivism is limited primarily to the sanctity of their domestic space—a luxury that CC's bandage reminds readers is not afforded to the Thompson family. The final panel of this scene recalls the memoir's opening sequence, which closes on a similar panel. In that instance, the domestic bliss represented by their suburban home is violated by the realities of the Vietnam War, brought into their home via television. Ironically, in their encounter with Mark and CC, the Long children fail to recognize the presence of the domestic war on the African American children they have just befriended.

In a larger sense, this division between public and private, diegetic and extradiegetic, recalls how Foucault delineates the unity of history and its fragmentation over space. We might think of the fictive diegetic re-creation of the Longs' home as the sort of utopian no-space that Foucault positions as "a general relation of direct inverted analogy with the real space of Society" ("Of Other Spaces," 24). In other words, the racial utopia represented by the children's exchange in their backyard is made legible because of its antithetical relationship to the society to which this utopia is responding. Therefore, the Long family's home represents an inverted analogy for the racist society that contains it, and acts as a diegetic counter to the extradiegetic history represented by consensus memory. In Foucauldian terms, the Long family's home "present[s] society itself in a perfected form, or else society turned upside down" (24). Unfortunately for the Long children, it will only be a matter of time before they discover that "these utopias are fundamentally unreal spaces" (24). While the space represented by their home may be "unreal," the children's constructed utopia, "society itself in a perfected form," initially seems insulated from the terrors that lie outside its fences.

The fictive diegesis of the memoir recalls Nora's romantic, even utopian description of memory: "Memory installs remembrance within the sacred . . . takes root in the concrete, in spaces, gestures, images, and objects" ("Between Memory and History," 9). But here we are met with something of a contradiction, even a paradox. How can Long's memories of Houston and the TSU Five be both fictive and rooted in concrete reality? Seemingly, *The Silence of Our Friends* posits that the mere act of commanding a diegetic space in order to transcribe memories prevents their slow consumption at the hands of history. But the memoir warns of the unavoidably vulnerable nature of these memories in the face of the force of history, which, as Nora cautions, works to obliterate them. In regard to *The Silence of Our Friends*, this threat manifests in the quiet encroachment of the extradiegetic space of history into the diegetic space of memory: first, symbolically by television motif, and later by the physical violence directed against African Americans like the Thompson family. Ultimately, the memoir urges, it is the silences of the Long family, both as neighbors and as media figures, that permit the suppression and destruction predicted by Nora to proceed and persist.

LONG SILENCES REDEEMED

The Long children's newly formed racial progressivism comes at a social and physical cost—a hard lesson they learn once they leave the safety of their suburban home and express their progressive racial views outside their protected diegetic space. In a pivotal scene, Mark receives a black eye for espousing his new racial politics (157). When confronted with the opportunity to stand up for the civil rights struggle after Bubba mocked his father's coverage of the TSU demonstrations, Mark meekly shied away from the confrontation, even as his little sister did not (61). Later, after his friendship with the Thompson children was forged, Mark returns home with a black eye, which he attributes to having fallen down—but which we soon learn was given to him by Bubba. The actual moment of violence goes undepicted; rather, the reader encounters the attack's aftermath as Mark's mother tends to his wound. Afterward, Mark goes to the backyard and runs the hose over his hair, a silent and meditative scene that suggests the young boy's attempt to wash away the trauma, a baptismal image that ushers the boy into a consciousness of a public world uglier and more harrowing than the easy racial harmony of his backyard. Even the safety of his home is violated when Mark is approached by their racist neighbor, the one who refused to express any sympathy for the "gook" executed on television in the memoir's opening scenes. This neighbor says that he knows Bubba gave Mark the black eye, and that he is not surprised, since "your folks really should have known that was gonna happen," to which Mark does not respond (158). Gone is the hopeful naiveté of the previous scenes, replaced by the young boy's silencing. The final panel again features a distant shot of the Longs' home, this time focused on the view from the street. In the center of the panel, their troublesome neighbor saunters away, mockingly singing "Soul Man," the same song that earlier brought together the Long and Thompson families. The hard lesson learned is that the easy separation of the family's domestic-diegetic space from the extradiegetic racism that envelops it cannot be long maintained.

Despite these challenges, the Long children are undeniably courageous, particularly when compared with their parents. As happened with their children, the influence of the Thompson family pushes the parents past their self-imposed social silence, and their growing friendship proves to be politically transformative. This is perhaps best shown when Mrs. Long confidently boasts to a perturbed Avon lady that she was hungover after a delightful night "with a lovely negro family" (111). Despite her initial hesitation, the Avon lady cheerfully enters the Long family's home, despite her obvious discomfort at Mrs. Long's beaming integrationist pride. Still, these kinds of moments, few in number, occur exclusively in the private space of the Longs' home. The public silence of white allies like the Longs preoccupies much of the memoir's narrative, and John Long struggles to voice his disapproval of the ubiquitous racism of his suburban Texas community, a narrative track that culminates with Long's testimony at the trial of the TSU Five.

The Silence of Our Friends goes to great lengths to characterize the Long family as committed antiracists. It features John Long repudiating his children for their casual use of the phrase "nigger knocking" (16), ranting about his racist station manager (59), and even expelling an old army buddy from his house after he uses racially charged epithets in front of his children (121). But these moments of resistance occur exclusively within the safety of the Longs' family home. The Long parents remain largely silent when confronted with the racist realities represented by the larger white community. For example, when Patricia discusses the execution of Văn Lém with her neighbor, she ignores the man's casual use of the word "gook" and meekly diverts the conversation toward the Geneva conventions, a counterargument that is quickly dropped (24). When discussing how to cover a case involving a local African American activist charged with issuing death threats to a police officer, John Long's station manager pressures him to exclude the perspective of the defendant from the nightly news report, a demand to which Long quietly acquiesces (58). Long repeatedly fails to stand up to his manager, even when the station's owner insists they investigate the everyday violence on Wheeler Avenue (96), or when the same manager refuses to air Long's eyewitness account—an account that would exonerate the TSU Five (143). Long's refusal to break his silence is doubly damning when one considers both his privileged position as a white man and as a television personality with mass media access. Long's greatest silent sin, however, occurs at the Wheeler riot, when Long (who is filming the mayhem) fails to assist Thompson as he pleads for help while being violently beaten by HPD officers (137). This moment is juxtaposed with Mark's black eye, an image chastising the cowardice of the father via the courage of the son. This final betrayal drives a deep wedge between Long and Thompson, one that is healed only at the trial of the TSU Five when Long testifies that he witnessed the death of Officer Kuba at the hands of a fellow officer's ricocheted bullet (169). Long's testimony leads to the acquittal of the TSU Five and eventually reconciles Long and Thompson.[10]

Before the trial, the narrative sets the thematic stakes in a pivotal scene in the family home. Bill, an old army buddy of John's, arrives unexpectedly at the Longs' home one evening, looking to reconnect. He asks John if he can stay the night; struggles with alcoholism have cost him both his job and his marriage (116). Bill decides to join the Long children in the living room, where they are playing one of their favorite games—mimicking their father's nightly news broadcasts by using a cardboard box as a television set (fig. 4.4). The middle two panels are bordered by the blackness of the paper behind them, which isolates the images of Mark crawling into the cardboard box. The box becomes something of a frame, marking the edges of the symbolic diegetic space where Mark can create his

4.4. Long, Demonakos, and Powell, *The Silence of Our Friends*, 118

own media narrative. But his awareness of the viewer—in this case, Bill—causes Mark to pause, and he hesitates before beginning his report. Acknowledging the "accident" that caused his friend CC's head injury, Mark states, "Today, a little black girl almost got run'ed over at Wheeler Street." Before he can continue, Bill interrupts the newscast. In the final frame of the left page, Bill's drunken response drifts across the page: "That's not news! Y'all do something funny. Act like some niggers or something." He follows up with a racist pantomime on the next page. This final frame on the left page shows Mark in profile, framed not by his cardboard television but by the family's cathode-ray television set. Mark and Julie resist Bill's demands, and Mark tells him, "We ain't supposed to say that no more." Before Bill can compel them to comply, their mother shepherds the children away while John kicks Bill out of the house (120).

The performative aspects of this scene continue to undermine the division between the Longs' private diegetic space and their extradiegetic public lives, thereby drawing together many of the memoir's thematic threads. Mark's attempt to script a newscast that addresses the racialized violence on Wheeler Avenue both accesses the symbolic diegetic space of the family home and reminds the reader of John's failure to address that violence on an actual newscast. Staging it in the family home implies the agency of authorship, one that must find both outlet and expression in the extradiegetic space of the public sphere. The image of the cardboard box as both a stage and a stand-in for a newsroom recalls the repeating chronotope of the television set. Mark previously struggled with materializing history over which he had no control or experiential proximity; here, he attempts to commandeer the medium of television to bring it in line both with his own politics and as a reflection of his experiences in inner-city Houston. Playing a newsman like his father functions as a corrective, since the children's commitment to breaking the silence that forbids action on racial injustice continues to outpace that of their parents. But Bill's presence disrupts the ease with which the Long family can move from the diegetic space of their home to the extradiegetic space that frames it. Bill's insistence that the children's make-believe newscast adhere to the kind of racialized stereotypes of African Americans that he expects to encounter on television, rather than focus on the tribulations of families like the Thompsons, implies complicity—on the part of both the viewer and the performer (should he acquiesce).

In his delineation of the relationship between diegetic spaces, Lefèvre notes that the diegetic space of the comic rarely acknowledges the presence of the extradiegetic space in which it operates ("Construction of Space," 160–161). But within the parameters of the symbolic diegetic space of the Long family's home, Mark is keenly aware of how the extradiegetic space of the public sphere contains and even shapes his ability to function as the author of his newscast. Furthermore, the extradiegetic elements represented by Bill as the audience not only contain the domestic-diegetic space represented by the cardboard box (an appropriately flimsy symbolic element), but also exert pressure on the narrative to conform to certain expectations of what should be expressed and what elided. Bill's dialogue balloons appropriately drift in from the right of the page, from outside the more literal diegetic space of the page, directing the authorship from without. The television set in the final frame of page 118 draws our attention to this same dynamic playing out at KRRC, where John works. This arrangement of the dialogue balloons echoes how the voice of John's station manager is displayed when he forces John to remain silent on the racial troubles plaguing Wheeler Avenue. And while Mark's resistance to Bill's insistence that he similarly ignore the everyday racial terrors on the campus of Texas Southern University may feel meek in comparison, what matters (as far as the memoir is concerned) is that even these meager words break the silence that permits such injustices. More importantly, Mark refuses to perform the role assigned to him by a US media culture that prefers to be entertained by racial injustice rather than being confronted by it.

This scene leads directly to the conflagration on Wheeler Avenue that claims the life of Officer Kuba and leads to the arrest of the TSU Five, a sequence in which the television motif plays its most critical role. As Long and Thompson express concern that "it feels like there's more police here than protesters" at the sit-in, the HPD silently advances on the students (127). Without warning, the officers begin to violently suppress the protesters, in a scene all too familiar to those with even a passing familiarity with the iconography of the civil rights movement. When Long hoists his television camera to film the chaos, a police officer clubs him in the back and demands that he stop filming or he will be arrested. For a moment, Thompson, Long, and the protesters are scattered, but they regroup and recommence the protest. The scene quickly descends into chaos as officers begin to club, cuff, and haul off the student protesters. In the midst of the riot, Thompson is beaten in the street. He asks Long to help him, but the latter is preoccupied with filming the conflict (and potentially afraid to intervene). Throughout the sixteen-page sequence of the riot, we "see" the violence through the lens of John's camera as the panels take on the now-familiar frame of the cathode-ray television panel. At the bottom of page 131, a television panel shows a police officer aggressively arresting a protester as he looks at the camera (fig. 4.5).

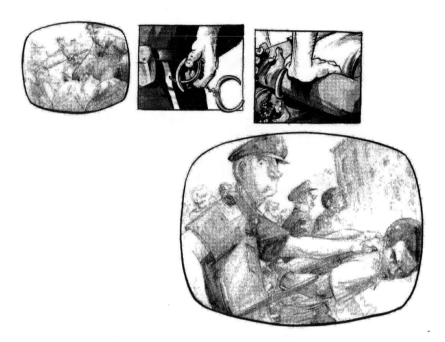

4.5. Long, Demonakos, and Powell, *The Silence of Our Friends*, 131

In this moment, the television chronotope violates the imposed division between diegetic and extradiegetic spaces in multiple ways. The first is literal: the officer's gaze causes the extradiegetic space in which the reader is situated to be "integrated by means of a character seemingly looking the reader straight in the eyes and addressing the reader" (Lefèvre, "Construction of Space," 161). This silent address challenges readers to consider their own potential complicity in the silences that prompted the production of the memoir they hold in their hands. Furthermore, John's perspective collapses into the extradiegetic space of Wheeler Avenue, "integrated," as Lefèvre puts it, through the recurrent television motif. The next set of images is on a two-page spread featuring television panels, traditional panels, and unpaneled images scattered across pages (fig. 4.6). This chaotic structure vacillates between television panels and more traditional comic panels, the two messily integrated on the page after the violation of the division between diegetic and extradiegetic spaces on the previous page. The images are united by the unbordered image at the bottom, which shows John filming the riot and an officer firing on a dormitory in response to the injuring of an officer, shown at the top of the page. The two men represent clashing perspectives on the

—

chaos, perspectives that will be integrated if John chooses to conform to the same expectations of media complicity that Bill sought from Mark, or that will counter each other. The spread represents this conflict, a struggle between the forces each man represents.

John's use of the camera to film the riot arguably creates the same paradox of simultaneous distance and nearness experienced by Mark in the opening scene—a final division between symbolic diegetic and extradiegetic spaces, which the memoir will erode. It permits John to ignore Thompson's pleas for assistance when he is being beaten during the riot, contented to film the assault rather than intervene in it—a common criticism of journalists of the period, particularly in regard to Vietnam. Yet it is because he is filming that he is able to witness the death of Officer Kuba, even though he failed to capture it on film. John tells his station manager that he can attest to the innocence of the TSU Five, but his station manager rejects his claims and airs the state's narrative of the students' presumed guilt (143). Again, John acquiesces. But his ability to hide behind the camera ends once the state subpoenas John to testify against the TSU Five, with his video recording entered as evidence on the side of the prosecution. As a result, John's control over his diegetic narrative of events is challenged, and he is thrust into the extradiegetic space of the courtroom. Here, the "truth" of his testimony is contested, even manipulated, to suit the needs of a state apparatus hostile to his integrationist politics. As the easy division between his private life and the public sphere collapses, John is forced into a choice that he has been avoiding during the entire narrative—speak out and face the potential consequences, or silently comply with the racial injustice he privately condemns. Prompted by Thompson (who serves as counsel for the defense), John contradicts the prosecution's framing of his testimony, and his eyewitness account ultimately exonerates the wrongly accused TSU Five.

Foucault believed that in contemporary historiography, space shapes "the horizons of our concerns, our theory, our systems" (Foucault, "Of Other Spaces," 22). While he contends that this idea is not an innovation, he maintains its pertinence to the contemporary world: "The present epoch will perhaps be above all the epoch of space. We are in the epoch of simultaneity: we are in the epoch of juxtaposition, the epoch of the near and far, of the side-by-side, of the dispersed" (22). Graphic narrative seems especially equipped, with its ability to arrange time in space on the page, to astutely represent the simultaneous, the juxtaposed, and the dispersed. In this regard, *The Silence of Our Friends* treats the dominant

4.6. Long, Demonakos, and Powell, *The Silence of Our Friends*, 132–133

narrative of civil rights consensus memory like an extradiegetic space, that is, as a context that surrounds and threatens to consume its own memories—a dynamic that its authors cannot exert control over. Rather, they choose to acknowledge this extradiegetic space and symbolically pull it into the diegetic space of the memoir. In doing so, the memoir highlights the distance between the spaces and attempts to collapse that distance and unite the story of the TSU Five with the master narrative of the movement. In this regard, the memoir participates in what Nora calls "commemorative vigilance," an active process that requires us to "deliberately create archives, maintain anniversaries, organize celebrations, pronounce eulogies, and notarize bills because such activities no longer occur naturally" (Nora, "Between Memory and History," 12). In this sense, *The Silence of Our Friends* reclaims memories forgotten by history, restoring them to a form "no longer quite life, not yet death, like shells on the shore when the sea of living memory has receded" (12). I invoke this final passage from Nora specifically, since in this context it comes to represent the physical bodies with which history both writes itself, and later discards.

This passage also allows me to meditate on perhaps the most anachronistic—as well as the most troublingly problematic—chronotope in the memoir, which appears in the book's epilogue. As Julie Long sits with her elementary school teacher and beams that she finally learned how to compose her name in Braille, a harried teacher interjects to distressingly report, "They shot King" (184). What follows is a long symbolic funeral procession featuring the characters of *The Silence of Our Friends*, closing with the quotation that lends the memoir its title. Martin Luther King's assassination occurred on 4 April 1968, nearly a year after the riot on Wheeler Avenue that set the memoir's events into motion. Given that the novel opens with the phrase "Houston, TX, 1968," we are symbolically returned to the beginning of the narrative, a gesture that collapses the time-space of the novel neatly into the year, even the moment, of MLK's death. In so doing, the memoir symbolically marks the end of the civil rights movement with the assassination of King, ostensibly extending the frame of the classical era of the movement from the passing of civil rights legislation to the passing of its most prominent leader. This new frame places the events of the memoir squarely within the parameters of this classical era, even as it reiterates the faulty and arbitrary logic that claims the movement begins and ends with King's career.

More troubling still is what the inclusion of this epilogue reveals about the construction of civil rights consensus memories—namely, the need for a black body. In every memoir so far discussed, the death of a martyred, typically male activist sets the story in motion and lays bare the stakes involved for the community that mourns the loss. The lone exception might be John Lewis's *March*, which integrates its body count to include martyrs from both the black and white communities. I do not mean to suggest that these narratives should shy away from the deaths that haunt civil rights consensus memories. Such an admonition would result in the sort of historical erasure that *The Silence of Our Friends* attempts to redress. But what does the inclusion of MLK's death reveal about the legibility of civil rights narratives that are not built on the bodies of murdered black men?

CHAPTER 5

Tropes, Transfer, Trauma

THE LYNCHING IMAGERY OF *STUCK RUBBER BABY*

H oward Cruse's celebrated *Stuck Rubber Baby* (1995), his fictionalized coming-out story set in civil-rights-era Alabama, opens with a meditation on bodies on display. From the outset, Cruse signals to his reader the importance of bodies either recalled from his coming of age in 1960s Alabama, imagined through fiction or, more (im)precisely perhaps, emerging from the murky waters of the consensus memory that joins the two. Cruse reconstitutes these bodies on the comic's pages, a sort of mournful display that posits the 1990s LGBTQ movement as the natural inheritor of legacies of 1960s civil rights activism. The novel opens with Toland Polk, Cruse's fictionalized protagonist, speaking from the inky shadows of memory to reflect on these bodies, specifically "the ones [he] saw stuck in [his] mind" (1). Speaking from the 1990s, Toland's memories are neatly organized across the title page; images of John and Jackie Kennedy are juxtaposed with images of racist southerners picketing the burning bus of the Freedom Riders. These two illustrations function chronotopically, situating the reader in a specific epoch of American history.[1] The images are unbordered, bleeding across the title page, suggesting a continuation of this history to the unbordered image of Toland narrating his story from the background.

In three neatly contained panels arranged in parallel on Toland's right, Cruse depicts the imagined death of his babysitter, Miss Violet, and his attendance at her funeral. As young Toland stands before the casket of poor Miss Violet, the adult Toland tells the reader, "As a rule, the expert hands of our best local morticians had the remains spruced up by the time I got my look at whoever was lying in state . . . so there was never any gore on display" (1). The sanitized nature of both Miss Violet's death and the manner in which her body is publicly displayed for the purposes of closure and catharsis is juxtaposed with a much more violent display when young Toland discovers the brutal lynching of Emmett Till via the famous issue of *Jet* magazine (fig. 5.1). Unlike the face of Miss Violet, who is framed in the top-left panel, the mutilated face of Emmett Till and the "gore" of his grisly murder are fully displayed only to Toland. The reader sees Toland's reaction to the "bashed, lynched, and dumped" body of the Chicago teenager, whose death galvanized US antiracists and is often remembered as having ignited the civil rights movement. In the three-panel sequence in the middle of the page, Toland tells the reader, "Something in my brain permanently blew a fuse when I saw that picture. I had nightmares. I was worried about my skull" (2). Toland's fear that his skull would end up like Till's connects the plight of one to the other, casting the murder of Till at the hands of white supremacists as a common threat to both marginalized young men. Bracketed with the images of the Kennedys and the assailants of the Freedom Riders, Cruse asks us to read Toland's struggles with his burgeoning homosexuality through the lens of the civil rights movement.

In this context, Cruse links the implicit, even if imagined, sexual threat represented by Emmett Till (who was murdered "because he said something flippant

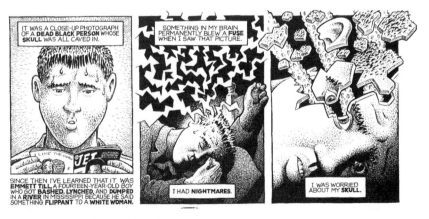

5.1. Howard Cruse, *Stuck Rubber Baby*, 2

to a white woman") with Toland's fear that he will likewise be brutally dispatched for the threat that his male homosexual identity represents. In effect, Cruse links the death of Emmett Till with the plight of the homosexual male community via a common enemy—the white hetero-patriarchal episteme that threatens both their bodies. Accompanying Toland's narration is a fragmented visual motif that appears throughout the narrative, particularly in moments of oppressive violence. In this opening sequence, Toland's traumatizing viewing of Till's body finds visual expression as we see his mind shatter across the page, a figurative reenactment of the literal shattering of Emmett Till. Through this fragmentation, Cruse's novel climaxes with the symbolic transfer of the brutal lynching of African Americans like Emmett Till to the body of Toland Polk's best friend, Sammy Noone, a homosexual civil rights activist lynched in the final scenes of the novel. This visual strategy reinforces the linkage between the marginalization of African Americans and that of the similarly threatened homosexual men who populate the underground subcultures of Clayfield, Alabama. But a key aspect undermines the pat intersectional logic of *Stuck Rubber Baby*: Toland Polk and Sammy Noone are white.

The fragmentation motif that accompanies Toland's reaction to seeing a photo of the body of Emmett Till appears throughout *Stuck Rubber Baby* but represents only one of the many narrative strategies Cruse employs to frame the story of the 1990s-era LGBTQ rights movement as the natural inheritor of civil rights pathos. The invocation of Till in the opening pages, alongside the familiar faces of the Kennedys and the Freedom Riders in the title's banner, deliberately invokes a familiar set of classical civil rights images. This invocation in many ways summons a now-reified historical narrative enshrined in the annals of consensus memory, emblematized perhaps by the inauguration of Martin Luther King Jr. Day as a national holiday.[2] And as with any established cultural narrative, the reification of civil rights consensus memory was accompanied by an incumbent set of stereotypes, stages, and tropes—many of which appear throughout *Stuck Rubber Baby*. The memoir uses immediately recognizable 1960s tropes—thinly veiled analogues of Martin Luther King Jr. and Coretta Scott King, a wide cast of interchangeable white supremacists, and familiar civil rights settings—to frame Cruse's 1990s LGBTQ-rights allegory in order to capitalize on the movement's social mobilization and sense of moral urgency.

In so doing, Cruse's novel participates in a wider debate among a number of groups across the political spectrum, each making similar claims in the hope of accessing the sociohistorical cache of civil rights legacies for their own sociopolitical ends. However, my work here does not seek to verify or invalidate the veracity of any group's claim to the legacies of the civil rights movement. Rather, it approaches *Stuck Rubber Baby* as reflecting an emergent form of consensus memory, one based on a stabilizing set of historical and narrative tropes concerning the movement. Cruse positions the movement as pivoting toward LGBTQ issues in the 1990s, a view pioneered by many of the original movement's leaders, such as Congressman John Lewis and Coretta Scott King—a rhetorical strategy employed by a bevy of rights groups in the 1990s. Thus, *Stuck Rubber Baby*'s political dimensions are contingent on the legibility of its civil rights tropes, particularly those related to its use of stock African American secondary characters, who are employed largely to validate its political purpose. In this vein, Cruse's memoir astutely represents the civil rights movement as it is remembered, a set of consensus memories that, in turn, continue to have political valence. After all, the civil rights movement is often invoked as morally righteous and is endlessly emulated—unlike, say, its more direct progeny such as the ethnic liberation and antiwar movements of the 1970s. It has become a historic watershed in the trajectory of American moral progressivism, one whose specter is often invoked to legitimize the forthrightness of contemporary sociopolitical causes.

This chapter explores the narrative strategies that Cruse employs to transfer both the agency and the traumas of the African American protagonists of the civil rights narrative onto the primarily white homosexual characters of his novel, which invariably reduces the overlap between these marginalized communities to a naively utopian fantasy. The novel culminates with the lynching of the homosexual activist Sammy Noone, a white man—a symbolic choice that in any other context would, and rightfully so, lead to condemnation of such an outright act of sociohistorical appropriation. But rather than openly chastise either Cruse or the many admirers of *Stuck Rubber Baby*, *Graphic Memories* ponders the questions, To whom have we conceded our memories of the civil rights era and to whom does this history belong?

STUCK RUBBER BABY AND A POLITICALLY USEFUL CIVIL RIGHTS PAST

We might think of Cruse's novel as attempting to integrate concomitant LGBTQ struggles with the master narrative of civil rights—an ethos that shapes the way he imagines the fictional town of Clayfield, Alabama. In an early scene in the novel, Sammy Noone treats Toland, his girlfriend, Ginger, and two of their friends to a "tour of Clayfield's underbelly" (47). Sammy, whose open homosexuality makes him welcome in all these spaces despite any potential anxieties his race might cause, takes them to the predominantly African American Melody Motel, to the town's underground gay night club, the Rhombus, and finally to the Alleysax, an integrated jazz club on the edge of town. In Clayfield's underbelly, the imagined social landscape on the margins of this fictionalized Alabama town and its social politics are laid bare. Homosexuals and heterosexuals, blacks and whites, intermingle openly, far from the oppressive gaze of the town's white hetero-patriarchy. It is in these spaces that Cruse introduces a large cast of African American characters that fill out the chorus of his civil rights drama. First, in the Melody Motel, known around town for housing the local Freedom Chorus, Toland discovers heterosexual and homosexual citizens of Clayfield openly interacting. Initially apprehensive, Toland is relieved that "most everybody there seemed fairly ordinary," with the exception of Esmereldus, an African American drag queen who, despite Toland's condescending reaction, is openly accepted and celebrated (24). The Rhombus offers a space where only racists (regardless of orientation) feel unwelcome; its patrons hide in plain sight as gay and lesbian couples switch partners to fool the intrusive Clayfield police (44). At the Alleysax, a racially and sexually integrated jazz club on the literal and figurative margins of Clayfield, the African American and homosexual communities commune openly with their more normative white heterosexual allies.

The sequence in which we encounter these spaces matters. We move from the predominantly racialized space of the Melody Motel to the somewhat closeted gay space of the Rhombus and finally to the intersectionally integrated space of the Alleysax. Symbolically, Cruse moves the reader through three spaces that represent three activist paradigms—the first predominantly African American, the second predominantly LGBTQ, and finally, the blended, integrated space that reflects the novel's interweaving of these parallel histories of marginalization. In each location, Cruse highlights the permeable nature of the supposed and imposed social boundaries separating these spaces: the act of moving from a social setting defined by a particular aspect of identity treated in isolation to one that embraces an intersectional dynamic is significant. Ultimately, the novel argues, it is in the fusion of these supposedly disparate sites of identity formation that the individual communities find their greatest strength. The whole, it would seem, is much greater than the sum of its parts, despite the efforts of the Clayfield police to fragment these marginalized groups. Symbolically, Cruse intertwines the histories and the constituents of these communities rather than treating them as socially, or even temporally, distinct, by reassembling the fragments into a cohesive whole. Even the name of the town—"Clayfield"—suggests the sort of plastic social terrain that Cruse can mold into his vision of the civil rights movement's historical legacy.

—

This represents only one of the many symbolic strategies Cruse employs to link the historical plight of African Americans and homosexuals—a discursive act largely informed by the mid-1990s debate over homosexual marriage rights. In 1996, John Lewis railed against the Defense of Marriage Act (DOMA), a federal law that before being ruled unconstitutional in 2013 and 2015, withheld federal recognition of (and federal benefits to) same-sex marriages, among its most far-reaching provisions.[3] DOMA defined marriage as the union of one man and one woman and permitted states to refuse to recognize same-sex marriages granted under the laws of other states. It passed with overwhelming bipartisan support and was signed into law by President Bill Clinton, a Democrat. In a fiery speech opposing the bill delivered on the House floor on 11 July 1996, Lewis, the former Freedom Rider, denounced the bill, making explicit the parallels between the drive for LGBTQ rights and the civil rights movement. Asserting his civil rights credentials, Lewis condemned the legislation, reminding his fellow legislators, "I have known racism. I have known bigotry. This bill stinks of the same fear, hatred, and intolerance" ("Civil Rights Hero"). Going further, Lewis invoked his friendship with Bayard Rustin, a gay man, a fellow civil rights activist, and an organizer of the March on Washington. Rustin was nearly pushed out of the movement, considered a liability because of an arrest nearly a decade earlier on trumped-up "morals charges"—an exclusion that Lewis condemns in *March*. Lewis reminded his colleagues about Rustin's plight: "He was pushed aside. He was brilliant, but they thought it would hurt the movement—that certain senators would use it against the march. It was wrong." Lewis added that DOMA "was an affront to the man, to what he stood for, and to the contributions he made" (quoted in Tucker, "Rep. John Lewis"). By invoking Rustin's near ouster from participation in the movement on the grounds of his homosexuality, Lewis implies an overlapping oppression faced both by the black and LGBTQ communities—compounded, of course, for figures like Rustin, who belong to each. It should come as little surprise, then, that Lewis has been a reliable ally and legislative champion of marriage equality, fighting against LGBTQ discrimination for his entire congressional career. Additionally, Lewis's rhetoric fosters a sense of political inheritance echoed by other prominent progressive voices—that the legacies of the civil rights movement might naturally be passed down to a historically concomitant LGBTQ movement that was rising in both efficacy and urgency in the 1990s.[4]

Congressman Lewis's rhetoric was challenged by legislators, politicians, and religious leaders from across party and racial lines. Congressman Bill Lipinski (D-IL), Congressman Tom Coburn (R-OK), and General Colin Powell refuted analogies establishing an equivalence between racial identity and sexual orientation regarding civil rights protections, and they argued that DOMA affected all orientations equally—ironically, the same logic that was used to prop up miscegenation laws just a generation prior.[5] In their diehard opposition to same-sex marriage, prominent white Christian leaders sought alliances with black churches. Chris Bull and John Gallagher astutely highlight the irony of leaders of the conservative Christian Right "aggressively courting blacks, even though many of the leaders, such as Jerry Falwell and the Reverend Lou Sheldon, had been opposed to many of the civil rights gains blacks had made in the 1960s" (*Perfect Enemies*, 170). Many of these anti-gay-rights voices took umbrage at the linkage between the LGBTQ rights and civil rights movements, and many of their arguments evoked the explicit threat to hetero-patriarchal society posed by gay marriage. As David Hirsch pointedly discusses, homosexual marriage was often cast as a deviant, even monstrous threat to normal heterosexual society, terms that, Hirsch contends, forced many into an unsatisfactory position of having to "advocate for either family or monstrosity" ("De-familiarizations, De-monstrations," 55). Of course the multifaceted debate over DOMA specifically, and gay rights generally, extended well beyond these political arenas, as evinced by AIDS activism and contemporaneous debates over "Don't Ask, Don't Tell." The rhetorical aspects of the gay rights movement's claim to civil rights legacies, both in *Stuck Rubber Baby* and in the 1990s generally, elucidate the need to come to terms with the concession of this status to one group by another. After all, the moral authority of the civil rights movement is never called into question, its social righteousness treated as sacrosanct, especially in the sanitized version of consensus memory. The only matter remaining, it seems, is to establish who may lay claim to its usable past in the political present.

Since *Stuck Rubber Baby* was published in 1995, it would be difficult not to read the novel's primary personal narrative and its frame narrative in the context of the debate over DOMA, and over the validity of the LGBTQ civil rights analogies that accompanied it. Reading the novel in this context elucidates Cruse's motivations to make such civil rights connections, which in many ways addresses the contestations made by conservative critics. Much of Toland Polk's coming-out narrative centers on his failed heterosexual relationship with Ginger Raines, a local folk singer and civil rights activist in Clayfield. As Gary Richards notes, their failed relationship is a trope in that it brings the novel in line with many other works in the coming-out genre ("Everybody's Graphic Protest Novel," 163). The title of the novel refers to the broken condom that results in Toland impregnating Ginger midway through the novel, producing a child the pair ultimately decides to give up for adoption. Given the climate surrounding the issue of same-sex marriage in the mid-1990s, it would be difficult to read this failed relationship and attempt at heterosexual parenting as anything but a resistive choice that points to failed heterosexual family units, rather than stable homosexual unions, as the true threat to the values of traditional marriage. Almost as a bulwark against a potential counterargument that Toland's homosexuality is to blame for this failed family formation, Cruse's frame narrative depicts an older Toland with his unnamed but emotionally supportive partner in a stable domestic setting. The AIDS activism posters that adorn the walls of their home remind readers that, as Simon Dickel notes, "Toland's coming of age is inextricably connected with the politics of the civil rights movement, and it is through this focal character that AIDS activism is linked to the civil rights movement" ("'Can't Leave Me Behind,'" 631). The elements of *Stuck Rubber Baby* that push back against anti-LGBTQ discourses have been noted by critics in both popular and academic circles; I will not reiterate those dimensions here.[6] Rather, it is the visual and narrative tropes that Cruse employs, their narrative consequences, and their connection with the reification of a particular set of consensus memories that motivate the rest of this chapter. Through these tropes, Cruse legitimizes his claims to the civil rights legacy, which in turn ultimately authorizes his use of the history of lynching in the novel's closing argument.

THE FRAGMENTATION OF CIVIL RIGHTS TROPES AND CONSENSUS MEMORY

The use of allusions to the civil rights movement reveal a series of tropes—a pattern of recurring images, motifs, and symbols—linked with the historical narrative of the movement in our consensus memories. As the novel's opening pages make clear, images, settings, and characters familiar to a particular version of a decades-past civil rights narrative are central to the legibility of the novel's sociopolitical project. Many of the novel's key events are staged at familiar, even stereotypical civil rights locations such as black churches, public protests, and racially mixed social gatherings on college campuses. Some of these spaces allude to specific moments in civil rights history, such as the bombing of the predominantly African American Melody Motel, which, as Dickel notes, "must be understood as a direct reference to the 16th Street Church Bombing in Birmingham" ("'Can't Leave Me Behind,'" 163). Similarly, the constant police surveillance of the gay nightclub Rhombus deliberately echoes the Stonewall Inn's confrontation with law enforcement on 28 June 1969 as well as signaling a longer history of police surveillance of gay and lesbian bars well into the 1970s.[7] The characters that fill these spaces can likewise be seen as allusions to familiar civil rights personas, such as the kindly, African American preacher and activist Harland Pepper, an obvious analogue of Martin Luther King. There is also the good reverend's wife, Anna Dellyne Pepper, clearly modeled after Coretta Scott King. Like Coretta, Anna Dellyne forsook a promising musical career to be at her husband's side in the pulpit and at protest marches. Mabel Older, the Rhombus's aging lesbian owner and piano player, who routinely bamboozles the Clayfield police, represents a classic trickster figure drawn from a larger African American literary tradition. In certain instances, these allusions take visual form. For example, when white supremacists tail Ginger and another folk singer–activist, Shiloh Reed, a member of the African American Freedom Chorus, Toland's heterosexual roommate Riley stands guard, in a shot that closely resembles a similar photograph of Malcolm X. Despite Riley's whiteness, his relationship to the peaceful activism of his friends can be thought of as mirroring the way in which many remember Malcolm X's relationship to the "mainstream" civil rights movement—distant, militant, uncomfortably gendered, yet committed.

It is through the use of these familiar characters, settings, and thinly veiled allusions that Cruse maps the experiences of Toland Polk onto the challenges faced by African Americans in the midcentury United States. In many ways, *Stuck Rubber Baby* relies on the same sort of iconic but sanitized version of civil rights politics outlined in chapter 1, and ultimately appropriates that history for its own ends. Motivated primarily by issues of political enfranchisement, the lone protest depicted in *Stuck Rubber Baby* shows an integrated group of activists protesting the closing of the public park that hosts their rallies (65). The rhetoric of nonviolence permeates the protest. A volunteer from the "Equality League" disseminates information while Shiloh Reed and the Freedom Chorus, a local African American boys choir, lead the crowd in freedom songs (67). They are met with a crowd of white, predominantly male antagonists—a familiar roster filled with belligerent college-aged counterprotesters and indifferent police officers resolutely looking the other way as protesters are assaulted. This faction of the town's citizenry is led by the violent police chief, Sutton Chopper, Clayfield's resident "Bull Connor" figure, and his snarling police dogs. The use of civil rights iconography functions primarily to establish the concomitant and intersecting narratives of Toland Polk's sexual coming of age and his political redemption. In many ways, civil rights activism lends meaning and purpose to the rudderless Toland, who makes these inspirations explicit when he comes out publicly at the end of the novel at the funeral of the lynching victim Sammy Noone.

Much like *The Silence of Our Friends*, these aspects bring the novel in line with Fred Hobson's concept of the "white southern racial conversion narrative," as Richards has noted ("Everybody's Graphic Protest Novel," 162). This narrative unavoidably reduces the African American characters to simple tropes in the service of validating the novel's linkage between black and homosexual struggles for equality in the 1960s and the 1990s. As Richards writes: "Always prone to melodrama, the novel seems to emerge from a guilt-infused white perspective that, in its efforts to interrogate and indict the dominant culture of the 1960s South for its racism and homophobia, consistently romanticizes the region's black culture, crafting a set of idealized African Americans who, in their near-perfection, ironically lose validity as characters in a novel ostensibly committed to representing historical reality" (169–170). Take, for example, the bombing of the Melody Motel, a predominantly black motel that hosts Clayfield's Freedom Choir, a group of young male gospel singers who perform at Harland Pepper's church. This event is clearly an allusion to the bombing of the 16th Street Baptist Church, which claimed the lives of four young girls in the church choir. The bombing takes place as retaliation for the attendance of the choir and its allies at the March on Washington, shown on the preceding page.

In the pages that follow, Toland and his friends are left to contend with the significance of their white skin and what it says about their potential allyship. This point is emphasized when the younger brother of one of the murdered choirboys regards Toland's presence at the hospital with suspicion, insisting, "They killed him, Mama! Some white men went an' killed Joab" as he looks directly at Toland (Cruse, *Stuck Robber Baby*, 107). But rather than investigate how this reality might problematize Cruse's equating LGBTQ struggles and civil rights activism, the novel moves to a conversation between the Reverend Pepper and Toland, wherein the reverend acknowledges Toland's secret sexual orientation before praising him for his help with the local protests—thereby quelling the tension of the prior scene. From here, the narrative moves on to Sammy Noone, who is berating the racist local newspaper, the *Dixie Patriot*, for encouraging a culture of violence that contributed to the bombing of the Melody Motel. Eventually, Toland, Ginger, Sammy, and the rest of their friends decide to attend the funeral services for those killed in the blast, despite any anxieties their skin color might entail, and they are openly welcomed. Cruse uses allusions to the 16th Street bombing to explore to what extent Toland's and Sammy's skin color interferes with their commitment to civil rights ideals (it does not).

These moments are a few of the instances that function largely as disclaimers, assuring readers that not only do the white characters recognize their privilege, but also that the African American characters recognize that recognition. Rather than explore how these moments of racial violence might problematize the novel's equation of race and sexuality, the novel uses the acceptance of its white characters by African American activists to largely sidestep any potential conflicts their racial identities might incur. Gender swapping the victims from young girls to young boys shifts our attention away from matters of race toward matters of gender and provides another thematic link with Emmett Till. Placing the bombing after the March on Washington, which is often remembered as the culminating moment of the civil rights movement, suggests a shift in priorities from racial matters to the LGBTQ struggle, since the novel shifts its attention to Toland's and Sammy's narrative arcs. The victims of the bombing are pushed into the background, their narrative function essentially completed by offering the opportunity to dissipate Toland's anxieties about his racial identity (thanks to his conversation with the Reverend Pepper). This dynamic is reinforced by the depiction of the bombing, framed by Toland's self-doubt and depicted in the background of the page's layout (fig. 5.2). The image echoes the fragmentation motif seen in the opening pages, the bombing of the hotel echoing the imagined fragmentation of Toland's skull. As the fallout clears, Cruse's narrative sleight of hand transfers the victimization of the children killed at the 16th Street Baptist Church to Toland and the other white characters of his novel, whose reactions to the murders are privileged over those of its tertiary black characters.

Perhaps a more telling example takes the form of the character Les Pepper, an openly gay black activist who inspires Toland's sexual awakening toward the end of the novel. During their first interaction at the Rhombus, Toland asks Les how his parents—the Reverend Harland Pepper and his wife, Anna Dellyne—feel about the "open secret" of his homosexuality. Les responds: "Mama knows. It's cool. She's always had 'sissyboy' friends. An' Papa knows—which ain't to say he's ever said the first word about knowin'. He used to push me to get married, but he's learned that ain't in the cards. Papa's the preacher in the family an' I'm the faggot. Martin Luther King himself could walk up to me an' say to me, 'Les, you gotta quit bein' gay!' . . . And I'd say to him, 'Sure thing, Dr. King—just as soon as you stop bein' Negro!'" (47–48). In many ways, Les functions as Cruse's mouthpiece in this scene, the bravado of his response revealing much of the novel's core message. His insistence that marriage "ain't in the cards" slyly reminds contemporary readers of the larger stakes at play during the DOMA debates of the 1990s. The final line makes the novel's focus on the overlap between racial and sexual oppression clear, linking the biological certainty of blackness (an exceedingly problematic claim) with the notion that homosexuality is an inborn trait. Les's open condemnation of his father's silence indicts the civil rights past that Cruse hopes to capitalize on, condemning its silence (and rightfully so) on issues of sexual equality and

5.2. Cruse, *Stuck Rubber Baby*, 103

tolerance, the same sort of silence that marginalized Bayard Rustin. Directing Les's declaration toward his reverend father and Martin Luther King can also be read as a chastisement of the black church as a social institution for failing to protect its LGBTQ parishioners to the same extent that it rallied around its heterosexual congregations.[8]

But Cruse's equating of the African American campaign for equal rights with LGBTQ struggles flattens both, a reductive choice that presses the former into the service of the latter. Had Cruse pursued Les's narrative arc as part of a larger interrogation of the intersectional nature of Les's oppression, this might have been avoided. Unfortunately, Les is left in a supporting role, either making enigmatic but underdeveloped connections between homosexual identity and racial passing (33) or assisting Toland in coming to terms with his sexual desire by giving him his first gay experience (138). We might think of these tropes as fragments, pieces of a larger historical truth whose summation exceeds the total value of its individual parts—not unlike the way graphic narrative functions by connecting a series of discrete fragments. By breaking the complex historical reality of the civil rights movement down to its narrative and visual tropes, *Stuck Rubber Baby* reveals how our consensus memories are based on politically useful reductions arranged into a carefully curated vision of the past. The graphic narrative form that Cruse employs, then, can both reflect this and re-form these memories into the vision of the present the novel endorses. The use of these narrative tropes and their reductive nature expose the composition of our consensus memories as well as their contemporary political function. The reduction of the complexity of the movement is often, perhaps always, a political act; in this instance, the movement's rhetorical force is used as a blunt instrument to hammer away at the social injustices facing the LGBTQ community in the 1990s.

THERE MUST BE BLOOD: THE LYNCHING IMAGERY OF *STUCK RUBBER BABY*

The most forceful iteration of the novel's use of civil rights tropes in fusing African American and LGBTQ histories comes at the end of the novel with the lynching of Sammy Noone. This trope reveals the seeming need for bodies to be destroyed—as in the bombing of the Melody Motel—for a civil rights narrative to gain legibility and legitimacy. Specifically, these depictions of violence demand that such a narrative culminate with a martyr—a sacrificed body that sanctifies the martyr's politics, motivates his or her community, and firmly establishes the justness of a civil rights cause. All the graphic memoirs discussed in this study prominently feature multiple scenes of violence against activists and protesters, which is not surprising, considering how many of the gains of the civil rights movement were tied to televised images of these acts of violence. But martyrs proliferate in these works, too, and their inclusion reveals much about how the civil rights movement is remembered—as a clash between the perpetrators of violence (white

—

supremacists) and their victims (African Americans), an easy political narrative that, though true, further elides the movement's historical complexity. All the narratives in this study are centered on these pivotal acts of violence, even if they manage to frame these events in a manner that does not reduce the martyrs to hapless victims devoid of agency. Anderson changed the original ending to *King*, which interrogated the efficacy of MLK's legacies in the modern era, in order to focus more on the moment of his death.[9] Much of *Darkroom*'s urgency follows the unarmed death of Jimmie Lee Jackson at the hands of police in Marion, Alabama. The *X-Men* martyred the group's founder and MLK corollary, Professor X, at the hands of his increasingly militant star pupil, Scott Summers.[10] Even *The Silence of Our Friends*, whose protagonists are acquitted of murdering a police officer, feels an obligation to shoehorn the assassination of Martin Luther King into a civil rights narrative occurring hundreds of miles from the major sites of his career. These are topped only by John Lewis's *March*, which avoids the limitations of the single symbolic martyr in favor of an increased body count that features multiple martyrs, both black and white.

I am not objecting to the inclusion of activists who lost their lives in the name of racial equality—how could I? The desire to honor the lives of those that paid the ultimate price for freedom is, of course, an understandable and laudable one. Nonetheless, I find myself disconcerted by a narrative impulse that builds such stories on the displayed bodies of the dead—black men in particular. There is something ineffably perturbing about these narratives' need to prominently feature such dire deaths, especially since the narratives open themselves up to voyeuristic readings by racists and antiracists alike. Perhaps this is the question: What is it about civil rights consensus memory that demands a body?

Given these tendencies, it should come as no surprise that *Stuck Rubber Baby* ends with the lynching of Sammy Noone, Toland's gay white activist mentor. With a narrative blueprint that demands its claim to civil rights pathos end in blood, Cruse's course was arguably set from the beginning. This speaks to what Jacqueline Goldsby refers to as the novel's "cultural logic." Goldsby notes that actual lynchings and representations of lynching invoke a set of "interpretative facets" that in turn are "indicative of trends in national culture" (*Spectacular Secret*, 5). Goldsby's work looks to situate lynchings and their representations in specific historical circumstances and contexts of power and modernity in order to liberate discussions of these issues from the notion that "the violence is largely resistant if not immune to historical change" (5). In this vein, I situate Cruse's choice to end the novel with the lynching of Sammy Noone as "indicative of trends" in 1990s political discourse that promoted the logic of race and homosexuality as parallel forms of marginalization. So while the other narratives in this study focus on the killing of real-world African American victims, Cruse invents a white victim (Sammy "No One," in a sense) in order to (re)construct his vision of the movement's history. In so doing, Cruse capitalizes on the rhetorical force of lynching imagery, which Amy Louise Wood describes as "the primary representation of racial injustice and oppression as a whole" (*Lynching and Spectacle*, 1). But to maximize this effect, Cruse must first deracialize the violence in order to transfer it to his white martyr, which Cruse accomplishes through a bevy of graphic narrative strategies. So while many of *Stuck Rubber Baby*'s claims to civil rights legacies often ring true, the novel's breakdown of civil rights consensus memories into tropes to be reassembled to suit its political purposes unavoidably amounts to historical appropriation. What results is not parallelism or allegory, but the complete annexation of one history (in this case, the African American history of the civil rights struggle) in support of a distinct, even if allied, social movement. In this context, *Stuck Rubber Baby*'s treatment of lynching appropriates a history of racialized violence against African American bodies to depict the very real threat to LGBTQ life, even as traditionally African American victims are often replaced by white homosexual victims.

This transfer of tragedy happens subtly throughout the novel. Take, for example, a scene of violence at the public park protest early in the narrative. Sammy Noone attempts to stop a white supremacist from beating a peaceful African American protester. The beating is shown in a single panel, while Noone's heroic intervention dominates the page. Noone is then beaten by a police officer, and a crowd gathers to assist him. Mabel distracts Noone from his injuries by relating a story of how she used to ride in the front of the bus by faking a disability. The story itself, which alludes, of course, to the activist career of Rosa Parks, acts as another tacit connection between the gay rights and civil rights movements through Mabel, the black lesbian owner of the Alleysax. Members of both communities rally around the fallen Sammy Noone for the following five pages. This scene is followed by Toland viewing the park at night, reflecting on the day's events. A police officer approaches him menacingly and tells Toland, "You're in the wrong neighborhood, seems to me," before demanding he "move on"—an interaction one would expect between an officer and an African American rather than a middle-class white man (Cruse, *Stuck Rubber Baby*, 76). And the unnamed black victim that inspired the entire incident? He does not appear again in the narrative. Cruse is hardly setting out to deliberately relegate African Americans to the background of arguably their greatest political movement. On the other hand, *Stuck Rubber Baby* goes to great lengths to praise the inspiration that the

LGBTQ movement has drawn from African American civil rights activists. Yet when that inspiration is coupled with a consensus narrative that fetishizes those same activists' bodies, what results is an outrageous act of cultural and historical appropriation that takes visual form via the motif of fragmentation. The lynching trope has gone largely uninterrogated by book critics and academic scholars alike.

I do not mean to suggest that that the novel has gone entirely unnoticed. Far from it in fact, since *Stuck Rubber Baby* has been lauded by many popular and academic outlets. Many applaud Cruse's ability to avoid reducing the period's historical complexity to a set of platitudes while praising the complexity of the artwork.[11] Others praise the redemptive nature of Toland's coming to consciousness as a modern allegory for political action.[12] Rarely do these articles discuss the lynching scene directly, often alluding only to the book's frank depiction of violence (broadly defined); Dennis Drabelle of the *Washington Post* refers to the lynching as a "hanging" that traumatizes Toland (review). The 2010 edition of the novel features a foreword by the graphic narrative artist Alison Bechdel that neatly sums up all of these themes: "Toland lives in a place and time where not just black people but 'white niggers' are routinely terrorized, and where being a 'nigger-loving queer' has dire consequences. The landscape is very different half a century later. The achievements of the Civil Rights and LGBT movements appear monumental, given our African-American president and the escalating moral urgency of the battle for same-sex marriage—neither of which I had any expectation of seeing in my lifetime" (introduction). Like the novel, Bechdel equates the historically concomitant movements for civil rights and same-sex marriage rights, insisting that the time-space that Toland comes of age in posed equal threats to both black Americans and the white homosexual allies who supported them. While this may be true, Bechdel remains silent on the novel's boldest statement of these intersecting marginalizations even while alluding to it; the "nigger-loving queer" slur refers to a placard left at Sammy Noone's feet by his murderers. The invocation of Barack Obama has a distinct postracial overtone to it, further endorsing an ideological stance that posits the LGBTQ movement as rising in "moral urgency" while African American concerns become historically resolved—over a decade removed from the 1990s discourse that inspired Cruse's novel.[13]

Treatments of the novel from academic sources fare no better, since the few published articles on *Stuck Rubber Baby* do not engage directly with the deracialized narrative politics of Sammy Noone's lynching. When they do, they follow similar patterns as those in popular press. For example, Paul Buhle's oft-cited "History and Comics" praises Cruse's novel as "the classroom Gold Standard" for its brilliant exploration of "the intersection of race and gender" (318). David

Bordelon's intertextual reading of southern print culture in the novel discusses lynching by focusing primarily on the effect of Emmett Till on Toland ("Picturing Books," 114). Sammy Noone's lynching—referred to as a hanging—is treated largely in a summative description of the novel's climax (113). In his excellent treatment of the visual motifs and metaphors of the novel (which informs much of my own), Simon Dickel does engage with Sammy's lynching, but exclusively in relation to the threat his homosexuality poses to the hetero-patriarchy of Clay-field; Dickel insists that "Cruse is careful not to equate racism and homophobia" ("'Can't Leave Me Behind,'" 617). Even Gary Richards, who takes Cruse to task for relegating his African American characters to subservient roles in the novel's white redemption narrative, does not discuss Sammy's lynching, arguably the most egregious example of his criticism. I am not accusing Bechdel, Buhle, or any of these other authors of deliberate silence or erasure; such an act would be antithetical to the intersectional allegiances that I, and others, praise within the novel. Nor do I criticize the formalistic elements these critics praise (although I do avoid their laudatory tone). Yet I do not understand how the appropriative logic that underwrites Cruse's fictionalized depiction of lynching escaped their notice. Coming to terms with the appropriative nature of Sammy Noone's lynching remains a critical gap in this scholarship demanding to be filled, and it therefore dominates my interrogation of Cruse's work.

TRANSFERRING TRAUMA

Stuck Rubber Baby's adoption of narrative tropes works in concert with its social politics to connect the plight of civil rights activists in the 1960s with that of homo-sexual men in the 1990s, the murder of Sammy Noone functioning as the novel's crescendo. The killing of Sammy Noone transfers the literal trauma of lynching to the symbolic struggle of Toland Polk, and the secondary African American characters authorize this rhetorical appropriation. Sammy's murder is not the first lynching prominently featured in the novel. While the specter of lynching is intro-duced by the *Jet* magazine photos of Emmett Till, it is the grisly death of Sledge Rankin, an African American community organizer and Ginger's close friend, which prefaces the eventual lynching of Sammy Noone. The murder is narrated by present-day Toland, who speaks from the background of the sequence (fig. 5.3). The reader receives Toland's recollection of Ginger's version of events, whose version is a distillation of the account given by the murder's only witness—Sledge's young son, Wren. As a result, the version presented in *Stuck Rubber Baby* is filtered through multiple accounts decades later, an unavoidable truth reflected in the

5.3. Cruse, *Stuck Rubber Baby*, 53

skewed panel shapes, most of which are four-sided but never quite square, suggesting a certain inability to correctly position and place the murder in a coherent time line. These panels resemble panes of glass, scattered about the page like shards, suggestive of the shattering of Sledge's body. The panels depict a group of Ku Klux Klansmen performing an initiation rite of passage, one that demands they "chop off some nigger's balls 'fore they'll let us be members"—a fetishistic word choice that evokes the sexual threat implied by both African American and homosexual men (53). On the following page, Sledge Rankin agrees to go with the Klansmen to his death if they spare his son the same fate. Still, poor Wren is forced to watch the castration and eventual murder of his father in the grocery store where Sledge was employed. Sledge's body is left in the storefront for the public to view, a detail that readers discover only if they read the text of the fictional newspaper account of the murder. As with the killing of Emmett Till, the body is seen only by the characters in the story, not by the readers.

Although only Wren witnesses the murder, the murder of Sledge Rankin in many ways recalls the history of "spectacle lynching." And while the murder of Rankin may not feature the most recognizable elements of spectacle lynching—he is not hung, nor is his murder attended by the public—the ritualistic nature of the murder in the name of white supremacy echoes that history. As Dora Apel defines it: "Spectacle lynchings, however, transformed clandestine nighttime killings by men who disguised their identities into open murder in the public square. Spectacle lynchings, attended by small groups of people or crowds that sometimes swelled to fifteen thousand, often led by the town's most respected citizens, had become increasingly sadistic and ritualized by the 1930s" (*Lynching Photographs*, 44). Spectacle lynchings may commonly be associated primarily with their public nature, and while Sledge is not publicly murdered, his body is left in the public space of a commercial business. But it is the ritualistic nature of castration and dismemberment that I highlight here. After all, many of these lynchings ended with the dismemberment of the victim's body, a form of fragmentation that produced "souvenirs" for the perpetrators. As Apel notes, photographs of these events "only hinted at the excitement and the complex social and psychological effects of the ritualistic murders in which the lynch mob had participated, including beating, torture, castration, mutilation, shooting, hanging, dragging, and burning" (44). Furthermore, the emphasis such mobs placed on genital mutilation and castration was often explicitly connected with myths of black sexual prowess, the patrolling of potential miscegenation, and the fear of the uncontrollable nature of black sexual desire.[14]

Cruse chooses to highlight the mindlessly ritualistic and disturbingly sexual nature of the crime rather than its public setting, even though we learn from the *Clayfield Banner* that Sledge's body was left out in the open, fulfilling the intimidation explicit in a public lynching. These facets of Sledge's murder are not lost on the citizens of Clayfield. Shiloh Reed blames himself after he is menacingly tailgated for driving with Ginger, a white woman. Shiloh says, "Sheer fool recklessness is what it was! We were so lost in our thoughts about Sledge, we ignored the obvious" (Cruse, *Stuck Rubber Baby*, 52). Cruse leaves the murder undepicted, sparing readers the trauma of witnessing the horror experienced by Wren and the townsfolk of Clayfield. While Cruse's reluctance to display the body of Rankin (or Till) seems motivated by an urge to forestall the sort of voyeurism that displays of black victimhood often inspire, he does not spare us from multiple depictions of Sammy Noone's lynched body at the novel's climax. Ultimately, these choices work to erase African Americans from the history of spectacle lynching, replacing them with the white homosexual subjectivities that concern the novel.

In choosing not to depict the bodies of either Emmett Till or Sledge Rankin, Cruse participates in a larger social dialogue about the appropriateness of such displays. Take, for example, the small photography exhibition dedicated to lynching photographs held by the Roth Horowitz Gallery in New York City in January 2000. The exhibition was titled *Called Witness: Photographs of Lynching from the Collection of James Allen*, named after the private collector who assembled some sixty photographs over the course of his life (A. Lee, introduction, 1). For many who braved the New York winter and the three-hour wait to enter the small gallery, *Called Witness* (later renamed *Without Sanctuary*) offered their first horrifying glimpses into one of the most shameful aspects of American, even human, history. Treated as artifacts, the photographs were displayed without frames, matting, or captions; worn, tattered, and faded, the images were allowed to speak for themselves. As expected, the display generated tremendous controversy. Cassandra Jackson describes the debate: "Not surprisingly, 'Without Sanctuary' has also incited fierce controversy about the point of such a gruesome display. The reemergence of these photographs in the public space has left viewers with a crisis of vision. We are faced with both a fascination with and simultaneous repulsion towards the photographs, the crowds, the violence, and our own spectatorship. We marvel at the force of the atrocity, while also asking ourselves, how can we bear to look at this?" (*Violence, Visual Culture*, 77–78). Much of the anxiety surrounding *Without Sanctuary* was generated by the gallery's decision to present the photographs with little or no context, which in unfortunate ways replicated the circumstances in which they were produced, since, as Anthony W. Lee points out, visitors attended the event "because of the spectacle of the lynched body" (introduction, 4). In response, the New-York Historical Society offered a wealth of context, including information on antilynching campaigns, situating the heinous act in the context of America's troubling racial past, and offering digital workstations with supplemental materials (*Violence, Visual Culture*, 80). But the central concern remains: can one reproduce images of lynching without simply

—

reducing the tragic circumstances of African American anguish to little more than a consumable spectacle?

The debates stirred by *Without Sanctuary* and the larger questions posed by the controversy reflect an ongoing conversation in literary scholarship regarding the depiction of violence against African American bodies. For example, Saidya V. Hartman contends that replicating such scenes of racial violence and terror denatures them and thereby robs them of their ability to shock our ethical sensibilities into action or response:

> I have chosen not to reproduce Douglass's account of the beating of Aunt Hester in order to call attention to the ease with which such scenes are usually reiterated, the casualness with which they are circulated, and the consequences of this routine display of the slave's ravaged body. Rather than inciting indignation, too often they immure [*sic*] us to the pain by virtue of their familiarity—the oft-repeated or restored character of these accounts and our distance from them are signaled by the theatrical language usually resorted to in describing these instances—and especially because they reinforce the spectacular character of black suffering. (*Scenes of Subjection*, 3)

While praising Hartman's decision to not reproduce these accounts, Fred Moten contends that such well-motivated attempts to "disappear" the violence perpetrated on the bodies of slaves are ultimately doomed to fail. Moten counters that such accounts are reproduced simply by referring to them and that what should concern us is "the inevitability of such reproduction even in the denial of it" and the "politics of this unavoidably reproducible and reproductive performance" (*In the Break*, 4).

Hartman's and Moten's debate is much more complex than I have represented here, and their critical conversation is centered specifically on prose slave narratives. And to be clear, I do not invoke their disagreement in order to resolve it or to carve out critical terrain for myself on either side of this debate. But their concerns over the depiction, or "reproduction," of the violence enacted upon black bodies in the name of white supremacy nonetheless informs my project here, since *Stuck Rubber Baby* forces us to contend with the sight of a deracialized lynching that erases its traditionally African American victims. In this vein, I bring up these differing opinions in order to make clear the stakes involved in depicting lynching, particularly in the case of Cruse's novel. Like Hartman, Cruse avoids showing mutilated black bodies, particularly those subjected to torture for the express ritualistic demands of groups like the Ku Klux Klan. And yet the inclusion of such scenes unavoidably reproduces the acts that they refer to, even if the work avoids any direct depiction of the violence. And we must still contend with the straightforward reproduction of this violence later in the novel, this time enacted upon the body of a white homosexual victim. While focusing on the graphic narrative techniques that Cruse employs to make this transfer of trauma legible, I close, as Moten suggests, by focusing on the politics that this act of historical appropriation conjures—for both the novel and its readers.

Unlike most of the characters in *Stuck Rubber Baby*, Sammy Noone does not represent a civil rights trope. Rather, he represents an idealized version of Toland in many ways, which only heightens the tragedy of his death. Unlike the closeted Toland, Sammy's orientation is an open secret, he is committed to civil rights activism, and he is joyfully comfortable in all of Clayfield's alternate spaces, such as the Melody Motel, the Rhombus, or the Alleysax. In fact, it is Noone who introduces Toland to Ginger, Les, Anna Dellyne, and the rest of Clayfield's underground community. His death inspires Toland to come out to this community at Sammy's funeral, before a crowd of like-minded friends and family. The murder happens after Sammy comes out to his father—a paraplegic and geriatric patriarch who supports white-supremacist politics. After taunting his father with a copy of the *Dixie Patriot*—the local, white-supremacist newspaper, which outed Sammy as a "nigger loving queer" and cost him his job at a local church (Cruse, *Stuck Rubber Baby*, 123)—Sammy drunkenly berates the editors of the paper at their office. In apparent retaliation, unseen attackers come to Toland's home, where Sammy is staying, and knock Toland out with a pipe. It is later revealed that he was spared because the attackers did not realize that Toland was homosexual. Toland awakens, stumbles through the yard in a daze, and bumps his head against Sammy's dangling feet (fig. 5.4). He looks up, aghast to discover his friend hung by the neck in the front yard, a placard emblazoned with the phrase "NIGGER LOVING QUEER" lying beneath his feet (178).

The first image of Sammy's lynched body is largely obscured, and the reader encounters only fragments of Toland's memories of Sammy's shattered body. Appropriately, the structure of this page is jumbled and chaotic, without gutters or traditional panels to orient the reader in any immediately evident reading orientation. The top left depicts Toland's initial discovery; Sammy's face is obscured by Riley, who attempts to warn Toland but fails. This shot is overlaid on one of Toland lying on the ground, looking up at Sammy's feet, a shift in perspective that further confuses the orientation of the page. Four jagged, broken-glass-style panels—which recall a similar motif used to depict the murder of Sledge Rankin—lie scattered across the page. In these broken-glass panels, we see flashes of Toland's memories—a fragmentation technique that both hints at the unreliability of these

5.4. Cruse, *Stuck Rubber Baby*, 178–179

partial memories and visually represents the psychic trauma they (fail to) contain. The seemingly unorganized chaos of this memory recalls Cathy Caruth's definition of trauma: "The pathology consists [. . .] solely in the structure of its experience or reception: the event is not assimilated or experienced fully at the time, but only belatedly, in its repeated possession of the one who experiences it. To be traumatized is precisely to be possessed by an image or event" (*Trauma*, 4–5).

Needless to say, graphic narrative is particularly well equipped to represent both the unassimilated nature of the memory and the images of the event that possess the one who experienced it—a feature that has not gone unnoticed by literary critics.[15] The broken-glass panels scattered across the page signal both of these elements for *Stuck Rubber Baby*'s visceral and disturbing depiction of Sammy's lynching. The four broken-glass panels, "in order," depict an angled view of Sammy's body, a partial view of his face, an obscured depiction of the deplorable placard at his feet, and finally his boots. Closely resembling traditional rectangular panels, the broken-glass panels suggest a potential narrative configuration that never coalesces—they remain unassimilated across the page. The absence of discernible gutters or other pacing time structures likewise suggest a trauma, denying the possibility of either narrative or psychic closure. These jagged panels pointedly lead the reader's eye to three stacked images of Toland speaking from the future, the pain of recalling this moment easily evident on his weary, weathered face—clearly still possessed by the recalled image of Sammy's feet. The three faces of present-day Toland echo one another, leading us from the murder to Toland's inability to process the psychic pain that accompanies the memory. The three unchanging faces suggest both the trauma that Toland has carried throughout his life as well as the moment when Toland's political consciousness came fully into view, since this moment inspires Toland's public avowal of his sexuality at Sammy's funeral.

Yet it is the trauma of witnessing Sammy's displayed body that lingers with Toland, a sentiment reinforced by the dialogue of the scene, which spills off the page onto the next, uncontained by the depiction of the memory itself:

If I just hadn't—(Lemme start again.) If I just hadn't bumped my damn head into his shoes! That's the memory that stays with me: the clumsy weight of his calves thudding against my ear . . . and the smell of the dried sweat in his denim. I can close my eyes and feel his shoes rolling around the back of my neck . . . 'cause my stumbling into him had start him swinging . . . And there were clumps of mud and leaf steams that I can still taste, that had peeled off his soles and landed on my lips. (Cruse, *Stuck Rubber Baby*, 178–179)

Toland's attempts to narrate his trauma occur in fits and starts, and his focus on the tactile sensations of the lynching evokes the haunting presentness of the memory. The repetition of the first line, despite his attempts to revise it, hints at the repetitious and cyclical nature of the trauma. The multiple faces of Toland across this sequence suggest a fragmentation of his psyche, one that mirrors the fragmentation of Sammy's body across the broken-glass panels in which his murder is depicted. The haunting image of Sammy's feet forbids Toland from creating "a safe place in [his] memory" into which he might place the trauma and thereby escape or control it (179). The specific detail of Sammy's boots imbues them with significant power, an image that possesses Toland to the present day.

The broken-glass panels also work toward symbolically dismembering Sammy, recalling both the gruesome history of spectacle lynching and the castration and murder of Sledge Rankin. In this first image of Sammy's lynching, the reader does not see Sammy's full form. Rather, his body is figuratively dismembered by Cruse's fragmentation motif and spread across the page—a physical shattering suggested by the very shape of the panels that contain elements of his body. The visual dismemberment of Sammy's body, spread across multiple panels, and the power that the memory of "Sammy's ankles clunking against [his] cheek" holds over Toland, recalls Harvey Young's work explicating the power of the fragmented, lynched body. Young's work focuses on the dismembered parts of lynched black bodies that were used as souvenirs, a grotesque but commonplace practice at many early spectacle lynchings, particularly around 1900. Cruse certainly did not include the lynching of Sammy Noone to function as the sort of grotesque human sacrifice represented by the victims of spectacle lynching. Yet Cruse's choice to feature such a powerful and problematic image of martyrdom as a central part of the novel's climax, when combined with the symbolic fragmentation of Sammy's body, makes Young's work vital for unpacking the narrative consequences of that choice.

I use Young's work to illuminate Cruse's visual representation of the murder of Sammy Noone and the deracialization of the history of lynching. Young contends that the body parts collected at spectacle lynchings can be read as "the souvenir, the fetish, and the performance remains"—although the dismembered body of the victim ultimately exceeds any of these terms (*Embodying Black Experience*, 169). Of these three paradigms, the concept of "performance remains" bears the most resonance for my reading of the death of Sammy Noone. Yet the other two have striking relevance for Cruse's novel as well. "The souvenir," for example, "refers back to a larger experience, of which it is a fragment," one that requires "an accompanying narrative furnished by its possessor in order to fill in that which is missing and to allow the fragment to reflect the event of experience of which it is a part" (170). While Sammy's shoes may not be physically present in Toland's narrative, their haunting presence in Toland's memories, as well as their visual fragmentation in the narrative's artwork, mean they function much like a souvenir. They represent a fragment—both of a moment and of a person—that recalls an incomplete memory that demands an accompanying narrative, not unlike the fragments of a traumatic memory. Sammy's shoes also function as a fetish object, in that they "synthesize multiple elements in a single body," as Young puts it (170). In other words, Sammy's shoes come to represent Sammy's entire form—without the tactile sensation of Sammy's ankles on his cheek, after all, Toland might be able to process, or at least suppress, the trauma.

It is Sammy's shoes' function as "performance remains" that bears the greatest relevance for delineating Cruse's narrative sleight of hand, which transfers the trauma (and history) of lynching from the body of African American victims to a white homosexual one. Drawing widely from the field of performance studies, particularly the work of Rebecca Schneider, Young treats the lynching spectacle as a performance, and "performance as a medium in which disappearance negotiates, perhaps becomes, materiality" (Schneider quoted in Young, *Embodying Black Experience*, 186). In his distillation of the debate on the ephemeral nature of performance, Young surmises that performances do not necessarily disappear the instant the performance ends—material remains, or "performance remains," allow us "to re-member the performance event" long after it has concluded (185). Applying this notion to the dismembered body of George Ward, an Indiana lynching victim in 1901 who was literally butchered and his body parts dispersed among a mob, Young writes: "His death creates souvenirs of his life. Their presence, as a consequence of his absence, bestows meaning, value, and the perception of power upon them. More interestingly, these material remains testify to the lynching victim's former living status. They continually evoke the victim's body through a repeated underscoring of its absence. Ironically, Ward's newfound visibility anchors itself in the fact of his invisibility. This is the magic of the performance remain. It remembers its own disappearance and, as a result, renders the performance event whole again" (186). If the physical remains of an actual lynching victim, by underscoring the absence of the whole victim, evoke the original performance and thereby reconstitute it in present-day memory, then what are we to make of Sammy Noone—a fictional victim whose body is figuratively dismembered and "re-membered" at his funeral while the novel's black victims perish offstage?

Cruse's fragmentation technique, which symbolically dismembers Sammy Noone, features what one might consider some graphic narrative sleight of hand to transfer the traumas of lynching from African Americans by erasing them from the performance event altogether. Sammy's shoes, whose memory haunts Toland, function much like the performance remains highlighted by Young. The power they hold over Toland causes him to relive the event—a linchpin of trauma literature, according to Caruth—and also forces the same sort of remembrance engendered by the bodily remains of George Ward. In the first image of Sammy's lynched figure, the fragmentation technique symbolically dismembers Sammy and evokes the history of spectacle lynching. But we never are given a clear look at Sammy's full form—even his face remains largely obscured, only partly featured in a single panel. In this way, Cruse draws our attention away from the specificity of Sammy's face, a marker for all the facets of his identity and of his whiteness in particular. In his own reading of graphic narrative depictions of lynching, Michael Chaney writes, "faces . . . are tantamount to persons" (*Reading Lessons in Seeing*, 158).[16] By obscuring Sammy's face, Cruse obscures his personhood (hence, Sammy "No One") and the racial specificity that a face implies. Rather, Cruse has the reader focus on Sammy's feet, which come to represent Toland's traumatic discovery of his fractured form. In essence, Cruse dismembers the performance event of lynching to obscure, or even forget, its essential racial dimensions. Via this act of deracialization, achieved through the performance remain of Sammy's shoes, Cruse "re-members" lynching by rebuilding the event to speak to the terrors plaguing the homosexual community of Clayfield and further establish the parallel subjections of African Americans and LGBTQ people. And while the threat of violence haunts black and white members of the homosexual community, its ultimate martyr is a lynched white man whom the visuals contend should be remembered for his sexual orientation, not his racial identity. After all, the panel that contains the placard placed at Sammy's feet, identifying him as a "NIGGER LOVING QUEER," obscures the racial epithet in order to highlight the other one. Since the lynching of a white man might, and appropriately so, be met with accusations of cultural appropriation, Sammy's shoes as performance remain function to sidestep such concerns.

The second instance in which we see and don't see Sammy's lynched body, when it is re-membered through Toland's testimonial at his funeral, only reinforces this dynamic (fig. 5.5). The underground community of Clayfield gathers at Alleysax to publicly celebrate Sammy's life, since many of them were banned by his father from attending his formal funeral. When Toland approaches the stage to deliver his eulogy, he winds his way through a series of anecdotes about his friendship with Sammy, finding himself so nervous that he felt as if he "was going to pass out." Toland's eyes find Shiloh Reed, the director of the Freedom Choir, who was rendered mute by the bombing of the Melody Motel. Locking eyes with Shiloh produces the same effect, both visually and psychically, as viewing Emmett Till's body in the opening sequence. Toland draws inspiration from Shiloh and "imagined the explosion at the Melody Motel . . . and what it must've been like to be Shiloh . . . and see a flaming tornado of shattered beams and concrete blasting toward me . . . and then I was on the back steps of the Wheelery again . . . watching hard steel whiz out of blackness" (Cruse, *Stuck Rubber Baby*, 190). This narration is accompanied by an explosion and fragmentation motif similar to the one accompanying Toland's recollection of seeing Till's photos in *Jet* magazine. This time, the fragments scatter across the following page and transform into his memories of Sammy's lynching, expanding into the same broken-glass panels employed to depict both that murder and the murder of Sledge Rankin.

In this instance, however, the fragmentation technique that accompanies Toland's attempts to imagine what the destruction of African American bodies portends for his own reconstitutes into the performance event itself as Toland fully identifies with Sammy's lynching:

And then something really bizarre took over . . . and it was like I was Sammy . . . and I was feeling what Sammy felt . . . and strange men's hands were all over me, dragging me somewhere that I didn't wanna go. And I heard a scream trying to break out of my throat . . . but a callused hand had clamped itself across my face and the scream was as trapped as *I* was. And I knew that I might very well be about to die . . . and I very strongly didn't want to. (191)

The scene continues as Toland narrates Sammy's tragic murder, this time from a first-person perspective as Toland experiences the destruction of Sammy's body firsthand. The fragmentation of Sammy is now to be understood as the fragmentation of Toland across the page. The accompanying text is fragmented, too, linked together visually and verbally by a series of pauses (represented by suspension points) that confer a sense of hesitancy and trepidation on Toland's narrative. Suspension points look like ellipses, however, which evoke the elision of material—in this case, the "missing" body of Sammy Noone, as well as the absence of an African American victim.

As the glass shards of Toland's symbolic lynching coalesce near the bottom of the page, they spill on over to the next, where they begin to conform to the rectangular, neatly arranged layout of a traditional comics page. As the visuals stabilize, a powerful thought enters Toland's mind. Seeing himself through the eyes of the dead Sammy Noone, Toland wonders, "Why was Toland lying flat in the dirt by the Wheelery's back steps, unconscious but alive . . . and why was I, Sammy Noone, suddenly ten galaxies away? Was it because I was a . . . NIGGER LOVING QUEER . . . while Toland Polk, though reputedly a 'nigger lover' as well, didn't appear to be a queer one" (192). Toland's question identifies Sammy's homosexuality as the deciding factor in his murder—which ultimately inspires Toland to come out to their friends and family at Sammy's funeral. The epithet at the center of his self-recrimination recalls the placard placed at Sammy's feet by his murderers—a visual echo that, like Sammy's shoes, functions as performance remains that conjure the original event. The coalescing of the fragmented, broken-glass panels culminates in this sequence in the middle of the page. As the page returns from the chaos of memory to the certainty of the present moment, we encounter a fully formed (bodily and psychically) Toland Polk, now altered by the experience of having been symbolically lynched. The performance elements of this moment are heightened by its staging, literally, since Toland stands on the stage of the Alleysax. Dual performances are occurring: Toland performs his coming-out to his friends and family, and a lynching is performed symbolically, this time with Toland replacing Sammy, who was a replacement for an African American victim. On the following page, Toland can recall saying only four words of his rambling coming-out speech: "It could've been me" (192). He says this to Shiloh Reed, who silently authorizes this transfer of trauma, playing a role similar to that of the other African American characters by noting the difference between his racial experience and Toland's and simultaneously excusing it. Or as Toland insists, "I knew I'd find understanding in Shiloh's eyes." Through these visual techniques and narrative tropes, Cruse effectively transfers tragedies, traumas, and history from murdered black men to Toland Polk, a living white man. And as with the sequence depicting the bombing of the Melody Motel, the presence of African American characters in these scenes does little more than justify these narrative proceedings; the black characters, like Shiloh, are otherwise silenced. The fragmentation of the traumas depicted in *Stuck Rubber Baby* may effectively dramatize the plight of white homosexual men in the 1990s, but only by replacing the African Americans at the center of the historical pathos the novel hopes to access. In doing so, it effectively erases African Americans from this history. In the end, only the performance remains.

TO WHOM DOES HISTORY BELONG?

On 18 April 2012, the conservative firebrand Ann Coulter penned an editorial on her blog in defense of Florida's "stand your ground" laws following the shooting death of Trayvon Martin at the hands of George Zimmerman—laws that

WHEN MY TIME CAME TO **SPEAK,** I SURPRISED MYSELF BY WINDING MY WAY FAIRLY **ARTICULATELY** THROUGH THE **ANECDOTES** I'D MAPPED OUT IN MY HEAD **BEFOREHAND.**

I WON'T BOTHER **REPEATING** 'EM **NOW.**

MOST OF 'EM I'VE TOLD YOU ABOUT **ALREADY.**

ONCE I'D **FINISHED,** THE **CORRECT** THING TO DO, OBVIOUSLY, WOULD'VE BEEN TO TURN AND STEP **DOWN** FROM THE **PLATFORM.**

BUT TO MY **EMBARRASSMENT,** SOME **WEIRDNESS** TOOK HOLD OF ME. I COULDN'T GET MYSELF TO STOP LOOKING AT ALL THE FACES.

I FELL SILENT AND JUST **STOOD** THERE—**FROZEN!**

AND WITH EVERY **SECOND** THAT TICKED BY, I BECAME MORE **AWARE** OF HOW THOROUGHLY EVERYONE **ELSE** HAD FALLEN SILENT, **TOO.**

AND I WAS AWARE THAT THE **AMPS** WERE GIVING OFF A LOW **HUM.**

AND I WAS AWARE OF THE **CHILLINESS** OF THE STEEL **MIKE STAND** MY **FIST** WAS CLUTCHING.

AND I WONDERED IF I WAS GOING TO PASS **OUT...**

'CAUSE ALL OF THE **FACES** I WAS LOOKING DOWN AT WERE BEGINNING TO DROP **AWAY...**

LIKE THEY WERE SPIRALING HEADLONG DOWN A WEIRDLY LIT **SHAFT** THAT I WAS IN SOME **DANGER OF** TOPPLING INTO **MYSELF!**

EXCEPT FOR **SHILOH.**

FOR **SOME** REASON MY **EYES** LOCKED ONTO **SHILOH'S** EYES...

...AND IT CAME **BACK** TO ME, WHAT HAD **PUT** HIM IN THAT **WHEEL-CHAIR...**

...AND I IMAGINED THE **EXPLOSION** AT THE **MELODY MOTEL...**

...AND WHAT **IT** MUST'VE BEEN LIKE TO BE SHILOH...

...AND SEE A **FLAMING** TORNADO OF **SHATTERED BEAMS** AND **CONCRETE** BLASTING TOWARD ME...

...AND THEN I WAS ON THE **BACK** STEPS OF THE **WHEELERY** AGAIN...

...WATCHING **HARD STEEL** WHIZ OUT OF **BLACKNESS.**

190

5.5. Cruse, *Stuck Rubber Baby*, 190–191

ultimately led to Zimmerman's acquittal. Coulter, in her typically acerbic, out-landish, and disputatious manner, equates challenges to the Second Amendment motivated by the "stand your ground" laws with the methods of subjugation used against African Americans:

> We don't know the facts yet, but let's assume the conclusion MSNBC is leaping to is accurate: George Zimmerman stalked a small black child and murdered him in cold blood, just because he was black. If that were true, every black person in America should get a gun and join the National Rifle Association, America's oldest and most august civil rights organization. Apparently this has occurred to no one because our excellent public educa-tion system ensures that no American under the age of 60 has the slightest notion of this country's history. Gun control laws were originally promul-gated by Democrats to keep guns out of the hands of blacks. This allowed the Democratic policy of slavery to proceed with fewer bumps and, after the Civil War, allowed the Democratic Ku Klux Klan to menace and murder black Americans with little resistance. ("Negroes with Guns")

Anyone even marginally familiar with Coulter's politics would find her clothes rending and teeth gnashing over the threat to African American lives spurious at best. Yet I cannot help but see rhetorical similarities between the logic present in Coulter's article and Cruse's novel. Both capitalize on the tragic killing of a young black boy—Emmett Till in Cruse, Trayvon Martin in Coulter. Both use these deaths as a catapult to a revision of history less concerned with an accurate representation of the past than with how that history might function politically in the present. And both attempt to commandeer the social movements inspired by those deaths—the civil rights movement and Black Lives Matter —for political purposes having little to do with the African American lives on which those movements were built. I do not mean to suggest that *Stuck Rubber Baby* is somehow the political equivalent of "Negroes with Guns." If nothing else, Cruse's novel sides with the oppressed, while Coulter dismisses the death of a young black boy in a frankly baffling attempt to garner his community's political allegiance. Yet given the immediate (and warranted) outrage that Coulter's diatribe was met with, I cannot help wondering why Cruse's similar act of strategic appropriation and revision of history has not received comparable criticism.

No doubt, much of this is due to the sympathetic nature of Cruse's cause. Homosexual men, white or otherwise, have certainly been met with terror and destruction at the hands of white heterosexist culture. The murder of Matthew

Shepard, a young gay man beaten and tied to a barbed-wire fence outside Laramie, Wyoming, occurred only a few years after the publication of *Stuck Rubber Baby* and resembled a lynching in many respects. (Shepard died in a hospital six days after being attacked.) In this case, the use of the civil rights frame to draw attention to this threat to LGBTQ lives appears warranted. The novel's failing is in the move from parallelism and connectivity to full identification and appropriation. For example, on the second page of the first account of Sammy's lynching, Toland's struggles with the memories resemble something of a testimonial, a compulsive attempt to narrativize the event that possesses him. His partner's silent presence in the scene signals a supportive role for the reader, who is to bear the weight of Toland's trauma. As Anne Whitehead has noted, "The listener bears a dual responsibility: to receive the testimony but also to avoid appropriating the story as his or her own" (*Trauma Fiction*, 7).

Yet it would be difficult to argue against the idea that the central conceit of *Stuck Rubber Baby* is the appropriation of history via a level of sociopolitical identification promoted by allied discursive agents of 1990s political discourse. And while the focus of my critique remains these key scenes of (formerly) racialized violence, I do not mean to treat the novel in isolation. In many ways, Cruse's elevation of sexual orientation to the level of racial oppression ultimately flattens both, inadvertently dismissing racial issues even within the LGBTQ community.[17] The presence of black LGBTQ characters such as Les and Esmereldus does little more than provide fantasies of deviance and sexual desire, since even present-day Toland's domestic bliss is tethered to race through his white partner. In this vein, Cruse inadvertently reiterates the literary role of African American characters as little more than sexual conquests, a problem that writers such as Richard Wright, James Baldwin, and Toni Morrison have attempted to address. Ultimately, *Stuck Rubber Baby* may articulate a fascinating, even if limited, treatise on how LGBTQ people might find a usable past in the nation's storied history of protest and activism, but it does so at the expense of a very reductive and problematic racial politics.

That Cruse's novel engages in a deliberate act of historical appropriation for admittedly sympathetic political purposes can hardly be questioned. Yet despite this, my principal intervention in this chapter does not deal with this specific appropriation of consensus memory. Rather, my larger question—which I have only begun to answer—concerns to what extent our larger political culture contributed to and even authorized such an act of appropriation of civil rights rhetoric and African American history. Furthermore, my desire to address the impetus to intervene in how the civil rights movement will be remembered and activated in the present moment on the bodies of the dead has hardly reached a satisfying conclusion. I have settled for highlighting a specific iteration of this issue, doing little to illuminate to overall nature of the problem. Not that this by any means excuses Cruse's problematic narrative choices, but to treat him in isolation would miss the larger discursive context from which *Stuck Rubber Baby* emerged. Given how actors from the original movement such as John Lewis and Coretta Scott King often vocally encouraged a connection between the 1960s campaigns for African American rights and the LGBTQ struggles in the 1990s, is *Stuck Rubber Baby* an overreach more than out-and-out appropriation? Truthfully, no, but one wonders why it took more than twenty years for the lynching scenes in such a celebrated novel to be fully interrogated. The admittedly scant amount of academic criticism on the novel, a lack of attention likely tied to dismissal of much the graphic narrative canon by the academy until recent years, explains this to some degree. Yet the lynchings are rarely brought up in any context other than summation, even in discussions tackling the novel's reductive visions of race and racial difference. Popular reviews are no different; most of them praise its depiction of the plight of the LGBTQ community, even if most of the representatives of this group are cisgendered middle-class white men. It forces a consideration of what versions of history we as a culture have conceded and how we permit those consensus memories to operate politically.

Cyclops Was Right

X-LIVES MATTER!

Many of the X-Men's civil rights parallels were lost on me when I first read their adventures as a kid. Like many young Americans, my fascination with superheroes started early. I was enthralled by the adventures that filled the pages of *The Flash*, *The Teenage Mutant Ninja Turtles*, and, everyone's favorite, *Batman*.[1] But the *X-Men* comics began my unending and unyielding intellectual love affair with superheroes, comic books, graphic novels, and—though I didn't realize it at the time—the civil rights era. Even as I wince at my own corny sentiment, I swell with affection for these four-color melodramatic outsider rebels, who have shaped my literary and political consciousness in ways that I am still joyously uncovering. I was introduced to the 1970s "Silver Age" *X-Men Classics* by other Latino kids in my neighborhood (shouts to Davin, Jaime, and Javier), and the struggles of these mutant outcasts resonated deeply with my own experiences growing up on the mean streets of inner-city Houston in the 1980s. The son of Ecuadorian and Salvadoran immigrants, I was raised in the Hispanic enclave of the Houston Heights, where I did not have to learn English until I went to school (I still have nightmares about not knowing how to ask where the restroom was). Fearing the deteriorating public schools in our neighborhood, my parents elected to send my little sister Jessica and me to Irvington Christian

Academy (ICA), a small Pentecostal school that would have left even James Baldwin shaken. The little one-building schoolhouse was within walking distance of my tiny house in a neighborhood that was too dangerous to walk in. So small was the ICA student body that for many years I was the only kid in my grade level! Its strident Pentecostal codes posited the culture of the secular world that lay outside its walls as something dangerous and sinful, to be avoided at all cost—which only increased its fascination in my ever-curious (naive) young mind. The resulting cultural isolation created something of a social segregating effect, since I was *in* my neighborhood but hardly *of* its community. I felt unspecifically different, an outsider in an inner city. This isolation left me primed to adore the X-Men's adventures (X-ploits?), and in the rosy light of nostalgia I have rediscovered the delight I felt in my encounters with a veritable legion of superheroes similarly excluded. Even better—they had their own school! The foundational tenet of the Xavier Institute for Gifted Youngsters—to embrace your difference—still animates me. This pivotal lesson is quite possibly the reason I feel most at home inside a classroom, and it remains the central pillar of my self-conception. The X-Men taught me that what makes you different doesn't only make you special—it makes you powerful.

Much later I realized how much the X-Men's metaphorical resonance draws power from their origins in civil rights allegory. Created by those sages of American folklore Stan Lee and Jack Kirby, the X-Men (a gendered name for a group that includes a vast array of powerful and ethnically diverse female and queer superpeeps) are populated by "mutants"—humans born with additional (X-tra?) gifts that made "normal" humans hate and fear them.[2] When asked about their inspiration for the X-Men, Lee said:

> I couldn't have everybody bitten by a radioactive spider or zapped with gamma rays, and it occurred to me that if I just said that they were mutants, it would make it easy. Then it occurred to me that instead of them just being heroes that everybody admired, what if I made other people fear and suspect and actually hate them because they were different? I loved that idea; it not only made them different, but it was a good metaphor for what was happening with the civil rights movement in the country at that time. (Lee, quoted in Zubal-Ruggieri, "How the X-Men Reflected")

Since the X-Men's debut in *The Uncanny X-Men* #1 in 1963, the parallels with the civil rights movement have seemed evident. Charles Xavier, aka Professor X, trains his students to control their powers (which arise during puberty, adding some bildungsroman elements to the comic's baseline concepts) and to defend a human society that hates and fears them. With his desire to peacefully coexist with the society that has marginalized his charges, Professor X clearly functions as a Martin Luther King analogue of the way that MLK was understood by popular culture (and later by consensus memory). Even his mutant ability to read people's minds might be thought of as a form of superpowered empathy, a quality one might associate with King. In this vein, the mutant supremacist (some would say "terrorist") Erik Lehnsherr, aka Magneto, leader of the Brotherhood of Evil Mutants, and his propensity for violence can be thought of as representing Malcolm X as he is often remembered (which, it must be noted, is rarely historically accurate). Magneto's powers, which allow him to manipulate magnetic fields and shape metal with his mind, along with his ability to attract followers embittered by their treatment at the hands of normal humans, function as a physical manifestation of Malcolm's "magnetic" charisma. Bryan Singer's 2000 *X-Men* film adaptation turns this subtext into text; his version of Magneto quotes Malcolm X directly, telling Professor X, "The war is still coming, Charles. And I intend to fight it, by *any means necessary.*"

The most powerful iteration of this allegory I encountered while growing up came from Chris Claremont and Brent Anderson's 1982 graphic novel *X-Men: God Loves, Man Kills.* The graphic novel opens with an act of violence so shocking that it must have left even the most cynical fans of the 1980s "grim and gritty" superhero era aghast. In the first scene, two young African American children, Mark and Jill, are running for their lives after the murder of their parents. They are pursued by the Purifiers, villains introduced into the X-Men universe by Claremont in this comic. "Our intentions should be obvious," their white captain declares as she shoots Mark in the back and promises to cleanse the Earth of their kind (2). A second shot kills Mark as his dormant mutant powers begin to manifest (fig. 6.1). As Jill holds her dead brother's body, she looks up and meekly asks, "Why?" Her answer? A gunshot. The captain of the Purifiers tells the dead mutant girl that she had "no right to live" and then commands her underlings to hang their dead bodies from the swing set of their school, seemingly mocking the Xavier Institute, the school for mutants where Mark and Jill could have found sanctuary.

The layout of the first page features no gutters; all the panels overlap, quickening the pace, the terror, and horror of the scene. On the following page, gutters return, asking the reader to linger, reflect, and mediate on the scene. The first panel shows a close-up of Mark, a placard around his neck emblazoned with the word "mutie"—a genetic slur used against the mutant characters of the Marvel universe. In the next panel, bathed in the cold blue light of a seemingly

6.1. Chris Claremont and Brett Anderson, *X-Men: God Loves, Man Kills*, 9–10

indifferent universe, hang the lynched bodies of these poor children for the world to discover (an exceedingly problematic trope; see chapter 5). At the center of the page, Magneto—mutant separatist leader, Malcolm X corollary, and Holocaust survivor—uses his magnetic powers to bring their bodies down, refusing to allow their deaths to be used as a violent spectacle. He laments that the children were "so young . . . so innocent . . . to know such terror and pain. Their only crime—that they had been born" (Claremont and Anderson, *X-Men: God Loves*, 4). The violence of the scene, the unspoken yet clear racial dynamics at play, the allusions to Emmett Till (Mark) and the young girls killed in the 16th Street Baptist Church bombing (Jill), bring the X-Men's allegorical aspects to a visceral fore never before seen in the catalogue of X-titles. Claremont's graphic novel has left an indelible mark on the X-Men universe, shaping the metaphorical and sociopolitical elements of this staple superhero fantasy even today. Clearly, civil rights allegories, analogues, and commentary are baked into the conceptual DNA of the Madrox-level multitude of X-Men comics, films, television shows, cartoons, and videogames.[3]

Or is it?

I recently conducted a poll of a number of comics scholars on the University of Florida's Comix-Scholars email list about a 2012 *Uncanny X-Men* story line that culminates in the death of Charles Xavier at the hands of his star pupil, Scott Summers, aka the eye-beam-wielding X-Men commander Cyclops. Much to my surprise, there was no consensus on whether Lee and Kirby intended the X-Men to be civil rights allegories at all. Some suggested that the metaphors for marginalization we associate with the comic now are a product of the issues edited by Len Wein in the 1970s and the story lines directed by Chris Claremont in the 1980s. Orion Ussner Kidder of Simon Fraser University, whose opinion evolved during the group's conversation, perhaps summed up this viewpoint best early in the discussion:

> My understanding was that civil-right parallels weren't in the original comics. They were much more abstract outcasts than specifically standing in for African Americans [. . .] These associations crept in slowly as they built backstory; e.g., Magneto's experiences as a Jewish prisoner in a Nazi concentration camp. All that stuff—civil rights, the holocaust, etc.—is very much part of the narrative now, but it took time to coalesce and then build momentum [. . .] as is the case with any superhero characters that survive for decades because they've had layers of signification accrete over time. ("RE: Cyclops Was Right")

Kidder's point, then, isn't so much that the characters aren't civil rights allegories, but that these connotations formed over years of narrative development and were arguably not present at the X-Men's inception.

Inadvertently, Kidder raises another salient point. If this comic is indeed a civil rights allegory, then how to explain the fact that the original cast is entirely white? As Joseph J. Darowski notes in his stellar (X-cellent?) comics history *X-Men and the Mutant Metaphor: Race and Gender in Comic Books*, African American characters were introduced into the Marvel canon soon after the first issue of *The Uncanny X-Men*: "Eventually, Marvel would introduce the first black superhero, the Black Panther, but it would not be until 1966. The Falcon, the first African American superhero in mainstream comics, would not be introduced by Marvel until 1969. In 1963, with the X-Men's initial roster, the team that many interpret as representing minorities was entirely white and middle class. The only exception to this was Angel, who was still white, but upper class" (32). Compounding this confusion is the fact that Lee and Kirby did not shy away from overt racial themes in their other Marvel properties. *Sgt. Fury and the Howling Commandos, The Fantastic Four*, and *Captain America* all directly tackle the issues of racism in US society head-on.[4] Even more confounding is the fact that two of the original five members, Beast and Angel, have physical mutant manifestations that require elaborate disguises in order for them to blend into normal human society—an obvious, even if clumsy, metaphor for racial passing (fig. 6.2). And except during a few moments of tension with humans, these elements are more context than content; in its first year, the comic focused largely on straightforward, even clichéd superhero yarns rather than on overt racial or social commentary.

Perhaps a better approach would be to think of the X-Men as a larger marginalization metaphor, contextualized by the civil rights movement in which it

6.2. Stan Lee and Jack Kirby, *The Uncanny X-Men* #1, 17

arose, but untethered from it as well. As Marc DiPaolo notes: "Presumably, the super-powered mutants allegorically represent real-world people; otherwise, they would not have resonance in a world in which superpowers don't exist. The allegory is clearly there, but what makes it so compelling is that it is a flexible allegory. The story of the X-Men is the story of the oppressed and the disenfranchised striking back against their oppressors, so any reader who feels oppressed may relate to the X-Men, regardless of the nature of the oppression, or its level of severity" (*War, Politics and Superheroes*, 219). In our email discussion, Noah Berlatsky, author of *Wonder Woman: Bondage and Feminism in the Marston/ Peter Comics, 1941–1948* (2015), reminds us that any inspiration drawn from the civil rights movement should not necessarily be equated with outright support of its political project or goals. He writes: "My sense is that there is a difference between using mutants as a metaphor for marginalized people and drawing parallels with the Civil Rights struggle, or endorsing the Civil Rights struggle. The initial X-Men I think did the first, but not the second so much. Stan Lee in the quote above suggests that he was writing in sympathy with the Civil Rights Movement. I think that's a very dicey claim" ("RE: Cyclops Was Right"). And we must contend with the political censorship imposed by the Comics Code Authority on superhero narratives, as well as with prevailing US print cultures at the time of the X-Men's conception. To what extent were Lee and Kirby allowed to make overt gestures to the civil rights movement? As Tony Rose, a research fellow at the Sequoyah National Research Center, noted in the email thread, "I was one of those who bought them off the stands. The difference is that I did it in the southern United States. If a wholesaler had gotten the idea that it was a civil rights comic, it would not have been distributed down here" ("RE: Cyclops Was Right"). So should we really consider the X-Men to be a civil rights allegory? Although there seems to be some civil rights inspiration at the core of the comic's "flexible allegory," perhaps we shouldn't.

Or maybe we should?

Let's remember that comics as a medium require active participation to complete the narrative magic of sequential art, and we can extend those elements of reader negotiation to the metaphors and allegories present in the X-Universe. As Rachael A. Zubal-Ruggieri of Syracuse University notes in the email discussion: "The meaning of characters to the reader, or even the interpretation of the material, can be different than what the artist or writer intended. It is indeed constructed by the reader. Although many say that Professor X is representative of MLK and Magneto more of Malcolm X, they really don't—they are white. But there are other interpretations of themes explored in the X-Men narrative as a whole, especially gay rights, disability rights, and any other civil rights struggles that the reader might glean from its pages" ("RE: Cyclops Was Right"). Ivan Kocmarek of McMaster University, in Ontario, was even more pointed in his contribution to the thread, contending that the comic is indeed a civil rights allegory: "To those of us who bought these X-Men books off the stands and who lived through the civil rights movement in the '60s, even in Canada, the allegory was palpable no matter what Lee/Kirby intended" ("RE: Cyclops Was Right"). The notion that the authors' intention matters less than how their creation is understood by readers is hardly a new one. Roland Barthes stated in 1967 that the author is dead, just a few years after the initial creation of Lee and Kirby's merry band of mutants. In the decades-long process through which US superhero mythologies gather meaning, fan culture plays a direct role in determining what form superhero allegories and metaphors take, as well as how those forms are remembered.

Of course, the question of how to determine what readers in the 1960s thought about any potential civil-rights-oriented readings of these comics is a tricky one. As Charles Henebry of Boston University noted in the discussion thread, relying on what readers *today* insist they saw in the comic *then* is subject to the revisionist tendencies of all recalled memories. Henebry goes further, suggesting that "to find hard evidence of readers *in the sixties* thinking of the X-Men by reference to MLK and Malcolm X, you'd need to read the letters pages of X-Men or, even better, harder to find contemporary fanzines" ("RE: Cyclops Was Right"). Blessedly, we do have access to many of these letters pages, thanks to Marvel's extensive digital archive. I am mainly interested in what the archive represents in regard to consensus memory as refracted through X-Men fandom. As Ramzi Fawaz's fantastic *The New Mutants: Superheroes and the Radical Imagination of American Comics* demonstrates, the letters columns in the monthly installments of Marvel's properties showcase this meaning-making process in almost real time. As part of his larger argument concerning the "cosmopolitics" of comics fan culture (specifically for the *Fantastic Four*, but broadly applied), Fawaz writes:

> From the outset Lee and Kirby self-consciously framed *The Fantastic Four* letters column as a forum for discussing the transformations taking place in Marvel Comics, and U.S. culture more broadly, in the 1960s. It soon became a social laboratory for the production of a new counterpublic, the Marvel Comics readership. (95)

> Readers responded by developing sophisticated interpretive practices through
> which they linked the fantasy content of Marvel Comics to larger questions
> of political concern, consequently demanding new forms of conceptual
> innovation and political accountability from the creators of their favorite
> stories. (96)

In this context, we might think of the X-Men comics and their potential for civil-
rights-oriented readings as an emergent form of consensus memory happening
nearly in real time. If readers demanded that the authors of the X-Men map their
civil rights concerns onto the comic's flexible allegory, it offers a window into how
those readers understood the movement at the time. I am wary of overreaching
here—an assertion that this relatively small corner of popular culture could fully
capture the ever-shifting terrain of consensus memory is, to quote Berlatsky, "a
dicey claim."

Despite these caveats, I find myself still so convinced of the claim that the
story of the X-Men is a civil rights allegory at its core that I insisted on its veracity
in the discussion thread, and I do so again in this epilogue. My investment in
that reading is personal—the civil rights allegory has always been so central to
my adoration of Marvel's merry band of mutants that I find myself emotionally
allegiant to it. I may be guilty of a backward projection, imposing my reading
on the comic's past. It is, perhaps, telling that I opened this epilogue not with
scenes from the X-Men's original 1960s run, but with one from Chris Claremont's
1982 *God Loves, Man Kills*—the comic that fueled much of my initial love of the
entire series. *God Loves* draws power from its overt civil rights allusions, its direct
condemnation of supremacist violence, and its religious martyr motifs—Xavier
is crucified in one overly symbolic dream sequence. Claremont's graphic novel
might reflect the X-Men comic's core themes not as they were, but as how we wish
to remember them. *God Loves* served as the template for Bryan Singer's highly
regarded *X-Men* film franchise of the 2000s; X2: *X-Men United* (2003) adapted
the graphic novel's primary narrative and characters. In this sense, *God Loves* represents a form consensus memory linked with the civil rights movement through
the comic, even though its primary concern is the comic itself. Most crucially, it
is a form of consensus memory that fans across multiple eras have participated
in and continue to participate in.

God Loves, Man Kills continues to inform the X-Universe in multiple ways,
particularly in regard to the character of Cyclops and to the comic's relationship
to the Black Lives Matter movement, a modern extension of the civil rights movement. The novel's primary focus is the diabolical Reverend William Stryker, who

believes mutants to be satanic abominations that must be eradicated. He openly calls for a mutant genocide. After nearly murdering the X-Men, Stryker kidnaps Professor X and attempts to use Xavier's telepathic abilities to power a machine that can render every mutant on the planet brain dead—effectively killing them all with the push of a button. Joining forces with their former nemesis Magneto, the X-Men stop Stryker and his human supremacist group, the Purifiers. The comic repositions Magneto as a sympathetic, even if militant, ally of the X-Men, opposed to their integrationist politics but committed to the defense of mutant lives. While Charles remains a kindly MLK figure, Claremont's version of Magneto seems to echo (or even predict) contemporary pop-culture understandings of Malcolm X as having been similarly sympathetic to the cause of civil rights, even though critical of its tactics and rhetoric. More importantly, however, it positions Cyclops as the intellectual and spiritual heir of Professor X's "dream" of human and mutant peaceful coexistence.

Once freed from Stryker's clutches, Professor X begins to consider the possibility that Magneto's brand of violent militancy might be the only path toward mutant survival. Scott Summers talks Xavier back from the brink of radicalization: "You brought us together to fulfill a dream, Charles—one born out of hope and the noblest of human aspirations—and we've sweated and bled, and some of us have died, to make it a reality. I'm not prepared to give up. The means are as important as the end—we have to do this right or not at all. Anything less negates every belief we've ever had, every sacrifice we've ever made" (59). This speech does more than perfectly summarize Xavier's commitment to nonviolence; its rhetoric shaped much of my fledgling (teenage) political consciousness—and it didn't hurt that Cyclops's power, like my own, is channeled through his glasses![5] Cyclops's role as Xavier's ideological heir apparent suggests a continuum; the movement that Xavier started must one day be handed to the next generation of activists and dreamers—a symbolic suggestion that the civil rights movement, at least in 1982, never ended. Which, excruciatingly, only heightens the tragedy of Cyclops killing Professor X thirty years later. But what fascinates me today is the reaction of a large subset of fans, myself included, to the death of the X-Men's founder—namely, "Cyclops Was Right."

The phrase "Cyclops Was Right" refers to the finale of a nearly decade-long story line steeped in X-Men lore that focuses on Scott Summers, aka Cyclops, who inherits leadership of the team from his mentor, Professor X—and eventually kills him in battle. Professor X's death at the hands of Cyclops came after years of the new leader's increasing militancy. The story, beginning in 2007 and spearheaded by the ever-controversial Brian Michael Bendis, sees Cyclops slowly embrace proactive and preemptive methods of violence in response to increasing intolerance, terror, and death directed at the mutant community by human supremacists. Ultimately, I read "Cyclops Was Right" fandom in the light of the Black Lives Matter movement, which entered the national conversation near the story's climax and shaped story lines and themes after the death of Professor X.

First, a quick recap of this fictional history. Wanda Maximoff, member of the Avengers and Magneto's daughter, loses control of her reality-altering mutant powers and magically strips millions of mutants of their abilities (symbolically deracializing them). This event reduces the number of mutants in the world to a scant 198.[6] With the mutant population on the verge of extinction, Stryker returns and attacks the Xavier School for Gifted Youngsters, bombing a school bus and killing 44 students.[7] In response, Cyclops gathers the world's remaining mutants and establishes an independent island nation known as "Utopia" a few miles off the coast of San Francisco. The island is built from the remains of Magneto's former space base Asteroid M.[8] This act of self-segregation and self-determination is, predictably, met with hostility by Earth's governments. Exacerbating the situation, the first post-decimation mutant, "Hope," is born, and the X-Men race to find her before Stryker and the Purifiers can kill her in her crib. Cyclops establishes a clandestine mutant hit squad led by Wolverine, which is committed to preemptively killing every Purifier it can.[9] The move, which represents a stark departure from Charles Xavier's commitment to nonviolence, alienates Cyclops from the majority of Xavier's former students, who remain committed to his nonviolent, integrationist politics. Even Wolverine, a former assassin, eventually abandons Cyclops after the embattled mutant leader, fearing that the Purifiers will attack Utopia directly, decides to prepare his teenage students for combat duty—a decision that leads Wolverine to accuse Cyclops of training child soldiers.[10]

In many ways, the narrative of Cyclops's increasing militancy adheres to the larger schema of the X-Men's flexible allegory, folding in elements that can be read as echoes of the civil rights era without confining itself within the strictures of direct analogies to the movement. For example, the bombing of the school bus by the Purifiers echoes both the 16th Street Baptist Church bombing and the torching of the Montgomery Freedom Riders' bus. Cyclops's decision to move the world's remaining mutants to Utopia echoes Marcus Garvey's "Back to Africa" movement and represents a return of sorts to the separatist ideology of Magneto/Malcolm X, embodied by the use of Magneto's former base of operations. Cyclops's adoption of these militant strategies, coupled with his desire for a mutant-oriented political consciousness, suggests a rejection of Xavier/MLK's nonviolent rhetoric and an embracing of a militant stance that echoes popular black power figures like Stokely Carmichael or Fred Hampton (as they tend to be remembered). Yet the story line seems mainly interested in exploring forms of militancy and justified violence in ways incompatible with any legible civil rights frame (for example, Cyclops's preemptive-strike mentality reflects George W. Bush much more than Malcolm X). An extended exploration of how these comics represent militancy and radicalism would be incredibly valuable as an extension of how US culture participates in these same discourses. But I am more interested in fans' embrace of Cyclops's militant turn, even when the mutants of Utopia faced off against Captain America, the ultimate symbol of US righteousness and state authority, only two months after the death of Trayvon Martin in February 2012.

The first chapter of the serialized *Avengers vs. X-Men* crossover was published in April 2012. The story sees the return of the Phoenix force, a cosmic energy force that takes the shape of a giant bird of flame, to Earth—a force that needs a mutant avatar in order to fully coalesce. The Phoenix force represents the cosmic cycle of death and rebirth, since any planet it visits is razed to the ground so that life can be reset and begin anew. The Avengers resolve to defuse, deter, or destroy the Phoenix force before it reaches the planet. Cyclops, knowing that the Phoenix will choose a mutant host, sees its arrival as heralding the return of the mutant race from the brink of extinction. He decides to allow the Phoenix to possess Hope Summers—a choice that puts him in direct conflict with Captain America and the Avengers. The Avengers attack the X-Men on their island home and capture Hope, and in the ensuing chaos, Tony Stark, aka Iron Man, manages to disperse the Phoenix into five hosts—Cyclops and four of his lieutenants (Hope not among them). Over the following issues, the Phoenix Five begin a series of humanitarian missions across the world, ending famines, droughts, and providing free clean renewable energy to many countries on the fringes of modernity—and then attacking developed nations and stripping them of their military might and nuclear arsenals. Captain America, predictably, finds this unacceptable, so he leads his Avengers against the Phoenix Five in order to restore proper order to the planet (presumably with the United States in charge) and banish the Phoenix before it consumes Earth.

After a series of heroic battles and internal betrayals, Cyclops alone controls the Phoenix force, which drives him completely mad. He decides to destroy the Avengers to prevent them from undoing the prosperity he has brought the marginalized peoples of the world, which he will then rule. The Avengers dispatch Charles Xavier to stop Cyclops, but Cyclops accidentally kills his former mentor in a fit of uncontrollable cosmic rage. Eventually, Hope steals the Phoenix force from Cyclops and disperses the energy across the globe, awakening the dormant powers of many mutants around the world, effectively restarting the mutant race and undoing the effects of the decimation. Cyclops, however, is taken into custody for the murder of Charles Xavier, whose destiny as a martyr is fulfilled. Allegorically, it seems that regardless of how necessary or righteous turns to violence may feel, embracing such tactics ultimately means sacrificing the dream represented by Xavier/MLK. The values and intended meanings of this symbolic death seem clear.

Yet many fans of the comics sided with Cyclops over Professor X—insisting that Cyclops was right. The first appearance of the phrase "Cyclops was right" appears in the second issue of *AVX: Consequences*, the epilogue to the principal *Avengers vs. X-Men* story line. Wolverine confronts his imprisoned former leader, and Cyclops attempts to goad Wolverine into killing him before he stands trial. When Wolverine realizes that he is being played, and that Cyclops wants to die, Cyclops says: "Of course I do. I'm dead weight now. I've done everything I can do. I die now, and I'm a martyr. And in a few years, some rebellious little kid is going to turn up at your school with me on his t-shirt. 'Cyclops was right'" (Gillen, *AVX: Consequences*, 13). Drawn from the mythology of the comic, the phrase alludes to Quentin Quire, a rebellious student who wears a "Magneto is Right" T-shirt to class—a shirt clearly styled after the popular Che Guevara shirts of the 1990s. The comment seems to have been meant to be read ironically, revealing Cyclops's full alignment with the militant (i.e., violent) ideology represented by Magneto, who is typically depicted as being diametrically opposed to Xavier's nonviolent integrationist politics, even when sympathetic to Xavier's cause. Professor X's death, at least, was intended to be read as tragic. Take, for example, this excerpt from an MTV interview with the X-Men writer Brian Michael Bendis, Marvel's editor in chief Axel Alonso, and senior editor Tom Brevoort:

> Bendis told us that it wasn't even so much about not liking Xavier, as the entirety of the X-Men franchise had moved past him. So when it came time for "Avengers vs. X-Men," something needed to be done. "Xavier's dream is dying," continued Bendis. "He can't just stand there and say, well that sucks. He'd have to take action, and so the conversation turned to that, maybe that's the point of no return for Scott. Maybe that's the thing that happens that changes Scott's life forever."
>
> More to that, Brevoort added, "Professor X's death wasn't the goal, it was just where the story inexorably led us. Given his viewpoint and actions over the past few years, once he was empowered by the Phoenix it was pretty well inevitable that Cyclops was going to have to face Charles, his virtual father, at a certain point. And the son striking down the father in a moment of uncontrolled passion seemed very Shakespearian." (Zalben, interview)

———

These comments from the Marvel brain trust are very telling. The notion that Professor X's death was "inevitable," that "it was just where the story inexorably led us," takes on additional prophetic inevitability given that he is modeled after Martin Luther King, the most iconic martyr of racial politics in US history. (Ironically, the fact that Professor X is killed by his own people more closely resembles the fate of Malcolm X.) I am much more interested in what I consider the understated bombshell of the interview: the X-franchise and its fans had moved past Xavier and everything he represents. Following the end of *Avengers vs. X-Men*, the internet began to proliferate with Che-style "Cyclops Was Right" memes and merchandise, much of it without any official Marvel sanction (fig. 6.3). In this context, what does it mean to say that Cyclops was right? Right about what?

It should come as no surprise that there is little consensus in the online community about what exactly Cyclops was right about. What I present here is just a sampling.[11] Some fans, even those who disagree with Cyclops's tactics, focus on the plot, noting that he was right about the Phoenix force's potential to reignite the mutant population's decimated powers.[12] Others focus on the thematic transfer of the MLK/Malcom X dichotomy from the characters of Professor X and Magneto to Wolverine and Cyclops; or they focus on the controversy itself, without taking sides.[13] For example, Marius Thienenkamp expresses nothing but sympathy for Cyclops, noting that he was right to attack Captain America, since "at this point, nearly of the less than 198 remaining mutants were gathered on Utopia island, with Scott responsible for *all of them*" ("From Apocalypse to Revolution"). Others

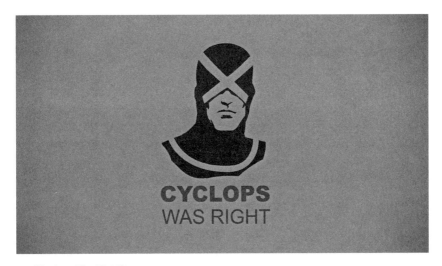

6.3. "Cyclops Was Right"

defend Cyclops's actions as an act of marginalized agency meant to strike back at mutants' oppressors. For example, Rogue Pryde (almost certainly a pseudonym) writes, "The stand that Cyclops takes is one that can easily be understood by any persecuted group, a simple message of 'this stops now!' informed by all the complexities inherent in struggles against oppression" ("Was Cyclops Right?"). Sean Ian Mills, who goes through the character's entire history, defending each action, worries about how Cyclops's legacy will be remembered by fandom: "Cyclops does the heroic thing, but the comic treats it like something villainous. History is written by the winners, after all" ("Cyclops Was Right Yet Again"). Clearly, some readers were enthralled by Cyclops's willingness to take matters into his own hands and go to war for the oppressed peoples of the world, often in defiance of US authority.

In *Avengers vs. X-Men*, Captain America, speaking symbolically for the United States, confesses that Cyclops was right—the nation had failed to protect its mutant population. In prison, Captain America tells Cyclops, "Back on Utopia, you were right about one thing: the Avengers should've done more to help mutants. I should've done more. I allowed the world to hate and fear them for far too long, I won't make that mistake again" (Bendis, *Avengers vs. X-Men*). For me, this admission took on added significance in light of the death of Trayvon Martin, six months prior. I could not help reading these stories in light of the emerging national conversation around the numerous shooting deaths of African American, Latinx, and Native American young men and women at the hands of law enforcement. In this sense, my response was emotional rather than rational: Cyclops was right—the United States has failed communities of color, and they must stand up for themselves.

To be clear: it would be irresponsible to suggest that fans' embrace of "Cyclops Was Right" represents some sort of deliberate allegiance to the Black Lives Matter movement. The dates don't match up. Cyclops began his militant path in 2007, and Trayvon Martin's murder occurred on 26 February 2012. *Avengers vs. X-Men*'s first chapter was published two months after the shooting and ended in October 2012—many months before Black Lives Matter began to coalesce online as a national movement. Cyclops was eventually freed from prison and given his own X-Men title in February 2013. The #BlackLivesMatter hashtag appeared later that summer in response to the acquittal, on 13 July, of George Zimmerman for the murder of Trayvon Martin. The movement, founded by Alicia Garza, Patrisse Cullors, and Opal Tometi, achieved national prominence after it took part in the political unrest in Ferguson, Missouri, following the shooting death of Michael Brown on 9 August 2014. These key dates do not support a reading of the original

Avengers vs. X-Men comic as commenting on any of these events directly. Nor can I really know to what extent (if any) the reactions quoted above are responses to the injustices confronted by Black Lives Matter.

Yet I am left contending with how the very public discourse concerning Black Lives Matter, the validity of its protests, and the accusations of its militancy shaped Cyclops's story in the aftermath of the death of Professor X. After all, a year after the events of *Avengers vs. X-Men*—and a full year after the death of Trayvon Martin—Cyclops was freed and starring in *The Uncanny X-Men*, Marvel's mutant flagship title and the comic in which the X-Men debuted. Titled "The Mutant Revolution," the story line opens with scenes of public protests by humans supporting mutant rights, with the Che-style image that accompanied the "Cyclops Was Right" memes and T-shirts front and center (fig. 6.4). The text of the scene, in which a captive Magneto claims, "*You* people hate him. People on the street *love* him," can, and perhaps should, be read metacritically—a nod to fan demands for more stories devoted to the mutant revolutionary. In regard to the comic, Cyclops embraces revolutionary rhetoric while abandoning his proactive violence; he limits himself to rescuing newly formed mutants detained without trial by S.H.I.E.L.D. (the Marvel universe's analogue for the Department of Homeland Security) and publicly supporting citizens' rights to protest. In fact, scenes of protest become stages for both commentary and plot as extremist factions of S.H.I.E.L.D. openly attack Cyclops at protests across the country (who is technically a fugitive).

A key moment comes in the August 2013 issue—exactly a year before the unrest in Ferguson, Missouri—during a pro-mutant rally organized by humans in Ann Arbor, Michigan (fig. 6.5). When the protest is attacked by US government operatives, Cyclops realizes that the attacks are designed to instill fear of his revolutionary movement in the hearts and minds of everyday Americans. He points out, "They're trying to taint the world's image of us. These violent displays are meant to compound people's fear of us," an accusation that was often levied at the Ferguson Police Department's violent suppression of the Ferguson protesters a year later (Bendis, *Uncanny X-Men*, vol. 1). The specific chapter, entitled "Mutant Power," harks back to the black liberation movements of the 1970s, which received similar treatment by state authorities and media outlets. In the same issue, Cyclops is inspired by seeing humans rally in support of mutant rights, a nod (perhaps) to the intersectional allegiances inspired by Black Lives Matter. As he battles S.H.I.E.L.D., Cyclops states, "All I can think about is these amazing humans who have come here to rally in support of us . . . and how they are being punished for doing so. In my lifetime, I never thought I would see the day that

6.4. Brian Michael Bendis and Chris Bachalo, *The Uncanny X-Men* #1, 7

6.5. Brian Michael Bendis and Frazier Irving, *The Uncanny X-Men* #10, 13–14

humans would stand up for us . . . for me" (Bendis, *Uncanny X-Men*, vol. 1). Public displays of support and allegiance across the country followed the acquittal of Trayvon's killer in July 2013, six weeks before the publication of "*Mutant Power*." Typically, superhero serials are produced month to month, which means the events of the comic *could* be a deliberate comment on the Trayvon Martin vigils—although I find it much more likely these comics represent a sort of zeitgeist moment rather than a deliberate allegory.

I do not believe the same can be said for the way the "Mutant Revolution" story line plays out. By August 2014, the tragedy of Michael Brown's death and the circumstances regarding his slaying had gripped the American consciousness. The ensuing unrest in Ferguson lasted from 9 August to 25 August 2014, and the predominantly peaceful protests were met by a fierce response from the militarized Ferguson Police Department riot squads.[14] The protests in the early issues of *The Uncanny X-Men*'s "Mutant Revolution" story line feel particularly prophetic in this case, which makes the absence of any scenes of protests after the unrest at Ferguson all the more glaring. It was not until eighteen months later in *The Uncanny X-Men* #36, which was renumbered to #600 to symbolically complete the first issue in 1963, that any images of organized protest or activism appeared in the pages of the comic again. Up until that issue, the story lines in *The Uncanny X-Men* featured fairly standard mutant fare: training sequences, clandestine missions, battling Sentinels, or ill-conceived time-traveling farces like bringing the original X-Men from the 1960s forward so they could witness what the world became.[15]

Published in November 2015, over a year after the unrest in Ferguson, *The Uncanny X-Men* #600 features the resolution of multiple subplots from the comic's three-year "Mutant Revolution" story line, culminating with Cyclops summoning all the world's most prominent mutants—villains and heroes alike—to the steps of the US Capitol (fig. 6.6). In a scene clearly designed to recall Martin Luther King's "I Have a Dream" speech, Cyclops addresses what he meant by "revolution" to the gathered mutants and their allies:

> Well, this is it. This is the Mutant Revolution. Here we are. All of us. Every single one of us. Every mutant in the world on the steps of the Capitol Building in Washington, D.C. In the heart of everything democratic and good . . . And do you hear that? Do you see that? Nothing. Nothing is happening. The humans' worst nightmare about mutants is that we would unite and attack. Unite and conquer. Unite and come after them. Well, here we are, united. And . . . isn't it beautiful? (30)

The scene closes with Magneto interrupting Cyclops to assure him that "Charles Xavier would love this," signaling some sort of redemption for the man who killed him.

It is hard to know how to interpret the finale of "The Mutant Revolution" as political commentary. Read through the national dialogue around Black Lives Matter specifically, as well as the role of public protest in national discourse generally, we might take Cyclops's affirmation that mutant unity need not be feared as a response to accusations of Black Lives Matter militancy. In this sense, Bendis and company cast the unity of the marginalized as something to be revered rather than reviled. Linking this back to the civil rights movement through Charles Xavier (via Magneto and Cyclops), the visual echoes of the March on Washington, and renumbering the issues so that they link back to the start of the X-Men casts Black Lives Matter as an extension of the civil rights movement. Yet this symbolic act is not without its problematic elements. A less generous reading would consider this corrective to target not media representations of the Black Lives Matter movement, but the movement itself, tacitly asking it to embrace the respectability politics associated with MLK's wing of civil rights activism. Further, it is hard to understand what is meant by "revolution" in this context, since neither of these readings feels particularly revolutionary, at least to this true believer. Revolution could suggest a cycle or a return to a previous state, or a journey around the sun—but those interpretations feel rather unsatisfying. Still, this much we can agree on—Cyclops was right. X-Lives matter.

Avengers vs. X-Men, the "Cyclops Was Right" trends, and the "Mutant Revolution" story line have a tenuous, unclear relationship at best (condescending at worst) to the Black Lives Matter movement, which was gathering energy at the time of their publication. Like the original X-Men comics, these stories might best be approached as functioning under the rules of a "flexible allegory" as outlined by DiPaolo. Bendis's X-Men run may draw narrative power from these discourses when it suits the story, but remains uncommitted to solely focusing on those elements, even when commenting on those initial inspirations. What matters more than the intention of the series' many contributors is how the stories were received both then and now. Only upon reflection will we know what, if any, consensus emerges regarding the allegorical content and value of these stories—as well as how they will be remembered. Nonetheless, these messily flexible allegories function as a sort of archive, and will eventually function as an artifact, that reflects how discourses surrounding racial justice and public protests shaped, stretched, and strained the X-Men's story lines. These flexible allegories can be taken as a form of emergent consensus memory that interacts with other sites of memory, even as it comments on those and itself. It will be left to future generations to contend with these future memories.

I found myself participating in the "Cyclops Was Right" trend from nearly the outset. My angst, trepidation, and fear, which were activated by the needless deaths of so many young people of color, found expression and catharsis in my old mutant friends. I am a committed ally of the Black Lives Matter movement, having attended a number of marches, demonstrations, and academic lectures on the issue. As a person of color in the United States, I have had frankly terrifying interactions with law enforcement. On the other hand, I am likewise committed to acknowledging good police work when I see it, having had as many affirming interactions with police officers as troubling ones—disparate experiences I have never been able to reconcile. Furthermore, I have many dear friends and family members working in law enforcement—including two of the same Latino men who introduced me to the X-Men in the first place. While I reject any suggestion that these two political stances are mutually exclusive, I would be lying if I insisted that the tension between these beliefs does not trouble me with frequent bouts

6.6. Brian Michael Bendis and Chris Bachalo, *The Uncanny X-Men* #600, 34–35

of cognitive dissonance. The X-Men comics have, at the very least, helped me process these often incompatible factions of my consciousness by dramatizing them through a variety of colorful personalities that have been dear to me since childhood. Even now, as I process my ambivalent emotions toward the end of the Mutant Revolution, I am relieved that it did not end in the sort of apocalyptic bloodshed that plagues too many modern superhero yarns. Perhaps imagining peace in times of tribulation is revolutionary in and of itself, even if it isn't revolutionary in any particularly satisfying way. After all, real history is traumatic enough—I do not need comic books to help me remember that.

Or do I?

A Conversation with Ho Che Anderson, Author-Artist of *King*

The Canadian graphic novelist Ho Che Anderson composes compellingly frenetic and socially engaged comic books whose content and styles are as diverse and energetic as the bevy of influences from which he draws inspiration. Born in London, but raised in Toronto, Anderson is named after the Vietnamese and Cuban revolutionaries Ho Chi Minh and Che Guevara. His work is likewise revolutionary, and he has risen to become one of the most prominent independent voices of the black North American comics scene. Moving from the narratively distant to the uncomfortably intimate, Anderson's oeuvre is characterized by more visual modes and graphic styles than can succinctly be listed here. Never content to be pinned down to any one tradition, Anderson's signature noir style is influenced by a bevy of other styles, drawing liberally from the Jack Kirby and Howard Chaykin comics that inspired him in his youth, and from the visual repertoires of the filmmakers Spike Lee and Oliver Stone. His subjects of interest are as varied as his influences: biography, science fiction, and explorations of eroticism, to name a few. His first title, *I Want to Be Your Dog* (1989), explored sadomasochistic themes, but the Seattle-based publisher Gary Groth had ambitious plans for the young artist. At the behest of Groth, Anderson broke ground on a project that in many ways catapulted his young career—a biography of Martin Luther King Jr. Anderson openly admits the pecuniary origins of the project, since he was eager to break into the comics industry in a big way. Over the course of the next ten years and three volumes, Anderson's sprawling and experimental *King: A Comics Biography* received increasing critical attention, becoming a staple of graphic narrative syllabi across college campuses. At the time of this interview, a third, updated edition of *King* was in the works from Fantagraphics.

Since the publication of *King*, Anderson's ambition and intellectual curiosity have taken his career into a multiplicity of new directions. In 1994, he published *Young Hoods in Love*, a collection of graphic short fiction exploring the urban life of 1990s Toronto. In a similar vein, he collaborated with Wilfred Santiago on the five-part *Pop Life* series, which focuses specifically on the lives of young women. *Wise Son: The White Wolf* appeared in 1996, a superhero-themed fantasy drama exploring the terrors of racism in America from the perspective of a Black Muslim hero. His chilling zombie fantasy *Scream Queens* (2005) has recently been recollected and rereleased by Fantagraphics. He has published a young adult graphic novel entitled *No-Boy Club* and the children's book *Steel Drums and Ice Skates*, with the writer Dirk McLean. Currently, Anderson is working on a long-standing dream project, *Godhead*, a science-fiction action adventure that explores themes of race and class struggle that arise when a corporation invents a machine that allows the user to talk to God. When he learned I was working on a chapter on *King*, Anderson graciously reached out to me and generously offered his insights. Our email correspondence grew into a full-fledged interview, conducted primarily over the summer months of 2017. This interview has been published largely intact, edited lightly for concision and clarity.

Jorge Santos: So, tell us about how your career got started. What inspired you to get into creating your own comics? What did you read as a young man?

Ho Che Anderson: This is a massive cliché at this point, but the reason we're talking here is because of *Star Wars*. I saw that movie in its original theatrical run, and the experience fundamentally changed me. Maybe I would have chosen this path even if I hadn't seen that film, maybe it would have been another audiovisual or purely visual entertainment that would have been the catalyst, but the fact remains I walked out of that cinema in summer '77 obsessed with mythology, science fiction, swashbuckling heroes, space travel, quests, and those obsessions over time filtered into a general love of storytelling, particularly visual storytelling, but storytelling in all its forms that I knew very early I had to try and turn into a career. Had I access to a camera as a child or a young person, I probably would have gotten into filmmaking much earlier than I did. At the time, all I had access to were pens and pencils, and I was always an artist. I don't remember when I started drawing, but it was pretty early on. Similarly, I don't really remember when I first got hooked on comics. To some extent, I might also have *Star Wars* to blame for that obsession as well, because the earliest comic I can actually *remember* reading is Howard Chaykin's *Star Wars* adaptation. My first five years were spent in England, so it's possible I was looking at stuff like *Beano* and *Topper* as a toddler—I definitely was by the time I was ten or eleven. But that *Star Wars* comic thrilled me. I hated Chaykin's art style, but the power of that story was such that I returned to it again and again. And in those days there was no streaming, no Netflix, no video stores, not even fucking VCRs, at least not for regular people. If you wanted to reexperience a movie you liked, you either hoped it got rereleased or waited for it to show up on TV, or you read the comic book adaptation. I still remember sitting in the kitchen with my mother reading the thing while eating a pizza at lunch before heading back to school. Such an innocent era.

After that, comics became a big part of my life, to the extent that my dad used to threaten to take them away from me because I always had my face buried in a comic book, usually while simultaneously consuming hours and hours of TV, because I watched every single show there was to watch in the '70s and '80s. I fell in love with the silver and golden ages of comics, anything published before 1975 was absolutely intoxicating to me. I fell in love with Jack Kirby and Steve Ditko, I spent forever aping Kirby images, painstakingly re-creating the panels from his comics as full-page sketchbook drawings. I've still got a lot of that stuff buried in a box in a storage space. My mom bought me an issue of *Heavy Metal* one day during a summer outing in 1977, and it was the first place I ever saw boobs in a comic—you know, there was *before* that day, and there was *after* that day, if you know what I'm saying. I still remember the thrill of it, and how weird it made me feel. Like I said, the '70s were a more innocent era. I read whatever I could get my hands on in that period without discrimination.

The next galvanizing force for me was Frank Miller's *Ronin*. I was thirteen. That book was just such a strange, compelling animal. I'd never seen anything like it at the time. I found the story confounding and the techniques used to tell it baffling, but the package as a whole excited me more than I could ever articulate, and I just had to plunder its secrets and figure out what Miller was doing and how he was doing it. Massive influence, that comic.

By the time I was sixteen, I'd decided I wanted to be a cartoonist, so I started taking my stuff around to publishers. Actually, I started at fourteen. I wasn't anywhere near ready, but I was hungry and inspired, and there was a comic I loved called *Mr. X* that I discovered was published locally. I knew that was my way in. At sixteen I still wasn't ready, but I was sufficiently evolved that I could at least get people to look at my work. By that point, I was also starting to take the work of being a writer very seriously. I used to write stuff just so I'd have something to draw, at least as it pertained to comics. But I was starting to realize there were things I wanted to say, and that I wanted to perfect the craft of saying them. I fell in love with reading plays—Tennessee Williams was a very early writing inspiration, followed by August Wilson. Yeah, I was really into plays for a while before my interest turned to screenwriting and movies in general.

JS: Moving to your own comics, the original volumes of your *King* biography took near nearly ten years to publish. What inspired you to take on such an ambitious project, and what kept you engaged with the material over such a long span?

HCA: *King* was an assignment. Fantagraphics publisher Gary Groth approached me very early into our relationship about doing the comic. I was excited to be offered a book, so it was an assignment I was happy to take. The comic was three volumes long. Doing the first volume took a year, and by the end of it I was kinda burned out and seriously starting to lose interest. The second volume was a struggle because I was more engaged with the other projects I had gotten involved in. I don't remember how long it took to do, but it had to have been at least six or seven years. By the time I got to the last volume, things had changed in my personal life, and I found myself reengaged by the work. But it took a radically new approach to producing the material for me to find my groove again. That results in something of a chimera of a book, but at least the thing exists.

JS: Can you tell us a little bit about this "radically new approach"?

HCA: It was on multiple fronts. The most obvious is that I was compelled to switch from black-and-white to color. Going into detail about why would take too long and not be that interesting, but I suddenly saw a way to get excited about producing those images, and that got me started. But it was deeper than that. My life was in turmoil, and the book was a lifeline, which it had never been before. It had been more lightweight up to that point. I started to do new research and learn new details, and my whole philosophy changed on that last chapter. I rewrote the last chapter script and started from scratch. The way I thought about King the man, the way I chose to cover scenes, for lack of a better word. There was a kind of distance to my approach, as though I were examining the events as a clinician would. I'm not really explaining it properly. I was just a different person by that point and was examining the material through a different lens, and I was seeing different things than I had before, and as a result was seeing new ways of presenting the material. If I had to quantify it, it would be, as I said, the use of color, it was using two-page spreads throughout. And I tended to present King at a remove. I'd often find myself putting him deep in the background and focusing on the other characters and their interactions or the landscape itself. I had to keep reminding myself that he was the star and needed a hero shot from time to time. I became less interested in the myth and more interested in the larger story being told, which I guess is the story of a movement, of a society in crisis and revolution, the story of an entire era.

JS: King biographies are nearly a cottage industry, with dozens of full-length books and thousands of academic and popular essays. Did any particular writers or biographies especially shape your vision of MLK?

HCA: Back in 1992, King bios weren't quite the cottage industry they have become. Back then, the pickings were a little slimmer. At the time, I was reading mainly for facts [rather] than for point of view. I didn't discriminate. I read articles, bios, children's books, watched documentaries. I read stuff about King directly, and stuff relating to the times at large. My research material is too long to list here, but a few of the major ones were *Let the Trumpet Sound* by Stephen B. Oates, *And the Walls Came Tumbling Down* by Ralph David Abernathy, and the book and documentary series *Eyes on the Prize*, by Juan Williams. Also, for info about the assassination itself, *Murder in Memphis* by Mark Lane and Dick Gregory, and *Orders to Kill* by William F. Pepper. But I read and watched a ton of stuff. There have been several books that have come out or that I have become aware of in the years since that I would dearly loved to have read during my initial research, like *Bearing the Cross* by David J. Garrow. But these are the realities of dramatizing real-life events.

For the next edition of the book, I'm going to be doing a brand-new story called *Caroline*, which is my deep dive into the assassination itself, something I didn't want to cover in the biography. I'm taking a character I created for *King* and using her to explore the various theories and facts about the assassination, *JFK*-style, and I'm very excited about it. It's going to be a gritty '70s-set paranoid thriller, the kind of stuff I grew up on.

JS: A new edition? That is very exciting! What can you tell us about it?

HCA: Not much other than it containing a new story and featuring a new cover. It will be pretty much the same material from the last edition, though I think I'm going to strip out the behind-the-scenes material. I'm not sure yet. Gary said he thinks it should be a perennial, and I couldn't agree more. Not sure when it'll be hitting the stands just yet, but it's next in the queue.

JS: Given the inky and occasionally erratic style of *King*, your vision of MLK is often obscure, even elusive, and yet personal and intimate. Can you give your readers some insight as to how to read your depiction of this significantly well-known pillar of the civil rights movement?

HCA: Yeah, the book is lacking a certain point of view, and I attribute that to several factors. One, I was young and inexperienced. I knew I wanted to avoid the presentation of King as saint, but beyond that I had no particular mandate. Another factor was that the comic was done over so many years, in so many fits and starts. Something I started pursuing during one phase would be forgotten or have lost its appeal when it came time to gear up for a next round of pages. By then a new inspiration would have taken hold. Ideally, I would have started and finished the book with no breaks between. Instead, since I kept starting and stopping, my interests kept shifting over the years—art styles, narrative techniques, what have you—so now when the work is viewed as a whole, it is difficult to find a central theme or core idea to hang onto. I've often said if I were to do this project again, it would begin with the March on Washington, King's greatest public triumph, and then go on to tell the story of his lowest moments, his time in Chicago. It would be lean and mean and laser focused, not a sprawling, somewhat rudderless epic. But like the old song says, this is what you want, and this is what you get. I can't advise a reader about how to engage with the book or the character of King created for it—that has to come entirely on their own terms.

JS: [By the time this interview is published], it will have been twenty-five years since the initial publication of *King*, volume one, and fifty years since the assassination of its principal subject—Dr. Martin Luther King Jr. Looking back, how has your estimation of your graphic biography changed?

HCA: I've always seen it as a profoundly compromised work, and that hasn't changed. But it took making the mistakes I made for me to develop a better methodology for my future work. That said, the thing has its merits, if only as a primer. If it's done its job, it's prompted at least one person to seek out the facts

———

on their own. Having seen death a lot more intimately since it was first published, I can say I think it succeeds in conveying the melancholy and the horror of the knowledge of impending death and then death's reality.

JS: Compromised? How so?

HCA: Just in the sense that its production was so spread out and so choppy, it resulted in an uneven work. It's compromised, but they were compromises imposed on it by my personal limitations, not by any external forces like publishers or lawyers or the King estate or whatever.

JS: Fans of *King* often marvel at the sheer variety of art styles it takes on, jettisons, recovers, and even forgets. You have mentioned in the past that the comic was something of a playground book for you, and have also listed a wide variety of artists across mediums that have influenced your oeuvre. Looking back, are there any specific artists or pieces that particularly influenced *King* that you would like to mention?

HCA: *King* has fans?! That's news to me. Oh God, too many artists to mention. There were the usuals for me, like Sienkiewicz, Chaykin, Miller. Dave McKean. Oliver's Stone's *JFK* was a massive influence. Scorsese's *Raging Bull* and *Goodfellas*. I'm endlessly fascinated by Bob Peak and Richard Amsel, and looked at their work a lot during the third volume, where I was really just saying, "Fuck it," and doing whatever the hell I wanted to on the page. It's really a long and varied list, but those would be some standouts. I'm a total sponge. I absorb and regurgitate everything appealing my eyes come across. I'm always trying to figure out how to apply lessons from other artists and integrate them into either my general approach or whatever specific thing I'm working on at that moment. And I have no shame or compunction about wearing my influences on my sleeve. I will proudly steal from anyone. As a result, I sometimes wind up going through a million styles in the search for whatever it is that I am natively. Probably none of that made any sense to anyone. There is a danger in going so hog wild with styles; some people will conclude you have nothing to say of your own and dismiss your work, and perhaps they would not be wrong to do so. Others will get burned out by the constant jumping from one mode to another. Others will be thrilled by it. You never know. Even when I dance between styles, I try to keep it to within a certain range, and usually the decision is motivated by an attempt to convey a certain state of mind or, say, to juxtapose frantic movement against stillness and calm. It's usually directed by purpose rather than just doing shit willy-nilly. Though I'm not above that either. Sometimes the decision to try a new technique is motivated simply . . . by boredom. If I have an idea that excites me about how to do a panel that conflicts with the one that came immediately before it, I'll just do it. I really don't care, because ultimately they're just comics and don't have that much true bearing on the real world.

JS: You've mentioned the influence that noncomics art has had on your work many times—books, documentaries, films, etc. From a creator point of view, what does the comics medium offer that some other mediums do not? Conversely, what are some of its limitations?

HCA: Comics offer a lot of freedom to go as grand and as epic or as intimate, even uncomfortably intimate, as you want. Their range is magnificent. For visual storytellers, this is an incredible luxury because you're not limited by budget or time constraints the way you are in film, on TV, or on the stage. On the other hand, comics don't and will never have the kind of overwhelming power that film and TV have. The combination of moving picture, sound, and music is pretty hard to beat. I'm not saying you can't be wowed by a comic book, because I'm here to tell you, you can, but I've never had my nerves frazzled and my senses tickled by a comic book in quite the same way that I've had walking out of your average blockbuster or even a really well-crafted arthouse movie. Another limitation is I don't think comics are the ideal medium to convey dense, complicated information, like if you want to take a deep dive into the minutiae of the Roman Senate or whatever, because the medium tends to be at its best when information can be conveyed in shorthand. But I'm open to being proven wrong on that one.

But comics have intimacy. You can curl up with them in bed. You can do that with your device too, I guess, but it's not quite the same. You can have a personal relationship with the object itself. I have a copy of Chaykin's *Time* that I flipped through a million times when I was younger and still look at a fair bit to this day. A friend gave me a mint-condition copy of it not long ago, and looking at that more pristine version was almost like looking at it for the first time. It had none of the scars, none of the history that my copy had. It wasn't the object I obsessed over when I was sixteen years old. This copy hadn't energized me when I needed inspiration, it hadn't comforted me when a romance ended.

JS: You have stated in previous interviews that you included photographs in *King* to remind readers that these events really happened, that there is a history that exists outside the biography that inspired it in the first place. Yet these images often appear with some level of distortion or overexposure. Can you comment on this element of the biography?

HCA: Simply importing an image as-is is often not enough to convey the kinds of textures and emotions I'm trying evoke or represent. I'm often going for an exaggeration of reality, an amplification of it. Also, using photographs as the starting point for my own imagery transforms it from simply a pic I cut and pasted—literally, back in those days—into a new piece of illustration I've created.

JS: I am fascinated by this notion of using photographs to "exaggerate reality." Can you expand on this for me?

HCA: It's not that I'm interested in using photos to exaggerate reality. It's more that I'm interested in a kind of exaggerated, operatic mode of storytelling, where the people and the events are larger than life. A technique I found to convey this with *King* was to add photos to my toolbox.

JS: You mention in the notes to the *King: Special Edition* that you initially sought a single iconographic image to represent MLK, like *Malcolm*'s silver "X," but failed to find one. What motivated this desire in the first place? Why do you think it was so difficult to develop such an icon?

HCA: Never underestimate the power of a single, simple icon. People die over icons. Icons galvanize people. Icons help to organize people, and the right icon can also generate interest and motivate sales. One of the reasons *Malcolm X* was such a cultural event when it came out was because of the power of that simple silver *X*. I saw that shit on T-shirts and baseball hats for *two years* before that movie came out and for a number of years after it had left the cinema. And it was obvious. Spike Lee, a major hero of mine, was a marketing genius in that era, but a chimp could have seen how cool the letter *X* looks as a graphic element. A few years previous, it had been the *Batman* logo that you couldn't get away from, not that I was trying to—I loved that image. I wanted something like that for *King*, but for the life of me I couldn't come up with anything interesting. Still can't.

JS: Many contemporary readers may not realize this, but your original ending to *King* closes with a scene of racial strife set in the present day. The ending was notably pessimistic, and you have said in previous interviews that you felt it was too negative, that it suggested King's career and sacrifices amounted to little or nothing. In the special edition, you changed the ending to focus more on King's assassination and removed the original ending altogether. In the context of what some may call a new civil rights movement, embodied by Black Lives Matter activism, do you feel any differently about the changes? How might you change the ending if you composed it today?

HCA: I'm still much more comfortable with the revised ending and wouldn't change it again today. It made me feel a little uneasy making those changes. There are certain luminaries in our culture, who shall remain nameless, who have famously tinkered with their own work after the fact—to diminishing returns, in this reporter's opinion—and engaging in similar behavior isn't something I'd recommend, having had the experience. Still, I stand by the decision, even given the world we're living in. It's a scary time. We've made some strides in the years since the original civil rights movement, but all you have to do is look around to see just how gossamer the veneer of equality really is. It's the mentally ill and people of color who get stuffed into prison in such disproportionate numbers. It's the mentally ill and people of color who get routinely murdered by the police. The police were designed to protect the state and to protect the elite, not to protect the masses, but to oppress them—specifically, the poor—so it shouldn't come as any surprise when they are given a license to murder those the state deems undesirable. Then there is a president in the White House who recalls the glory of "the good old days," where you could handle anyone who stepped out of line. I wonder to whom he's referring? Whatever gains were made during the civil rights era are in serious danger of slipping away. But that doesn't change the fact that King and the other fighters in the movement fought and bled and died and gained ground with their blood, and that original ending, as much as I believe in what it was saying, just shit all over that, in my opinion.

JS: You have worked as a solo artist and as a collaborator. What are the pluses and minuses of each?

HCA: Collaboration is something that I've always been interested in and have rarely gotten to participate in. Well, that's not totally true. I've done it many times as an illustrator—that's all about working with writers—and I've illustrated hundreds of articles and essays. As a comic book artist, I've also worked with quite a few writers, and while it's not my ideal way to work, it can be satisfying in its own way, being the interpreter of someone else's vision. As a writer, I've

—

always wanted to write for an artist, and I've always been interested in seeing the results of writing with a partner. With the former, I've only had the opportunity once, with Wilfred Santiago. With the latter, I've never had the opportunity, and I'm frankly not even sure it would work, because I'm not sure how good I'd be at giving in if I didn't like my collaborator's ideas. But I'm still really hoping to do it one day. I'm hoping with a project I have coming up that I can make both of those goals a reality. When I read the work of some of the great writer-artist teams like Claremont and Byrne, or Rizzo and Azzarello, or Gibbons and Moore (the Lennon and McCartney of comics), I would love to know the rush of producing work of a high caliber that could only come from the marriage of two minds. On the other hand, it's fun creating your own world and playing in it entirely by your own rules. In the movies, I've always been most attracted to writer-directors, and in comics I've always been most attracted to writer-artists. My biggest heroes were all writer-artists—Miller, Chaykin, Los Bros Hernandez, etc.—and ultimately that's always where my heart is going to be. But as I said, one of my biggest dreams is to be the writer on an ongoing series in collaboration with an artist, so there's no one good way to create a great comic.

JS: In what ways did your experiences on working on *King* inform the other works in your oeuvre that tackle issues of race, such as *Black Dogs* or *Wise Son*?

HCA: To be honest, those books made me not want to be so overt in my discussion of race. That was the tenor of the times, I was young and angry, and there were things I wanted to express. But that can quickly become a box, and a very narrow one. To this day, pretty much the only time I'm approached to do work is on race-based material. I would never be considered to do a "Spider-Man battles Doc Oc" arc, for example, which I would dearly love to do. Racial issues are important and need to be discussed, because race is a deeply toxic quantity in our society, and it's something we're loathe to have frank discussions on. But that's not all there is to my creative life. That said, in the wake of Donald Trump and the endless, endless police shootings, and the racism of the internet, sometimes casual, sometimes virulent, I'm feeling a need to tackle race head-on again, probably in a story involving the police. Not sure what form that will ultimately take, but it's in me at the moment. It would be interesting to return to that terrain with slightly more mature, more experienced eyes, because I was so young and naive when I was tackling those issues initially, more filled with fire than facts. Race still factors into my current stuff, but I like to think it's buried in the subtext rather than right there on the surface.

JS: Have you ever thought about returning to the biography business? Malcolm X perhaps, or some other titanic figure?

HCA: Not really. I mean, I have thought about it, but I haven't been so compelled by any one person that I'd want to undertake their biography. It's a lot of work, and you really have to be passionate about the subject you're portraying. My attraction to historical subject matter comes as a result of a love of world building, so I'd be more interested in tackling a specific period in history or a significant historical event than any particular individual. I wanted to do an adaptation of Bobby Seale's book *Seize the Time* for a while, but then a Panthers biopic came out in the '90s and I lost interest in the idea. I'm really more interested in selling out and doing more mainstream material. I like crime and science fiction and thrillers. I'm about to start pitching a superhero book called *Sol*. I want to go in the opposite direction of serious biography for a while.

You know . . . I just said all that, but one just popped into my head who would be cool: Hannibal. An action-based bio about Hannibal and Carthage against Rome could be badass. Like *300* or something, which I love. And I just remembered about ten years ago I was considering doing a story about Elvis. Not a major book, like, maybe a forty-to-fifty-page story. They did a radio documentary about the impact Elvis had when he first appeared, and the way people who were there described it got me thinking of doing something that examined the birth of pop culture and the effect it can have on both individuals and society at large. I planned to make it funny and do it in bright candy colors—I'm actually getting into the idea as I'm describing it. Not sure why that one fell away. One of a million ideas most artists get that they'll get around to "one day," I suppose. And maybe one day I'll actually do it.

Damn it, that question's got me thinking. Another interesting figure might be Tesla. That guy was fascinating. I've always wanted to tell a story about an engineer or an architect or an industrial designer, someone like that. Tesla or Frank Lloyd Wright or Vertner Woodson Tandy or Le Corbusier, even though I think his architecture was sort of ugly. A story about Tesla versus Thomas Edison might be really interesting. The thing is, biographies themselves are a little boring to me right now, but taking a historical figure and telling a story about them, either dramatizing a moment in their lives or putting a real figure in a fictionalized setting, that interests me. I have a story I very much want to publish called *The Renaissance* that is a mystery about a child searching for a painting in 1920s Harlem that takes many historical figures and inserts them into this kid's adventure. That kind of thing would be wicked fun.

—

JS: So we'll be expecting those soon?

HCA: From your mouth to God's ear, my friend. Isn't that what the kids say these days? If someone wants to publish a kick-ass Hannibal or Elvis story, I'm available.

JS: What can you tell us about your upcoming project, *Godhead*, for Fantagraphics?

HCA: *Godhead*! I am very excited about my new comic book. *Godhead* is a science-fiction action adventure about a corporation that invents a machine that allows the user to talk to God. When the Vatican find out about the machine, they are immediately threatened by it and send in a group of commandos to destroy it. My story follows the CEO of the corporation that creates the god machine and one of the commandos. It's a simple tale told in a complex way. It's about science versus religion. It's a commentary on class, as it juxtaposes the struggles of a plutocrat against the struggles of a former soldier, a grunt, part of the system designed to protect the plutocrats, and puts them in opposition to one another. It's part relationship melodrama, architecture porn, blaxploitation thriller, sci-fi adventure, robot cautionary tale, undersea adventure, and men-on-a-mission story. I first came up with the pitch in 2002 and tried to sell it in 2003. No takers. Got close several times, but couldn't quite get the trigger pulled—that DC rejection still hurts to this day. I finished a script and some artwork in 2005 and pitched it again in 2006. Still no takers. I shelved it and got into the movie business. But I couldn't get the thing out of my head. It was taking up too much valuable mental real estate, so I thought, I need to just do it and exorcise it from my soul. Fortunately, Fantagraphics rode to my rescue, and here we are. Part of me wishes it could have been published when it was originally conceived, because it is definitely based on 9/11 paranoia to a large extent. But for whatever reason, that wasn't its time, now is, and I couldn't be happier. Hopefully, it'll sell well enough to justify another story, because I have many adventures I'd like to tell in this world. We'd be going to Mars on the next one, then out into interstellar space. But we'll see.

JS: For a man who wants to talk about social issues less overtly, a space opera that draws from blaxploitation and class struggles seems delightfully counterintuitive!

HCA: Let's hope the buying public feels the same way.

JS: You mentioned your rejection from DC. Do you feel smaller and independent presses offer more avenues for publication today than they did in the past? What is your view of the publishing field from your vantage point?

HCA: There are two lists that get passed around to the editors at all the comic book companies. On the first list are the names of the people you give publishing deals to no matter what. Guys like Frank Miller, Jeff Lemire—they're on that list. Mike Deodato wants to do *Fecal Matter: The Musical*? Done! That's the list you want to be on. I'm not on that list. I'm on the *other* list. I knew for sure I was on that other list when DC turned me down, because I thought I had a solid pitch, I had an editor advocating for me, and I was coming off of *King*, which was getting a lot of attention at that moment. I wasn't asking for big money, and I wanted to be a team player. And they'd published a lot of comics a lot shittier than anything I was offering them. It didn't seem like they'd have much to lose by taking a chance on me. But they passed, and passed with extreme prejudice. I had pissed off another DC editor about seven years previous, so maybe that was keeping my name on the other list. I don't know. So I guess I'm an indie press guy, with aspirations to the big time. Smaller presses have always offered more avenues for publication in the sense of their willingness to tackle a more diversified subject matter than the larger houses—that was true when I was starting out, and I suspect it remains true today. Something to consider is that they need us as much as we need them. The perception is that the power is all skewed toward the publisher, and in some ways that's true, at least at the beginning of your career. But we always have the right to take our work elsewhere if we don't like the offer on the table or the treatment we're being given. And without work to publish, the people in those offices are just wannabes with a dream, same as the cartoonist. But if we're talking about backing your work and getting it out to as wide a range of people as possible, the smaller presses don't always have the resources and the branding power to make that happen. It's funny, though, when you consider the rise of a company like Image, when you consider the kind of branding muscle they possess and the wide range of material they publish. I can't imagine a publisher of their scale publishing and thriving off the kind of material they're putting out now back twenty, thirty years ago. The equivalent back then were publishers like Pacific or First or Comico, and I don't think any of them ever achieved what Image has. The rise of Image is going to make an incredible book one day, if one doesn't already exist. Anyway, I'm rambling. I'm not sure how to answer your question about the state of the publishing industry from my vantage point because I'm deep in it, yet sort of outside it at the same time. I just do my work. I'm not as plugged into the politics and the players in the industry as a whole as I should be. It feels like getting actually *published*, a printed book that winds up on a shelf, seems to be somewhat in peril due to the encroachment of the digital age. Maybe that's just old-man talk, but it seems like the preeminent avenue for young cartoonists is the cyber realm, with less emphasis on the printed book. Like if you get a book published, it's like putting something out on vinyl or something, or shooting a film on actual film, if you'll allow me to jumble my metaphors a bit. For me, the old ways are still the best, where getting a book published is the goal. I still think that that's an achievement, and the thought of physical publishing going away is something that scares me. I may be stuck on the other list, but I'm grateful I'm still in a position that I can make a living off my work and get a physical book onto a shelf, that I don't have to rely on posting my work to get it out there. And I say that with no disrespect to cartoonists who publish online. Just finishing a comic and getting it out into the world is a great and noble thing. But what can I say—I'm from the old school.

Notes

INTRODUCTION

1. For the books in the series, see Jeffery and Li, *The Little Rock Nine*; Jeffery and Boccanfuso, *Malcolm X*; Jeffery and Spender, *Martin Luther King Jr.*; Jeffery and Spender, *Medgar Evers*; Jeffery and Spender, *Rosa Parks*; and Jeffery and Aggs, *Thurgood Marshall*.

CHAPTER 1

1. References in this chapter are to the collected special edition released by Fantagraphics in 2010.

2. Bruyneel's excellent article traces the development of the MLK Memorial on the National Mall in Washington DC and how it functions as an iteration of the iconic MLK narrative; see Bruyneel, "King's Body."

3. For more, see the epilogue.

4. My application of iconicity here is potentially complicated by the implicit racial logics of identification. Race is often synonymous with specificity, while sites of projection are marked as universal, which, under the current racial aesthetic regime, means white.

5. For more on the relationship between graphic narrative, civil rights memory, and the contemporary logics of postracialism, see chapter 2.

6. For more on appropriations of civil rights history in the name of contemporary politics, see chapter 5.

7. For an in-depth analysis of the *Martin Luther King and the Montgomery Story* comic, see chapter 2.

8. Carson's overview of Martin Luther King–related scholarship breaks down the historical and thematic trends of the field in an extremely useful manner that I will not attempt to replicate here; see Carson, "Paradoxes of King Historiography."

9. For more on the role of symbolic witnessing in civil rights graphic novels, see chapter 3.

10. In his interview with Dale Jacobs, Anderson names over fifty comic artists, painters, filmmakers, and writers. He concludes by saying, "This is just a scratching of the surface; there are so many other artists and writers and musicians and filmmakers whose work has helped shape what I do." After making this comment, he named three more influences (Anderson, interview, 364).

11. Additionally, Douglas's cutout style incorporates Egyptian influences and designs, which "followed the most basic rule of stylizing the body by painting the figure as if it were being observed from several different viewpoints" (Kirschke, *Aaron Douglas*, 77). For Anderson, this sensibility manifests both orally and visually in "The Witnesses," since the simultaneity made possible by graphic narrative means that we encounter the multiplicity of perspectives offered by the witnesses both in sequence and (perhaps paradoxically) simultaneously.

12. For more on symbolic use of "bleeds," see chapter 2.

13. For more on the relationship between photographs and civil rights graphic memories, see chapter 3.

14. For more commentary on the claim of a postracial US society made by civil rights graphic novels, see chapter 2.

CHAPTER 2

1. The notion that the story must be "told" also hints at the manner in which oral culture has shaped African American history, art, and literature. A project that focuses on how graphic narrative can enact or represent the orality of African American intellectual culture (particularly in regard to its relationship to cultural memory) is long overdue.

2. For an excellent overview of the debate about graphic novels versus comic books, see the introduction to Hatfield, *Alternative Comics*.

3. Placing this concern at the end of the novel is odd, since, presumably, at this point a reader would have realized that *March* is anything but kid's stuff.

4. The boys, interestingly enough, are named Jacob and Esau, a nod to the heavy biblical influences that permeate the memoir. The names also gesture to ideas of inheritance and birthrights, since Jacob and Esau were the grandchildren of

Abraham via Issac. While I do not explore the religious elements of *March*, further study into this element of the text is warranted.

5. The Fellowship of Reconciliation is an international nonviolent group formed in the United States in opposition to World War I. In the late 1940s, FOR, alongside the Congress of Racial Equality (founded by the former FOR staffers James Orange and George Houser, with Bernice Fisher) sponsored the first Freedom Rides.

6. The Montgomery bus boycotts were landmark events in civil rights history. The campaign protested the racial segregation of the public transit system of Montgomery, Alabama, in response to the now-infamous arrest of Rosa Parks on 5 December 1955. The protest lasted over a year. The US Supreme Court declared such segregation laws unconstitutional on December 20, 1956.

7. For more on MLK's iconicity, see chapter 1.

8. For more on the minimization of Bayard Rustin's influence on civil rights memory, see D'Emilio, *Lost Prophet*.

9. The Teacher's March occurred on 22 January 1965 in Dallas, Texas, in response to voter registration suppression in the county. Over one hundred teachers marched two by two to the Dallas County Courthouse to demand voter registration for themselves and their 7,000 students, knowing full well the violent response they would receive from Sherriff Jim Clark. It has been referred to as the "forgotten march," overshadowed by the Selma marches of later that year. For more, see Fitts, *Selma*, chapter 8.

10. Interestingly, 52 percent is nearly identical to Obama's popular vote percentage of 52.9 percent, as tallied by the Federal Election Commission report on the election results (certified on 8 January 2009), suggesting that the postracial positivity expressed in the wake of his election fell along partisan lines.

11. Any cartoons referred to but not duplicated in *Graphic Memories* can be found in the extensive database maintained by PoliticalCartoons.com, by searching for the artist's name and a subject keyword. I used the word "Obama" and searched for cartoons published the day after the election (5 November 2008) and the morning of his inauguration (20 January 2009).

12. For more on satirical political cartoons featuring Barack Obama, see Conners, "Barack versus Hillary," and Selzer, "Barack Obama."

13. McCloud's assertion that single-panel cartoons should not be considered forms of sequential art in graphic narrative because they lack juxtaposition (and therefore closure) has been met with contestation (as has much of *Understanding Comics*). The best example perhaps is McCloud's interview with R. C. Harvey, who counters that the presence of speech balloons implies time across space, which in turn implies juxtaposition and closure (McCloud, interview). Additionally, a great deal of scholarship analyzes caricature, satire, and metaphor in political cartoons, including single-panel examples. For an exhaustive collection of related articles, see the Bonn Online Bibliography of Comics Research, www.comicforschung.uni-bonn.de.

14. The international cartoons in particular merit further investigation, particularly in regard to how American civil rights history is remembered abroad as an international version of consensus memory.

15. In *Morgan v. Virginia*, the Court ruled that Virginia's laws requiring segregation on interstate buses were unconstitutional. *Boynton v. Virginia* overturned a lower court's trespassing conviction of an African American law student for entering a "whites only" restaurant in a Virginia bus terminal. As a result of the decision, the Supreme Court held that racial segregation in public transportation facilities violated the Interstate Commerce Act, effectively allowing the federal government to regulate racial discrimination in the busing industry.

16. For more on the relationship between civil rights photography and graphic narrative, see chapter 3.

17. On 15 September 1963, four white-supremacist terrorists aligned with the Ku Klux Klan planted fifteen sticks of dynamite attached to a timing device beneath the steps of the 16th Street Baptist Church in Birmingham. The explosion injured twenty-two parishioners and killed four young girls of the church's choir: Addie Mae Collins, Cynthia Wesley, Carole Robertson, and Carol Denise McNair. No prosecutions occurred until fourteen years later, when one of the terrorists was convicted of first-degree murder. In 2001 and 2002, two additional terrorists were sentenced to life imprisonment. One of the bombers, who died in 1994, was never convicted of a crime.

18. At the 1964 Democratic National Convention, the Mississippi Freedom Democratic Party (MFDP) claimed the seats for the Mississippi delegates, on the ground that the official delegation had excluded African Americans. Presidential nominee Lyndon B. Johnson, who worried that seating them as the delegation would cost him the southern vote, resisted the MFDP's claims. Eventually, a compromise was reached in which the MFDP was given two of the sixty-eight seats—a clear dismissal of the African American vote and a slap in the face. In *March: Book Three*, Lewis says of the compromise, "We played by the rules. We did everything that was necessary—but when we arrived at the doorstep, we found the door slammed in our face. What's so tragic is that Johnson didn't have to do what he did. He still won re-election in a landslide, and he still lost the south" (125).

CHAPTER 3

1. In regard to the terminology used throughout this chapter, I use the inclusive term "Latinx" when referring to the community as a whole, but still employ the terms "Latino" and "Latina" as appropriate for individuals discussed in this chapter.

2. I do not mean to suggest that Latinx communities were generally inactive during this period. The Mexican American population in particular was quite active in the labor movement and the land grant movement, Cesar Chavez and Reies

López Tijerina most famous among them. Both the Chicano arts movement and Nuyorican writers produced novels, poetry, and art that explored what it meant to be Latino in a shifting US racial landscape. Yet for the isolated Quintero family living in Marion, Alabama, without a strong Latinx presence, allegiance with African Americans was presented as the only available avenue for activism. For more on Latino/a activity in this period, see Sánchez González, *Boricua Literature*; Caminero-Santangelo, *On Latinidad*; Vargas, *Crucible of Struggle*; Behnken, *Fighting Their Own Battles*.

3. As Clara E. Rodriguez writes in her contribution to *Hispanic New York*, Latinx communities and individuals in the United States were often forced to negotiate a "U.S. racial structure that assumed a white-notwhite division of the world" and were forced into an ambiguous "gray position" within this structure ("Puerto Ricans and Other Latinos," 184). Rodriguez is referring specifically to the experiences of Puerto Rican migrants moving to the mainland United States. But difficulties in articulating Latinx social identity in the post–World War II United States, particularly in relation to the individual's proximity to whiteness, permeates both Latinx ethnic memoirs and fiction. For example, the Nuyorican authors Piri Thomas and Edward Rivera attempt to articulate their identities on a black-white spectrum. Chicano authors such as Rudolfo Anaya and Nash Candelaria negotiate their potential whiteness against indigenous or Native American identity. Locating oneself on a spectrum with (unattainable) racial and cultural whiteness at the top of a racial hierarchy is a consistent theme throughout this body of literature.

4. The way that graphic narrative blends word and image makes it an ideal medium in which to write histories from otherwise omitted perspectives. From early work such as Jack Jackson's *Comanche Moon* trilogy (1977–1978) to more contemporary works such as Marjane Satrapi's *Persepolis* (2000), graphic novels offer an alternative literature and an intellectual space for the historically marginalized to write their own histories. In this sense, graphic narratives offer a space where the slivers (as Weaver puts it) of forgotten histories can be written into the larger collective narrative. In *The Writing of History*, Michel de Certeau claims that these slivers, elements of the past sacrificed by dominant narratives in order to maintain their own intelligibility in the present, always "come back, despite everything, in the edges of discourse or in its rifts and crannies: 'resistances,' 'survivals' or delays discreetly perturb the pretty order of a line of 'progress' or system, of interpretation" (4). Weaver addresses these "rifts and crannies" (or gutters?) in the dominant cultural narrative of the US civil rights movement as a black-white struggle by rendering her family's personal and political histories as inextricably linked with this moment in US history.

5. This sequence can be read as a subtle acknowledgment of the graphic narrative form's indebtedness to and mutually influencing relationship with film and photography; see Gardner, *Projections*.

6. This might also explain why the memoir is relatively silent on the subject of Juan Domingo Perón's brutal regime in Argentina in the 1960s—it receives only a single page of attention (Weaver, *Darkroom*, 113). Since Weaver's memoir serves as a form of documentation, even if imagined, of events the family was present for, there would be little to help them to account for this simultaneous dark time in Argentina's history. What little there is to know comes from correspondence from her grandparents, which includes their photographs.

7. The fact that Lila is specifically a *child* witness shapes the memoir as well, an element I do not cover here. For more on Lila as a child witness, see Breckenridge and Peterson, "Lila Quintero Weaver's *Darkroom*."

CHAPTER 4

1. For more on trauma theory and graphic narrative, see chapter 5.

2. According to the appendix, the names of many key characters, the Thompson family in particular, "have been changed for storytelling purposes" (Long et al., *Silence of Our Friends*, 198). Long is deliberately vague about the reasons for the changes, saying only that the book required a "balance between factual accuracy and emotional authenticity" (199). Long's blurring of the line between fact and fiction echoes a similar logic used in Weaver's *Darkroom*, in that it wants to blend personal histories and perspectives with official histories to create a more "authentic" vision of the civil rights past.

3. To what extent the political silences that the memoir addresses can be attributed to a Cold War culture that encouraged silent conformity in the name of capitalistic nationalism and discouraged all forms of political dissent is unclear (since the novel does not comment on it directly).

4. Alternatively, we might read the rocket not as representing optimism or futurity, but escape, since the United States symbolically runs from the problems of race rather than addressing them. In depicting Americans traveling to space and investing their efforts in that instead of learning to live in harmony where they are, *The Silence of Our Friends* could be read as accusing Americans of trying a high-tech method of running away from their problems, trying to leave them behind on Earth rather than to confront them directly.

5. Bakhtin's argument concerns the history of genres and the ways in which they are marked by genre-specific conventions of time. His essential argument covers how novelistic formulas enable us to situate works in their cultural milieus. It would typically be applied to a comparative reading of many works in order to pinpoint broad tendencies that could be used to identify a cultural process at work in the literature of a given tradition or movement. I invoke it here to connect graphic novels with such broad conventions, even if I do not explore it fully.

6. For more on John Lewis's civil rights graphic memoir, see chapter 2.

—

7. For more on public spaces as contested sites of consensus memory, see Alderman, "Street Names as Memorial Arenas," and Bruyneel, "The King's Body."

8. For more on symbolic uses of panel bleeds, see chapter 2.

9. The memoir's use of images of children as a vehicle for social change is one of the many strategies employed by *The Silence of Our Friends* to establish its civil rights narrative bona fides. As Katharine Capshaw puts it: "Picturing childhood became a powerful instrument of civil rights activism, because children carry an important aura of human value and potential, and threats to the young made the stakes of the movement palpable to individuals and to the nation. Undoubtedly, images of children under siege had generative effects for the civil rights campaign" (*Civil Rights Childhood*, xi). To Capshaw's point about "images of children under siege," the first thing Julie notices when touching CC's face is the bandage on her forehead, a visual reminder of a previous scene in which a local racist ran CC down with his car as she was riding her bike down Wheeler Avenue (Long et al., *The Silence of Our Friends*, 88). Going further, we might also read these scenes as evincing the sort of psychological freedom that Capshaw highlights; the photobooks she examines construct "a freedom of spirit," a generative tone that "articulates a new way of seeing themselves" (*Civil Rights Childhood*, 122).

10. The focus on Long's need for political redemption places *The Silence of Our Friends* squarely in the genre of the "southern conversion narrative," another aspect of the memoir that makes it legible as civil rights history. Fred Hobson traces the genre's roots to New England religious conversion narratives. The southern narratives, Hobson claims, are built around a rejection of the South's racial history and an embrace of the progressive racial politics that came out of the South in the mid-twentieth century. Hobson defines the genre according to its practitioners' motivation: "What these southern 'conversion narratives' have in common with the Puritan narratives, however, is a recognition and confession of the writer's own sins and the announced need for redemption, as well as a description of the writer's radical transformation—a sort of secular salvation. But the guilt that motivates the confession—the conviction of sin, as the Puritans termed it—is no less real, nor is the deep need to tell one's story, nor the changed lives that these narratives relate. The impulse is the same—to witness, to testify. Indeed, the writing of a conversion narrative is, to a great extent, the final proof of that conversion, the equivalent of testifying" (*But Now I See*, 4). In *The Silence of Our Friends*, the "impulse" to witness and testify is literal, since the courtroom drama in which the narrative climaxes leads directly to Long's redemption. It is only by breaking his silence through the act of testimony that Long achieves the "freedom from racial guilt" that Hobson claims motivates such narratives (*But Now I See*, 5). Hobson points out that the advent of the civil rights movement crystallized the genre of the southern conversion narrative, turning the genre into "a flourishing southern industry" (83). As a result, Hobson continues, southern conversion narratives of the 1960s and 1970s treated the civil rights movement as being about, in addition to race, "personal and cultural salvation in a broader sense," a problematic perspective that certainly informs *The Silence of Our Friends*. Although published a full generation after the texts Hobson highlights, Long's memoir can be grouped with other contemporary works such as Howard Cruse's *Stuck Rubber Baby* (1995) and Kathryn Stockett's *The Help* (2009), in that it is less invested in telling African Americans' history than in redeeming the white societies responsible for their marginalization. What sets *The Silence of Our Friends* apart from the literary tradition Hobson defines is that the epiphanic moment of conversion one might expect from such a narrative is largely absent, since the Long family is not encumbered by the racist attitudes exhibited by their neighbors. Rather than proclaiming a reformation of the spirit, *The Silence of Our Friends* seeks a public venue for Long's impulse "to witness, to testify."

CHAPTER 5

1. For more on chronotopes, see chapter 4.

2. For an excellent overview of controversies surrounding the placement of Martin Luther King memorials, see Bruyneel, "The King's Body."

3. After nearly two decades of controversy, the Supreme Court overturned the Defense of Marriage Act in a pair of rulings. *United States v. Windsor* (2013), ruled section 3 of DOMA unconstitutional under the Due Process Clause of the Fifth Amendment. *Obergefell v. Hodges* (2015) struck down provisions that disallowed same-sex marriages under federal jurisdictions. Combined, these rulings effectively legalized same-sex marriage in the United States.

4. Unsurprisingly, other groups, which ran the gamut from left to right, laid claim to the civil rights tradition. These groups included disability advocates, women's rights advocates, Second Amendment groups, the Christian Right, and many others—claims annually reiterated on Martin Luther King Jr. Day, down to the present. Many of these claims began in the 1980s with the Reagan administration's appropriation of MLK's rhetoric for its own ends. For some key examples, see Bostdorff and Goldzwig, "History, Collective Memory, and Appropriation"; Edwards, "Deaf Rights, Civil Rights"; Marley, "Riding in the Back"; Morgan, *What Really Happened to the 1960s*, chap. 9.

5. For more on the congressional dimensions of the DOMA debate, see Bull and Gallagher, *Perfect Enemies*; Eskridge, *Case for Same-Sex Marriage*; Smith and Windes, *Progay/Antigay*.

6. For more, see Dickel, "'Can't Leave Me Behind,'" and Bordelon, "Picturing Books."

7. On 28 June 1969, members of the Greenwich Village LGBTQ community responded violently to a police raid in the early morning hours at the Stonewall Inn in Manhattan, a club popular with the gay and transgender communities. The event is often cited as the birth of the modern gay liberation movement. I have often wondered why Cruse didn't have Sammy Noone die at the hands of a police raid in

order to establish a parallel between the African American civil rights movement and the LGBTQ movement, especially since confrontations with police permeate the novel. Such an ending would have been more logical narratively and would have avoided many of the pitfalls of historical appropriation that plague the novel, particularly at its climax.

8. Les's indictment of the black church of Clayfield proves largely unfounded, since the church is depicted as a largely tolerant, even if silent, space for the town's LGBTQ parishioners—almost naively so, since the black church has historically had an ambivalent, and often oppositional, relationship to LGBTQ communities. This antagonism has become something of a cliché and potentially overblown; works such as E. Patrick Johnson's *Sweet Tea* undermine the notion that gay black men in the South lived exclusively in fear. In some ways, we might think of *Stuck Rubber Baby* as attempting to revise this view of history. We can also read it in the context of rising black conservative politics in the 1990s, which in some instances made for strange political bedfellows, as when the Reverend James Sykes of the St. James AME Church in Largo, Florida joined a Ku Klux Klan antigay rally in 1996, claiming that "for all the bad the Klan does, they are right about gays" (quoted in Bull and Gallagher, *Perfect Enemies*, 171). Still, these impulses largely take a back seat to the novel's larger concerns. Further, one can't help but wonder what James Baldwin might have thought of the reductive, even utopian, relationship between Harland and his son and how it frames the black church's stance on LGBTQ issues.

9. For more on the different ending to *King*, see chapter 1 and the appendix.

10. For more on civil-rights-inspired superheroes, see the epilogue.

11. See Estes, "*Stuck Rubber Baby*"; Warmoth, "Comics We Love."

12. Burgas, "A Review a Day"; McBride, "Review: *Stuck Rubber Baby*."

13. For more on postracialism and consensus memory, see chapter 2.

14. For more, see Hartman, *Scenes of Subjection*; C. Jackson, *Violence, Visual Culture*; Simien, *Gender and Lynching*; Young, *Embodying Black Experience*.

15. There is a growing body of scholarship on trauma as treated in graphic narrative. Hillary Chute's work in *Graphic Women* is exemplary, particularly chapter 3. For a variety of approaches, see Jacobs and Dolmage, "Difficult Articulations"; Nabizadeh, "The After-Life of Images"; Køhlert, "Working It Through."

16. For more, see Chaney, *Reading Lessons*, chap. 5.

17. E. Patrick Johnson has done extensive work on the intersections and disconnections between race and gender in the queer community; see his "SNAP! Culture" and "'Quare' Studies."

EPILOGUE

1. Even today, my love for the X-Men is matched only by my deep affection for the Ninja Turtles. I attribute my deep connection to the lean, green machine to the turtles having no inherent racial identity—anyone can be a Ninja Turtle! That, and ninjas are cool.

2. Stan Lee recently revealed that the original name of the comic was "The Mutants," but his editor made him change it: "'Oh, I've got to tell you about my boss,' Lee said. 'My publisher said, when I brought him the idea, he said "yeah I like the idea but you can't call them the X-Men" and I said, "why not?" He said . . . no, I'm sorry, hold it. I wanted originally to call them The Mutants and he said, "you can't call them The Mutants" and I said, "why not?" He said, "our readers, they aren't that smart." He had no respect for comic book readers. He said, "they won't know what a mutant is." Well, I disagreed with him, but he was the boss so I had to think of another name. So, I went home and I thought and thought and I came up with the X-Men and I mentioned it to him the next day and he said, "that's okay" and as I walked out of his office I thought, that was very peculiar. If nobody would know what a mutant is how will anybody know what an X-Man is? But he had okayed the name and I used it'" (Drum, "Stan Lee Reveals Original Name for X-Men").

3. Jamie Madrox, aka the "Multiple Man," can create an unlimited number of clones of himself, each representing a particular personality trait associated with the original.

4. For more on the "uneven execution" of making Marvel's merry mutants parallel to their civil rights counterparts, see Darowski, *X-Men and the Mutant Metaphor*, chap. 2.

5. Even this is a bit of revisionist history—while growing up, everyone knew that Cyclops was an insufferable Boy Scout nerd. Like every other kid of the 1980s and 1990s, I found myself drawn to that former assassin and mutant James Dean—Wolverine!

6. For more, see Bendis, *House of M*.

7. For more, see Kyle and Yost, *New X-Men: Childhood's End*.

8. For more, see Fraction, *Utopia: Avengers—X-Men*.

9. For more, see Carey et al., *X-Men: Second Coming*.

10. For more, see Aaron, *X-Men: Schism*.

11. These are just a small sampling—something of a snapshot—of the reactions to Cyclops, most of them from blogs. To get a larger sense of the "Cyclops Was Right" trend, one would have to read tweets, forum posts, and fan letters.

12. For more, see Chan, "Why Cyclops Was Right"; O'Neil, "Blogathon 27."

13. For more, see Hunsaker, "AvX Consequences #2"; Truitt, "Hero or Villain."

14. It should be noted that there was some looting and violence, but such actions were committed by a small minority of the protesters at Ferguson and did not characterize most of them, despite the reports on Fox News.

15. Instead of bringing the past forward to address the shortcomings of the present, the stories disperse the characters into other comics.

Works Cited

Aaron, Jason. *X-Men: Schism*. New York: Marvel, 2012.

Aaron, Jason, Brian Michael Bendis, Ed Brubaker, Matt Fraction, and Jonathan Hickman. *Avengers vs. X-Men*. New York: Marvel, 2013.

Alderman, Derek H. "Street Names as Memorial Arenas: The Reputational Politics of Commemorating Martin Luther King Jr. in a Georgia County." In *The Civil Rights Movement in American Memory*, edited by Renee C. Romano and Leigh Raiford, 67–95. Athens: University of Georgia Press, 2006.

Anderson, Ho Che. Interview by Dale Jacobs. *International Journal of Comic Art*, Fall 2006: 363–386.

———. *King: A Comics Biography*. Special ed. Seattle: Fantagraphics, 2010.

———. *King*. Vol. 3. Seattle: Fantagraphics, 2003.

Apel, Dora, and Shawn Michelle Smith. *Lynching Photographs*. Chapel Hill: University of North Carolina Press, 2008.

Ater, Renée. "Creating a 'Usable Past' and a 'Future Perfect Society': Aaron Douglas's Murals for the 1936 Texas Centennial Exposition." In *Aaron Douglas: African American Modernist*, edited by Susan Earle, 95–114. New Haven, CT: Yale University Press, 2007.

Bai, Matt. "Is Obama the End of Black Politics?" *New York Times Magazine*, 10 August 2008. www.nytimes.com/2008/08/10/magazine/10politics-t.html.

Bakhtin, M. M. *The Dialogic Imagination: Four Essays*. Edited by Michael Holquist. Translated by Caryl Emerson and Michael Holquist. Austin: University of Texas Press, 1982.

Bechdel, Alison. *Fun Home: A Family Tragicomic*. Boston: Houghton Mifflin, 2006.

———. Introduction to *Stuck Rubber Baby*, by Howard Cruse. New ed. New York: Vertigo, 2010.

Behnken, Brian D. *Fighting Their Own Battles: Mexican Americans, African Americans, and the Struggle for Civil Rights in Texas*. Chapel Hill: University of North Carolina Press, 2014.

Bell, Derrick. "Who's Afraid of Critical Race Theory?" In *The Derrick Bell Reader*, edited by Richard Delgado and Jean Stefancic, 78–84. New York: NYU Press, 2005. Available at www.jstor.org/stable/j.ctt9qg47z.12.

Bello, Grace. "A Comic Book for Social Justice: John Lewis." PublishersWeekly.com, 19 July 2012. Accessed 6 September 2017. https://www.publishersweekly.com/pw/by-topic/authors/profiles/article/58354-a-comic-book-for-social-justice-john-lewis.html.

Bendis, Brian Michael. *Avengers vs. X-Men*. New York: Marvel, 2016.

———. *House of M*. New York: Marvel, 2006.

———. *Uncanny X-Men*. Vol. 1. New York: Marvel, 2016.

———. *Uncanny X-Men*. Vol. 2. New York: Marvel, 2016.

Berger, John. *Ways of Seeing*. London: Penguin, 1972.

Berlatsky, Noah. "RE: Cyclops Was Right." Comic-Scholars Discussion List, 19 September 2017. Accessed 21 September 2017. www.english.ufl.edu/comics/scholars.

Bordelon, David. "Picturing Books: Southern Print Culture in Howard Cruse's *Stuck Rubber Baby*." In *Crossing Boundaries in Graphic Narrative: Essays on Forms, Series and Genres*, edited by Jake Jakaitis and James F. Wurtz, 107–122. Jefferson, NC: McFarland, 2012.

Bostdorff, Dennis M., and Steven R. Goldzwig. "History, Collective Memory, and the Appropriation of Martin Luther King, Jr.: Reagan's Rhetorical Legacy." *Presidential Studies Quarterly* 35, no. 4 (December 2005): 661–690.

Boyd, Bentley. *The Civil Rights Freedom Train*. Williamsburg, VA: Chester Comix, 2005.

Branch, Taylor. *At Canaan's Edge: America in the King Years, 1965–68*. New York: Simon and Schuster, 1989.

———. *Parting the Waters: America in the King Years, 1954–63*. New York: Simon and Schuster, 1989.

———. *Pillar of Fire: America in the King Years, 1963–65*. New York: Simon and Schuster, 1989.

Breckenridge, Janis, and Madelyn Peterson. "Lila Quintero Weaver's *Darkroom: A Memoir in Black And White*: Envisioning Equality." *Confluencia: Revista Hispánica de Cultura y Literatura* 29, no. 1 (2013): 109–125.

Brown, Tina. "9/11 in Reverse." *Daily Beast*, 20 January 2009. www.thedailybeast
.com/911-in-reverse.

Bruyneel, Kevin. "The King's Body: The Martin Luther King Jr. Memorial and the
Politics of Collective Memory." *History and Memory* 26, no. 1 (Spring–Summer
2014): 75–108.

Buhle, Paul. "History and Comics." *Reviews in American History* 35, no. 2 (2007):
315–323. JSTOR, www.jstor.org/stable/30031655.

Bull, Chris, and John Gallagher. *Perfect Enemies: The Religious Right, the Gay
Movement, and the Politics of the 1990s*. New York: Crown, 1996.

Burgas, Greg. "A Review a Day: *Stuck Rubber Baby*." CBR.com, 19 June 2010.
Accessed 9 September 2017. www.cbr.com/a-review-a-day-stuck-rubber-baby.

Caminero-Santangelo, Marta. *On Latinidad: U.S. Latino Literature and the Construction of Ethnicity*. Gainesville: University Press of Florida, 2007.

Cantiello, Jessica Wells. "From Pre-Racial to Post-Racial? Reading and Reviewing
'A Mercy' in the Age of Obama." *MELUS* 36, no. 2 (2011): 165–183. JSTOR, www
.jstor.org/stable/23035286.

Capshaw, Katherine. *Civil Rights Childhood: Picturing Liberation in African American Photobooks*. Minneapolis: University of Minnesota Press, 2014.

Carey, Mike, Craig Kyle, Chris Yost, Matt Fraction, and Zeb Wells. *X-Men: Second
Coming*. New York: Marvel, 2012.

Carson, Clayborne. "Paradoxes of King Historiography." *Organization of American
Historians Magazine of History* 19, no. 1 (January 2005): 7–10.

Caruth, Cathy. Introduction to *Trauma: Explorations in Memory*, 3–12. Baltimore:
Johns Hopkins University Press, 1995.

Certeau, Michel de. *The Writing of History*. Translated by Tom Conley. New York:
Columbia University Press, 1988.

Chan. "Why Cyclops Was Right." Comic Newbies. Accessed 26 September 2017.
https://comicnewbies.com/2015/05/28/why-cyclops-was-right.

Chaney, Michael A. "Drawing on History in Recent African American Graphic
Novels." *MELUS* 32, no. 3 (2007): 175–200. JSTOR, www.jstor.org/stable/30029796.

———. *Reading Lessons in Seeing: Mirrors, Masks, and Mazes in the Autobiographical
Graphic Novel*. Jackson: University Press of Mississippi, 2017.

Chute, Hillary L. *Disaster Drawn: Visual Witness, Comics, and Documentary Form*.
Cambridge, MA: Belknap, 2016.

———. *Graphic Women: Life Narrative and Contemporary Comics*. New York:
Columbia University Press, 2010.

Claremont, Chris, and Brett Anderson. *X-Men: God Loves, Man Kills*. New York:
Marvel, 2011.

Conners, Joan L. "Barack versus Hillary: Race, Gender, and Political Cartoon
Imagery of the 2008 Presidential Primaries." *American Behavioral Scientist* 54,
no. 3 (November 2010): 298–312. EBSCOhost, doi:10.1177/0002764210381703.

Coulter, Ann. "Negroes with Guns." Townhall, 18 April 2012. https://townhall.com /columnists/anncoulter/2012/04/18/negroes-with-guns-n1179191.

Cruse, Howard. *Stuck Rubber Baby*. New ed. New York: Vertigo, 2010.

Darowski, Joseph J. *X-Men and the Mutant Metaphor: Race and Gender in the Comic Books*. Lanham, MD: Rowman and Littlefield, 2014.

D'Emilio, John. *Lost Prophet: The Life and Times of Bayard Rustin*. New York: Free Press, 2003.

Dickel, Simon. "'Can't Leave Me Behind': Racism, Gay Politics, and Coming of Age in Howard Cruse's *Stuck Rubber Baby*." *Amerikastudien / American Studies* 56, no. 4 (2011): 617–635. JSTOR, www.jstor.org/stable/23509432.

DiPaolo, Marc. *War, Politics, and Superheroes: Ethics and Propaganda in Comics and Film*. Jefferson, NC: McFarland, 2011.

Drabelle, Dennis. Review of *Stuck Rubber Baby*, by Howard Cruse. *Washington Post*, 21 August 2010. www.washingtonpost.com/wp-dyn/content/article/2010/08/20 /AR2010082005245.html.

Drum, Nicole. "Stan Lee Reveals Original Name for X-Men." Comicbook.com. Accessed 26 September 2017. http://comicbook.com/marvel/2017/09/11/stan-lee -x-men-original-name.

Dyson, Michael Eric. *I May Not Get There with You: The True Martin Luther King, Jr.* New York: Free Press, 2011.

———. "Race, Post Race." *Los Angeles Times*, 5 November 2008. www.latimes.com /opinion/la-oe-dyson5-2008nov05-story.html.

Earle, Susan, ed. *Aaron Douglas: African American Modernist*. New Haven, CT: Yale University Press, 2007.

Edwards, R. A. R. "Deaf Rights, Civil Rights: The Gallaudet 'Deaf President Now' Strike and Historical Memory of the Civil Rights Movement." In *The Civil Rights Movement in American Memory*, edited by Leigh Raiford and Renee Romano, 317–345. Athens: University of Georgia Press, 2006.

Eskridge, William N., Jr. *The Case for Same-Sex Marriage: From Sexual Liberty to Civilized Commitment*. New York: Free Press, 1996.

Estes, Jeremy. "*Stuck Rubber Baby* Brilliantly Illustrates the Complex Era of 'Kennedytime' in American History." Pop Matters. Accessed 9 September 2017. www .popmatters.com/review/127857-stuck-rubber-baby.

Fandel, Jennifer, and Brian Bascle. *Martin Luther King Jr.: Great Civil Rights Leader*. North Mankato, MN: Capstone, 2007.

Fawaz, Ramzi. *The New Mutants: Superheroes and the Radical Imagination of American Comics*. New York: New York University Press, 2016.

Fellowship of Reconciliation. *Martin Luther King and the Montgomery Story*. 1957. Reprint, edited by Israel Escamilla. CreateSpace, 2017.

Fitts, Alston, III. *Selma: A Bicentennial History*. Tuscaloosa: University of Alabama Press, 2016.

Forceville, Charles. "Conceptual Metaphor Theory, Blending Theory, and Other Cognitivist Perspectives on Comics." In *The Visual Narrative Reader*, edited by Neil Cohn, 89–114. London: Bloomsbury, 2016.

Foucault, Michel. "Of Other Spaces." Translated by Jay Miskowiec. *Diacritics* 16, no. 1 (Spring 1986): 22–27. JSTOR, www.jstor.org/stable/464648.

Fraction, Matt. *Utopia: Avengers—X-Men*. New York: Marvel, 2010.

Gardner, Jared. *Projections: Comics and the History of Twenty-First-Century Storytelling*. Stanford, CA: Stanford University Press, 2012.

Garrow, David. *Bearing the Cross: Martin Luther King, Jr., and the Southern Christian Leadership Conference*. New York: Morrow, 2004.

Gillen, Kieron. *AVX: Consequences #2*. New York: Marvel, 2012.

Goldberg, David Theo. *The Racial State*. Malden, MA: Wiley-Blackwell, 2001.

Goldsby, Jacqueline. *A Spectacular Secret: Lynching in American Life and Literature*. Chicago: University of Chicago Press, 2006.

Green, John. "Crash Course in U.S. History #39: Civil Rights and the 1950s." YouTube. Uploaded by Crash Course, 21 November 2013. https://www.youtube.com/watch?v=S64zRnnn4Po.

Groensteen, Thierry. "Narration as Supplement: An Archeology of the Infra-Narrative Foundations of Comics." In *The French Comics Theory Reader*, edited by Ann Miller and Bart Beaty, 163–182. Leuven, Belgium: Leuven University Press, 2014.

———. *The System of Comics*. Translated by Bart Beaty and Nick Nguyen. Jackson: University Press of Mississippi, 1999.

Hall, Jacquelyn Dowd. "The Long Civil Rights Movement and the Political Uses of the Past." *Journal of American History* 91, no. 4 (2005): 1233–1263.

Hartman, Saidiya V. *Scenes of Subjection: Terror, Slavery, and Self-Making in Nineteenth-century America*. New York: Oxford University Press, 1997.

Hatfield, Charles. *Alternative Comics: An Emerging Literature*. Jackson: University Press of Mississippi, 2005.

Heer, Jeet, and Kent Worcester, eds. *A Comics Studies Reader*. Jackson: University Press of Mississippi, 2009.

Henebry, Charles. "RE: Cyclops Was Right." Comic-Scholars Discussion List, 19 September 2017. Accessed 21 September 2017. www.english.ufl.edu/comics/scholars.

Hero, Rodney E., and Caroline J. Tolbert. "Race and the 2012 Election: A Post-Racial Society, More Apparent than Real Mini-Symposium." *Political Research Quarterly* 67, no. 3 (September 2014): 628–631. JSTOR, www.jstor.org/stable/24371897.

Hirsch, David A. H. "De-familiarizations, De-monstrations." "Queer Rhetoric." Special issue, *Pre/Text: A Journal of Rhetorical Theory* 13, nos. 3–4 (1992): 53–65.

Hobson, Fred. *But Now I See: The White Southern Racial Conversion Narrative*. Baton Rouge: Louisiana State University Press, 1999.

Hunsaker, Andy. "AvX Consequences #2: Cyclops Was Right." CraveOnline
.com. Accessed 26 September 2017. www.craveonline.com/site/198369-avx
-consequences-2-cyclops-was-right/amp.

Jackson, Cassandra. *Violence, Visual Culture, and the Black Male Body*. Abingdon,
UK: Routledge, 2013.

Jackson, Jack. *Comanche Moon*. Edited by Calvin Reed. New York: Reed, 2003.

Jacobs, Dale, and Jay Dolmage. "Difficult Articulations: Comics Autobiography,
Trauma, and Disability." In *The Future of Text and Image: Collected Essays on
Literary and Visual Conjunctures*, edited by Ofra Amihay and Lauren Walsh,
69–89. Newcastle upon Tyne, UK: Cambridge Scholars, 2012.

Jeffery, Gary, and John Aggs. *Thurgood Marshall: The Supreme Court Rules on
"Separate but Equal."* New York: Gareth Stevens, 2013.

Jeffery, Gary, and Emanuele Boccanfuso. *Malcolm X and the Fight for African
American Unity*. New York: Gareth Stevens, 2013.

Jeffery, Gary, and Nana Li. *The Little Rock Nine and the Fight for Equal Education*.
New York: Gareth Stevens, 2013.

Jeffery, Gary, and Nick Spender. *Martin Luther King Jr. and the March on Washington*. New York: Gareth Stevens, 2013.

———. *Medgar Evers and the NAACP*. New York: Gareth Stevens, 2013.

———. *Rosa Parks and the Montgomery Bus Boycott*. New York: Gareth Stevens, 2013.

Johnson, E. Patrick. "'Quare' Studies, or (Almost) Everything I Know about Queer
Studies I Learned from my Grandmother." *Text and Performance Quarterly* 21,
no. 1 (2001): 1–25.

———. "SNAP! Culture: A Different Kind of 'Reading.'" *Text and Performance
Quarterly* 15, no. 2 (1995): 122–142.

———. *Sweet Tea: Black Gay Men of the South*. 2nd ed. Chapel Hill: University of
North Carolina Press, 2011.

Kidder, Orion Ussner. "RE: Cyclops Was Right." Comic-Scholars Discussion List,
19 September 2017. Accessed 20 September 2017. www.english.ufl.edu/comics
/scholars.

Kirschke, Amy Helene. *Aaron Douglas: Art, Race, and the Harlem Renaissance*.
Jackson: University Press of Mississippi, 1995.

Kocmarek, Ivan. "RE: Cyclops Was Right." Comic-Scholars Discussion List, 19 September 2017. Accessed 21 September 2017. www.english.ufl.edu/comics/scholars.

Køhlert, Frederik Byrn. "Working It Through: Trauma and Autobiography in
Phoebe Gloeckner's *A Child's Life* and *The Diary of a Teenage Girl*." *South Central
Review: The Journal of the South Central Modern Language Association* 32, no. 3
(2015): 124–142.

Kurtz, Howard. "The Clock Is Ticking." *Washington Post*, 22 January 2009. www
.washingtonpost.com/wp-dyn/content/article/2009/01/22/AR2009012200822
.html.

Kyle, Craig, and Chris Yost. *New X-Men: Childhood's End*. Vol. 2. New York: Marvel, 2006.

Laird, Roland, Taneshia Nash Laird, and Elihu "Adofo" Bey. *Still I Rise: A Graphic History of African Americans*. New York: Sterling, 1997.

Lee, Anthony W. Introduction to *Lynching Photographs*, by Dora Apel and Shawn Michelle Smith, 1–8. Chapel Hill: University of North Carolina Press, 2008.

Lee, Taeku. "Somewhere Over the Rainbow? Post-Racial and Pan-Racial Politics in the Age of Obama." *Daedalus* 140, no. 2 (2011): 136–150. JSTOR, www.jstor.org /stable/23047457.

Lefèvre, Pascal. "The Construction of Space in Comics." In *A Comics Studies Reader*, edited by Jeet Heer and Kent Worcester, 157–162. Jackson: University Press of Mississippi, 2009.

———. "Some Medium-Specific Qualities of Graphic Sequences." *Substance*, 40, no. 1 (2011): 14–33.

Lewis, David. *King: A Critical Biography*. Santa Barbara, CA: Praeger, 1970.

Lewis, John. "Civil Rights Hero John Lewis Denounces DOMA." Available from the Gay and Lesbian Activist Alliance, www.glaa.org/archive/1996/lewis796.shtml. Accessed 26 May 2018.

Lewis, John, Andrew Aydin, and Nate Powell. *March: Book One*. Marietta, GA: Top Shelf, 2013.

———. *March: Book Two*. Marietta, GA: Top Shelf, 2015.

———. *March: Book Two*. Marietta, GA: Top Shelf, 2016.

Lewis, John, and Michael D'Orso. *Walking with the Wind: A Memoir of the Movement*. New York: Simon & Schuster, 2015.

Long, Mark, Jim Demonakos, and Nate Powell. *The Silence of Our Friends: The Civil Rights Struggle Was Never Black and White*. New York: First Second, 2012.

Marley, David John. "Riding in the Back of the Bus: The Christian Right's Adoption of Civil Rights Movement Rhetoric." In *The Civil Rights Movement in American Memory*, edited by Renee C. Romano and Leigh Raiford, 346–362. Athens: University of Georgia Press, 2006.

McBride, Clare. "Review: *Stuck Rubber Baby*." *The Literary Omnivore*. Accessed 9 September 2017. https://theliteraryomnivore.wordpress.com/2015/02/18/review -stuck-rubber-baby.

McCloud, Scott. Interview by Robert C. Harvey. *Comics Journal* 179 (August 1995): 52–81.

———. *Understanding Comics: The Invisible Art*. New York: Harper Perennial, 1993.

Miller, Connie Colwell, and Dan Kalal. *Rosa Parks and the Montgomery Bus Boycott*. North Mankato, MN: Capstone, 2007.

Mills, Sean Ian. "Cyclops Was Right Yet Again, Let Me Count the Ways." Henchman-4-Hire. Accessed 26 September 2017. https://henchman4hire.com /2016/12/02/cyclops-was-right-yet-again-let-me-count-the-ways.

Morgan, Edward P. *What Really Happened to the 1960s: How Mass Media Culture Failed American Democracy.* Jackson: University Press of Kansas, 2010.

Moten, Fred. *In the Break: The Aesthetics of the Black Radical Tradition.* Minneapolis: University of Minnesota Press, 2003.

Nabizadeh, Golnar. "The After-Life of Images: Archives and Intergenerational Trauma in Autographic Comics." In *Mapping Generations of Traumatic Memory in American Narratives*, edited by Dana Mihăilescu, Roxana Oltean, and Mihaela Precup, 171–191. Newcastle upon Tyne, UK: Cambridge Scholars, 2014.

Nora, Pierre. "Between Memory and History: Les Lieux De Mémoire." *Representations* 26 (1989): 7–24. JSTOR, www.jstor.org/stable/2928520.

O'Neil, Tim. "Blogathon 27: Cyclops was Right! Cyclops was Wrong!" *Graphicontent.* Accessed 26 September 2017. http://graphicontent.blogspot.com/2013/01/blogathon-27-cyclops-was-right-cyclops.html.

Peterson, Nancy J. *Against Amnesia: Contemporary Women Writers and the Crises of Historical Memory.* Philadelphia: University of Pennsylvania Press, 2001.

Poe, Marshall, and Ellen Linder. *Little Rock Nine.* New York: Aladdin, 2008.

Postema, Barbara. *Narrative Structure in Comics: Making Sense of Fragments.* New York: RIT Press, 2013.

Pryde, Rogue. "Was Cyclops Right?" Comics Amino. Accessed 26 September 2017. http://aminoapps.com/page/comics/8308161/was-cyclops-right.

Rancière, Jacques. *The Emancipated Spectator.* Translated by Gregory Elliot. London: Verso, 2009.

Redlawsk, David. P. "Introduction." *Political Psychology* 32, no. 6 (2011). JSTOR, www.jstor.org/stable/41407143.

Richards, Gary. "Everybody's Graphic Protest Novel: *Stuck Rubber Baby* and the Anxieties of Racial Difference." In *Comics and the U.S. South*, edited by Brannon Costello and Qiana J. Whitted, 161–183. Jackson: University Press of Mississippi, 2012.

Rodriguez, Clara E. "Puerto Ricans and Other Latinos." In *Hispanic New York: A Sourcebook*, edited by Claudio Iván Remeseira, 183–200. New York: Columbia University Press, 2010.

Romano, Renee C., and Leigh Raiford. "Introduction: The Struggle of Memory." In *The Civil Rights Movement in American Memory*, edited by Renee C. Romano and Leigh Raiford, xi–xxiv. Athens: University of Georgia Press, 2006.

Rose, Tony. "RE: Cyclops Was Right." Comic-Scholars Discussion List, 19 September 2017. Accessed 21 September 2017. www.english.ufl.edu/comics/scholars.

Roy, Oliver, and Justin Vaisee. "How to Win Islam Over." *New York Times*, 21 December 2008. www.nytimes.com/2008/12/21/opinion/21roy.html.

Royal, Derek Parker. "Introduction." *MELUS* 32, no. 3 (2007): 7–22.

Sánchez González, Lisa. *Boricua Literature: A Literary History of the Puerto Rican Diaspora.* New York: New York University Press, 2001.

Saraceni, Mario. "Relatedness: Aspects of Textual Connectivity in Comics." In *The Visual Narrative Reader*, edited by Neil Cohn, 115–128. London: Bloomsbury, 2016.

Satrapi, Marjane. *Persepolis: The Story of a Childhood*. New York: Pantheon, 2004.

Selzer, Linda F. "Barack Obama, the 2008 Presidential Election, and the New Cosmopolitanism: Figuring the Black Body." *MELUS* 35, no. 4 (2010): 15–37. JSTOR, www.jstor.org/stable/25759556.

Simien, Evelyn M. *Gender and Lynching: The Politics of Memory*. New York: Palgrave Macmillan, 2011.

Smiley, Tavis. *Death of a King: The Real Story of Dr. Martin Luther King Jr.'s Final Year*. New York: Back Bay, 2016.

Smith, Ralph R., and Russel R. Windes. "The Progay and Antigay Issue Culture: Interpretation, Influence, and Dissent." *Quarterly Journal of Speech* 83, no. 1 (1997): 28–48.

Smithers, Gregory D. "Barack Obama and Race in the United States: A History of the Future." *Australasian Journal of American Studies* 28, no. 1 (2009): 1–16. JSTOR, www.jstor.org/stable/41054118.

Sontag, Susan. *On Photography*. New York: Picador, 1973.

Steele, Shelby. "Obama's Post-Racial Promise." *Los Angeles Times*, 5 November 2008. www.latimes.com/opinion/opinion-la/la-oe-steele5-2008nov05-story.html.

Thienenkamp, Marius. "From Apocalypse to Revolution: The Many Trials of Scott Summers." Comicsverse. Accessed 26 September 2017. https://comicsverse.com/apocalypse-revolution-many-trials-scott-summers.

Truitt, Brian. "Hero or Villain, Cyclops Is Center of 'Uncanny X-Men.'" *USA Today*, 12 February 2013. Accessed 26 September 2017. https://www.usatoday.com/story/life/2013/02/12/uncanny-x-men-marvel-comics-series/1912997.

Tucker, Karen Iris. "Rep. John Lewis on *Selma*, Civil Rights, and LGBTQ Equality." *Slate*, 13 January 2015. Accessed 26 May 2018. www.slate.com/blogs/outward/2015/01/13/john_lewis_on_selma_bayard_rustin_and_lgbtq_civil_rights.html

Vargas, Zaragosa. *Crucible of Struggle: A History of Mexican Americans from Colonial Times to the Present Era*. New York: Oxford University Press, 2011.

Warmoth, Brian. "Comics We Love: Howard Cruse's *Stuck Rubber Baby* in Print Again at Last." Comics Alliance. Accessed 9 September 2017. http://comicsalliance.com/stuck-rubber-baby-review-preview.

Warren, Robert Penn. *Who Speaks for the Negro?*. New Haven, CT: Yale University Press, 2014.

Weaver, Lila Quintero. *Darkroom: A Memoir in Black and White*. Tuscaloosa: University of Alabama Press, 2012.

Whitehead, Anne. *Trauma Fiction*. Edinburgh: Edinburgh University Press, 2004.

Witek, Joseph. *Comic Books as History: The Narrative Art of Jack Jackson, Art Spiegelman, and Harvey Pekar*. Jackson: University Press of Mississippi, 1989.

Wood, Amy Louise. *Lynching and Spectacle: Witnessing Racial Violence in America, 1890–1940*. Chapel Hill: University of North Carolina Press, 2011.

Young, Harvey. *Embodying Black Experience: Stillness, Critical Memory, and the Black Body*. Ann Arbor: University of Michigan Press, 2010.

Zalben, Alex. "Interview: Brian Michael Bendis, Tom Brevoort, and Axel Alonso on Today's Big 'Avengers vs. X-Men' Death." MTV.com. Accessed 26 September 2017. www.mtv.com/news/2626430/interview-brian-michael-bendis-tom -brevoort-and-axel-alonso-on-todays-big-avengers-vs-x-men-death.

Zubal-Ruggieri, Rachael A. "Bibliography: Sources for Martin Luther King, Jr." *Organization of American Historians Magazine of History* 19, no. 1 (2005): 11–12. JSTOR, www.jstor.org/stable/25163734.

———. *The Civil Rights Movement and Vietnam*. Irvine, CA: Saddleback, 2009.

———. "How the X-Men Reflected the Fight for Civil Rights." *Root*, 4 April 2014. https://www.theroot.com/how-the-x-men-reflected-the-fight-for-civil-rights -1790875215.

———. "RE: Cyclops Was Right." Comic-Scholars Discussion List, 19 September 2017. Accessed 21 September 2017. www.english.ufl.edu/comics/scholars.

Index